# ENCYCLOPEDIA OF MUNICIPAL BONDS

Since 1996, Bloomberg Press has published books for financial professionals on investing, economics, and policy affecting investors. Titles are written by leading practitioners and authorities, and have been translated into more than 20 languages.

The Bloomberg Financial Series provides both core reference knowledge and actionable information for financial professionals. The books are written by experts familiar with the work flows, challenges, and demands of investment professionals who trade the markets, manage money, and analyze investments in their capacity of growing and protecting wealth, hedging risk, and generating revenue.

For a list of available titles, visit www.wiley.com/go/bloombergpress.

# ENCYCLOPEDIA OF MUNICIPAL BONDS

A Reference Guide to Market Events, Structures, Dynamics, and Investment Knowledge

## Joe Mysak

**BLOOMBERG PRESS**
An Imprint of
**WILEY**

Published by John Wiley & Sons, Inc., Hoboken, New Jersey.
Published simultaneously in Canada.

For general information on our other products and services or for technical support, please
contact our Customer Care Department within the United States at (800) 762-2974, outside the
United States at (317) 572-3993 or fax (317) 572-4002.

Wiley also publishes its books in a variety of electronic formats. Some content that appears in print may
not be available in electronic books. For more information about Wiley products, visit our web site at
www.wiley.com.

*Library of Congress Cataloging-in-Publication Data:*
Mysak, Joe.
    Encyclopedia of municipal bonds : a reference guide to market events, structures, dynamics, and
investment knowledge / Joe Mysak.-1
       p.   cm.— (Bloomberg financial series)
    ISBN 978-1-118-00675-7 (cloth); ISBN 978-1-118-17803-4 (ebk);
    ISBN 978-1-118-17843-0 (ebk); ISBN 978-1-118-17847-8 (ebk)
       1. Municipal bonds–Encyclopedias.  I. Title.
HG4726.M94   2012
332.63'23303—dc23
                                                                                    2011032160

Printed in the United States of America
10  9  8  7  6  5  4  3  2  1

# Contents

# L                                                    111

laddering · last looks · lease financings · legal opinion · letters of credit · liens · limited obligation

# M                                                    115

market activity · Marks-Roos · Mello-Roos · mini bonds · moral obligation · mortgage bonds · MSRB · Municipal Assistance Corporation · municipal utility district · mutual funds

# N                                                    122

negotiated sale · net asset value · net interest cost · New Jersey pension obligation bonds of 1997 · New Jersey Turnpike scandal of 1993 · New York City financial crisis of 1975 · NRO

# O                                                    131

official statement · OPEB · open-end funds · Orange County, California · original issue discount · out-of-state authorities

# P                                                    142

par · pay-to-play · pension obligation bonds · pensions · "People don't buy municipal bonds to get rich; they buy municipal bonds to stay rich" · Philadelphia trial · PIT bonds · preliminary official statement · premium bonds · premium laundering · prerefunded bonds · price to the par call · pricing · principal · private placements · Proposition 2½ · Proposition 13 · public–private partnerships · Puerto Rico · pyramid bonds

# Q                                                    162

Qualified School Construction Bonds; Qualified Zone Academy Bonds

# R                                                    163

ratings · the ratio · Recalibration of 2010 · redemption · refunding · repudiation · reserve fund · retail order periods · revenue bonds · RFPs · risk factors · rollover · Rule 15c2-12 · rum bonds

# S                                                                      174

# T                                                                      181

# U                                                                      197

# V                                                                      200

# W                                                                      203

# Y                                                                      209

# Z                                                                      213

# Acknowledgments

The *Encyclopedia of Municipal Bonds* is the work of a career rather than of a few months or even years, and I am pleased to acknowledge here the contributions of some of the people who helped make my career.

In December 1980, I interviewed with a soft-voiced gentleman then building the staff of a newspaper that covered the municipal bond market, called *The Daily Bond Buyer*. He didn't find my lack of financial expertise to be a drawback; if anything, he said, that was a plus. He wanted people who could write clear English. When could I start? To John H. Allan I owe my career in this odd little market. I was his first hire at the newspaper, and was soon joined by scores more, many of whom are still in the profession. John was the father of us all.

Editors are fired when their bosses get tired of them. When that happened to me in 1994, Jim Grant, founder of *Grant's Interest Rate Observer*, invited me to come and work for him. I have on my desk five bound volumes of *Grant's Municipal Bond Observer* and two of *Grant's Municipal Bond Issuer*, and consult them to this day. My idea for the publication, I see now, was that the municipal market was, in general, a safe place, and that what investors really needed was a guide to what not to buy. I am pleased to say that almost every nutty, unrated, high-yield deal we wrote about went bust. This perhaps was not a formula for success as measured in terms of circulation, however. Jim was a patient man. So was publisher Jay Diamond. I am fortunate to count them as my friends.

In May 1999, my old boss John McCorry called me while I was on vacation and said there was a big job awaiting me at Bloomberg. When I returned, I sent an e-mail to Matt Winkler, then, as now, famed as the editor of a hard-driving, fast-expanding news service. Over lunch, Matt offered me a job as a columnist. It has been my good fortune to work for him since then, and in a variety of jobs.

Their bylines appear numerous times among the sources for the entries here, but I would be remiss if I did not mention writers past and present on the states and municipalities beat at Bloomberg: Tom Cahill, Darrell Preston, Martin Braun, William Selway, Brendan McGrail, Jerry Hart, Michael McDonald, and Mike Quint, as well as managing editor William Glasgall and executive editor Susan Goldberg. Then there are the colleagues here who ornament the hours and make the days nicer: Reto Gregori, David Wilson, Tom Keene, Caroline Baum, Manuela Hoelterhoff, Laurie Muchnick, Lisa Kassenaar, Lisa Wolfson, Joyce Kehl, and Beth Williams.

In August 2010, Ted Merz spotted me in the office on a Sunday and told me all about his new venture, Bloomberg Briefs, a series of newsletters, and suggested I start one on municipal bonds. And so, the world coming full circle, since February 2011 I have been editor of a daily publication all about the municipal bond market. Thanks to Ted and Brian Rooney, and to all who make up the early-morning world of Bloomberg Briefs: Jennifer Rossa, Rose Constantino, Katie Porter, Ian Maready, Rob Williams, Mike Nol, Deirdre Fretz, Nathaniel Baker, Nicole Allen, Doug Simmons, Mike McDonough, Joe Brusuelas, and Richard Yamarone.

The *Encyclopedia* would not have been possible without the unflagging efforts of our librarians: Michael Novatkoski, Nick Tamasi, Mike Weiss, and Anita Kumar.

Bloomberg provides its users with ease of access to information. And so I must mention all those in Data who have helped me gain access to their world: Mike Olander, Joe Helmlinger, Sowjana Sivaloganathan, Bert Louis, and Andy Peszka.

Thanks here to Steve Isaacs of the Bloomberg Press imprint, who asked me whether I wanted to update my 1998 *Handbook for Muni-Bond Issuers*, and at John Wiley & Sons, my thanks to Evan Burton and Meg Freeborn.

The current mania in MuniLand not to comment for the record about anything, ever, is a disturbing one. Journalists are lost without sources. I have been blessed to have many good ones over the years.

James B. G. Hearty was a source, both as an issuer and as a banker, and is a friend. Thanks, pal.

Kit Taylor, executive director of the Municipal Securities Rulemaking Board (MSRB) for three decades, was both an early source and a patient teacher—a guide, if you will, to MuniLand and its history.

He wasn't alone. Among the analysts who have helped me are Jim Cusser, Richard Ciccarone, Austin Tobin, J. B. Kurish, Natalie Cohen, Tom Doe, Dennis Farrell, Robert Kurtter, Robin Prunty, George Friedlander, John Hallacy, Tom Kozlik, Richard Larkin, Sylvan Feldstein, and Parry

Young. Richard Lehmann of the *Distressed Debt Securities* newsletter has been a reliable source on an often inscrutable topic, defaults.

Municipal bond lawyers have played a special part in my education. Since 1994, I have been a speaker at the annual Bond Attorneys Winter Workshop at the invitation of John L. Kraft, whom I have known since at least 1985. That is, the first time I quoted him in a story was in 1985, on the New Jersey Turnpike's then-record $2 billion bond issue. I suspect we go back even further than that. It has been a privilege to speak before this group, and I am pleased to acknowledge it here. In particular, I'd like to thank Robert Dean Pope, John VanDuys, Bob Jones, Dave Franklin, Fredric Weber, Brad Waterman, Ken Haynie, Rick Weiss, Don Howell, Jerry Turner, Fred Rosenfeld, Margaret Pope, Phil Genetos, Tim Frey, Bill Danhof, Glenn Floyd, Deborah Winter, Gary Walsh, Griff Pitcher, Tony Stemberger, and Todd Meierhenry. Bankruptcy specialist James Spiotto is not part of this group, but I'd be remiss if I didn't mention his help.

The market's regulators have always been kind. I'd especially like to thank Paul Maco, Martha Haines, Cliff Gannett, Charlie Anderson, Lynnette Kelly Hotchkiss, Hal Johnson, and Jennifer Galloway.

Financial advisers have walked me through many a deal that would otherwise have been indecipherable. Thanks to Peter Shapiro, Robert Doty, Lori Raineri, Freda and J. Chester Johnson, Doreen Frasca, John White, and James H. White III.

A few issuers have provided me with immeasurable assistance over the years. These include Ed Alter, Patrick Born, Frank Hoadley, Patrick Foye, Ben Watkins, Bob Bowman, and T. Spencer Wright. At the Government Finance Officers Association, I would like to thank Jeff Esser and Susan Gaffney for their assistance and guidance.

I was almost afraid to mention bankers who have helped me for fear they'd be fired, but I really do wish to thank Dave Andersen, Bob Downey, David Clapp, Michael Geffrard, Roger Hayes, Mike Crofton, George Marlin, Greg Finn, Ray Kljajic, Bud Byrnes, Mitch Asch, David Kotok, Chris Emmet, and Tim Davis.

Those on the other side of the equation, the buyers and money managers, have been especially good to me. Thanks to George Calvert, Eddie Horner, Hugh McGuirk, Chris Dillon, Ken Woods, Ron Fielding, Gary Pollack, Joe Deane, Evan Rourke and John Flahive, and John Wilen.

Thanks to my friends for all their support and for listening to too many stories about municipal bonds: Jack Doran, Steve Dickson, Pat Fitzgibbons,

Ted Hampton, Mike Ballinger, Andy Ferguson, John Dougherty, Parker Bagley, Steve Gustavson, Mark Reed, and Howell Mette; Philipp, Julia, Katharina, Anna, and Amelia Windemuth; Ken Lindley and Clay Schudel.

Only my in-laws, Rob Merett, Bob Loughrey, and Jim Merett, have heard more of those stories, and even their patience pales in comparison with my wife's. Thanks, Sue!

J.M.

# Introduction

Welcome to MuniLand.

If I didn't coin the term, I know I was one of its early adopters, featuring a map of the place in the first issue of a short-lived fortnightly I edited called *Grant's Municipal Bond Observer*, in 1994. The idea behind "MuniLand"—and I refer to the term, not specifically the map—was a simple one: Here was a market that was particular and specific to an almost absurd degree. Calling it MuniLand was the usual attempt to bring order out of chaos. I used the word when attempting to explain the municipal market to those steeped—as most people are—in the culture of equities. I wanted them to, as the poet says, suspend disbelief. They were entering a new world, as strange and idiosyncratic as any uncharted island nation.

There is a 1937 short story by Thomas Wolfe—no, not that one, the other one, who wrote the novel *You Can't Go Home Again* (1940)—called "Only the Dead Know Brooklyn." The story touches on the impossibility of knowing the vast borough east of Manhattan Island, and that is a good way to think about MuniLand. Only the dead know munis. I have been covering this market for more than 30 years; I know I am the only person to have read the first 100 years' worth of *Bond Buyers*, and I still discover things I didn't know.

Ah, yes, the *Bond Buyer*. The year I began covering the municipal market for the newspaper then known as *The Daily Bond Buyer*, states and municipalities sold $46 billion in bonds, the last time annual issuance was below $50 billion. More than half was sold through negotiation, and revenue bonds far outnumbered general obligation bonds, as they had since 1976. Those are the only characteristics that market had in common with today's.

For the rest of it, the municipal market in 1981 was not so very different from the market of 1961, or even 1941. Bond insurance, whose spectacular blowup in 2008 and 2009 stunned the world, had at that point been in existence for a decade, yet covered less than 1 percent of the year's bonds.

Almost all the bonds sold were fixed-rate, and almost all were sold to raise new money, as they say, rather than to refinance existing issues. The market was still a very staid place.

MuniLand was, I also learned, a very mysterious place. For one thing, there was no physical market, like, say, the New York Stock Exchange. It traded, they told me, but there was no way to verify that. You could see the primary market—new issues being priced, and those prices coming over the Munifacts machine—but the secondary market was something of a fiction. I helped perpetrate that fiction when the time came for me to learn how to write "The Column," an adornment of page one of *The Daily Bond Buyer* for decades. As instructed, I called four or five traders and asked them how five or six "dollar bonds," large, recently priced issues, were "trading," and they told me, and I duly figured out where things stood using a Monroe calculator. Things often seemed to be up an eighth when they weren't down an eighth, and more often than not "unch" (unchanged).

There was no actual trading, and there were no prices. Or, as I say, prices were what someone on the other end of a telephone told me they were. It made no difference that I was a reporter. An investor would have been told the same thing. There was a publication called the Blue List, so-called because it was printed on a sort of blue tissue paper, and which one trader advised me was "like a municipal bond novel," if only I would learn how to read it. The Blue List showed dealer inventory in state after state. Sometimes it showed prices; more often, just coupons and yields.

As for other data about "the market," I found that I was now at the very center of it. Yields, the amount of bonds sold this week, last week, last month, last year, last century, who underwrote the most—those numbers were all gathered by *The Daily Bond Buyer*, and had been since 1891. Having put a couple of publications out of business right out of college, I liked the sound of that.

I also thought I would be at the paper for about six months. What I really wanted to do was write for magazines, like Tom Wolfe (yes, that one). I was there for 13 years.

MuniLand in 1981 was about to be transformed, and I was there to witness it, at New York City headquarters, with very occasional forays out into the bush. These were usually conferences held at various swanky hotels and resorts featuring bankers, bond lawyers, analysts, financial advisers, issuers, and buyers, all the denizens of MuniLand. As a journalist, I fanta-sized about being assigned to a bureau, preferably in San Francisco, London, or Mustique, but being at headquarters, of whatever publication I actually worked for, gave me a certain advantage. I got to see all parts of the market at once, sort of a bird's-eye view.

The first thing I learned was that there was no single market at all, but six or seven state markets and perhaps another three or four regional ones. And then there was Washington, DC, which, while a marginal issuer of municipal bonds itself, happened to be very important to what occurred in all those other markets. I took what seemed like years of dictation from reporters on Capitol Hill on the subject of tax reform. As I write these words, it seems that once again tax reform seems likely to be visited upon MuniLand.

I also learned that time in the municipal bond market, with the perhaps singular exception of Orange County, California's bankruptcy in 1994, which happened in a heartbeat, is marked with a calendar, not a stopwatch. Even the simplest story, like a bond default, almost never seemed to end. It was a rare thing to watch a reporter lay the last clip in a file and put it away, certain that the last bondholder had been paid, or not, and that the case was closed.

Hysteria was the municipal bond market's portion in 2010 and 2011, fed by people who didn't know what they were talking about, talking and writing and, especially, blogging. Yet now that I think about it, it seems that the biggest lesson I've learned is that just as this market resists generalization, so does it fight off periodic calls for Armageddon.

In 1995, for example, one very knowledgeable bond buyer who did know what he was talking about nevertheless said that Orange County, California, then still dithering its way through bankruptcy, might lose access to the capital markets for a generation. In fact, Orange County was back selling bonds within six months of its Chapter 9 filing.

That little story says many things. For example, of course, it says that bond buyers are also that old *Saturday Night Live* character, Mr. Short-Term Memory. For another, though, it says that hyperbole and hysteria are always with us.

The chief reason people get MuniLand wrong is that they think of the municipal market in equity terms. States and localities are not corporations. What's more, there is no reason they should be more like corporations, much to the apparent annoyance of those people who think they should. Again: Welcome to MuniLand. Just because they do things differently here does not mean that what they are doing is wrong.

Take a municipal bond's reaction to bad news: there isn't any. This confounds critics used to the ups and downs of the stock market. Why don't the bonds react? Why don't bonds trade off? The answer is because the typical muni bond doesn't trade at all much beyond the first 30 days after its birth (see the entries for "All bonds go to heaven" and market activity).

Or take bankruptcy. States cannot enter Chapter 9 municipal bankruptcy. This infuriates those who, wrongly, see bankruptcy as a perfectly acceptable tool that incidentally could be used to gut the public labor unions and reduce states' pension and benefit obligations. They see it, or some heretofore unimagined version of it, as a simple and elegant solution to some states' seemingly intractable pension burdens. It is neither of those things, neither simple nor elegant, yet that does not stop the proponents of state bankruptcy from insisting that it is a viable solution to states' budget woes. These people also invariably have an issue with politics and politicians, and with public officials both elected and appointed. I'm not sure who they expect to run the nation's states and localities, unless they also intend to replace democracy with—what, exactly? Corporate governance?

I seem to have become known, in some circles, as a harsh critic of the municipal bond market. In fact, I consider it one of the wonders of the world, allowing for the ultimate in local independence and control. Reviewing my columns and stories over the years, I see that I have taken a stand against only two things.

The first: I didn't think the entire market should go negotiated. This has been a consistent position of mine, and I wrote columns back in the 1980s about the subject, predictably angering those on Wall Street who thought that every last municipal bond issue should be sold through negotiation, and not at auction. My own thought on it was: Here you have this old-fashioned, perfectly acceptable way of selling municipal bonds. Why not use it? Competitive, or auction, or, as the old-timers used to call it, advertised sale makes underwriters bid for bonds and divorces the proceeds from favoritism and pay-to-play, which have been prominent features of the modern market.

The other thing I have advocated against on a consistent basis, again angering a certain swath of the professional community, has been the use of swaps. Just too much about them—their pricing, their design, their risks— would prove inaccessible to the citizen financiers in charge of most of the municipal bond market. Because, of course, swaps (like negotiated finance, come to think of it) were one of those things that at first weren't for everybody, but very quickly became so. Wall Street pounds every idea into the ground, as James Grant put it so well, like a tomato stake.

Neither of these positions was designed to ingratiate me with those proposing that every deal, no matter how small and no matter who was the issuer, even the smallest school district, should be sold through negotiation and with a swap. Yet who now can argue against the eminent reasonableness of these positions? Even those municipalities that embrace negotiation should sell an issue at auction from time to time, in order to gauge the acceptance of their securities in the market. As for swaps, it ought to be a while before municipalities engage in their use again. If the $4 billion and counting in termination payments issuers had to make after the financial crisis doesn't dissuade them, perhaps the bid-rigging trials will, or maybe it will be the numerous studies slated to emerge from Washington officialdom in the coming months.

I also wrote stories about the subject of yield burning, after Michael Quint of the *New York Times* broke the story. Yield burning can be described in a shorthand way as overcharging issuers for the various products they use when they have to reinvest their bond proceeds. These stories did not make me popular with those who evidently engaged in this most obscure and yet seemingly ineradicable of all municipal market behaviors. By the time I started to write about the subject, of course, the Securities and Exchange Commission (SEC) was already deeply involved in its investigation into and, ultimately, settlement with the securities firms that thought it was okay to cheat issuers because no one was looking.

For a brief period, I perhaps even kept the story alive, as a legitimate journalistic subject, and even broke news in a publication that came out fortnightly. But how could I not? I was surprised that so few of my brethren elected to sit down and hear out Michael Lissack, the Smith Barney banker who blew the whistle. He had a lot of good stories to tell, supported by a lot of evidence. It broke my heart when my old newspaper carried a front-page story with a headline reading "Refunding Issuers Say Deals Did Not Involve Yield Burning: Survey," and I almost felt it a sort of personal rebuke. Their readers' cheer proved short-lived. As I wanted to tell the banker who took an empty chair at a conference lunch and who found to his evident horror that he was sitting next to me: I didn't invent yield burning.

Yield burning, in both its past and its present manifestations (see the entry on bid rigging), has taken up more than half my career. The industry did not handle it very well the first time around, which may be why there is a second time around. It may be my imagination, but the old industry, I think, would have admitted it had a real problem and then come up with a plan to fix it. The new industry, or the one that existed in 1995, when

Lissack spoke first with the FBI and the SEC and then with Mike Quint, denied there was a problem at all and stuck to the somewhat arrogant if novel defense: prices are what we say they are.

The yield-burning business marked, sadly, the last time you could pick up the telephone and talk to bankers, traders, salespeople, analysts, and underwriters. Nowadays few of them will give even the most innocuous quote without a publicity person listening in, if they allow for it at all, which means most municipal market stories are festooned with ridiculous denials, rejections, and refusals to comment—on anything. I don't know what irritates me more: the fact that they don't comment or the rote refusals to comment that so lard up all the stories.

I wasn't the first reporter to write about yield burning. But I was the first to describe flipping in MuniLand, which works in much the same way as it does in the world of initial public offerings. That is, a few big investors get allotments of bonds, and then quickly sell them at a profit. The higher price means a lower yield, which leads this taxpayer to wonder why the issuer didn't get that rate in the first place. It doesn't happen all the time or on every bond issue, but the selection of certain favored investors to act as wholesalers converting municipal bonds into a retail product seems to fly in the face of what the negotiated method of sale was supposed to be all about. That was, award us your business and we will get you the best price on your bonds, because negotiation gives us the time to get your bonds into the hands of final investors. If there is flipping—and until the Municipal Securities Rulemaking Board (MSRB) began listing trades in 1995, there was no way of knowing—then negotiation isn't all it was cracked up to be. And issuers who decide to use it, as so many will, should be smart about it. Please, no more "leave the driving to us" in your dealings with underwriters.

MuniLand is no longer as mysterious as it was, no longer the unknown and unknowable enigma of the capital markets. Those who use the word *murky* to describe it are writing yesterday's story. Anyone who wants to can find details of prices and trades, complete copies of official statements, and all manner of material-event notices, online and for free (see the entries for escrowed to maturity and EMMA). MuniLand is accessible. I was surprised to discover that the chief reason it is so is a little incident that occurred at the end of 1986, when the Kansas City, Kansas, Board of Public Utilities sold bonds that would result in the calling of some of its other bonds that had been escrowed to maturity. That was my story, but until I chatted with Kit Taylor recently, I didn't quite understand its significance. I remembered that when I had called him for a comment a quarter-century ago he responded, as always, with alacrity. But even his response was a little too quick. It was almost as if he had known this would happen. The existence of calls on escrowed-to-maturity bonds were "a material fact," the then-executive director of the MSRB told me. "It looks like underwriters assumed that escrowed-to-maturity bonds were not callable, and that's a big mistake. Somebody did not do their homework," he said. "The industry is supposed to disclose material facts at the time of sale, and it seems it is being faced with a tremendous information problem."

I asked him about that answer, and then he stitched the whole story together for me, about how dealers that summer had rejected the MSRB's proposed amendment to its Rule G-15, which would have required dealers to deliver to customers written information about the call provisions on bonds they purchased within five days, upon request. In a series of comment letters to the board, the dealers said they couldn't possibly tell their customers what all the calls on a bond might be, because they did not have access to all of the official statements for the bonds they might sell. That story was probably written out of the D.C. bureau. I can see now I didn't pay it much attention.

That excuse sounds a little improbable, today, even unimaginable—we can't tell you what the calls to the bonds we sold you are, because we don't know ourselves—and yet that was the situation at the time. The dealers gave what they regarded as a plausible answer. But they also suggested that maybe the MSRB could do the job, and that, with a few false starts and modifications, is where we are today. There is no excuse for bond buyers not to be intimately acquainted with the securities they have purchased or intend to purchase.

In the *Encyclopedia of Municipal Bonds*, I have attempted to define terms and tell stories that may be unfamiliar to most people not in the market. I also thought it important to list the sources of the information, because so much of it is based on original documents, contemporary newspaper and news service accounts, ratings company reports, and securities firm comments—primary sources. Most of the history I tell here has not been put between hard covers before in any kind of comprehensive way (there are exceptions, of course, like New York City's financial crisis of 1975, which has not lacked for chroniclers). I know I have left some good stories out, and perhaps overemphasized some at the expense of others. I look forward to hearing from those who have something to add, and suspect that this *Encyclopedia* will be about double the size in five years or whenever it is next updated. In many ways, this is the kind of reference book I wish I'd had on my desk as a reporter and columnist (along with these two pieces of advice right up front: Laws governing the issuance of municipal bonds and conflicts of interest are different in each state, and watch out for *m*'s for *b*'s in stories and headlines). Serious students can go back and at least begin to research any of the topics here. I hope I have given them a place to start.

Joe Mysak

# ENCYCLOPEDIA OF MUNICIPAL BONDS

## ability to pay

Municipal bond analysts make two assessments when considering a government's creditworthiness: its ability to pay its debts and its willingness to pay. Ability refers to an issuer's relative financial condition. If a municipality is open for business and can levy fees and taxes, investors expect it to pay its bills and to repay its loans, even if it has to raise those taxes and fees to do so. Willingness to pay is far more difficult to judge, as it deals with political will at a point in time.

See also Orange County, California; willingness to pay.

## acceleration

A provision, normally present in a bond indenture agreement, mortgage, or other contract, that the unpaid balance is to become due and payable if specified events of default should occur. These include failure to meet interest, principal, or sinking fund payments; insolvency; and nonpayment of taxes on mortgaged property.

*Source:*

Mysak, Joe. *The Handbook for Muni-Bond Issuers.* Princeton, NJ: Bloomberg Press, 1998.

1

## additional bonds test

A legal requirement that new additional bonds, which will have a claim on revenues already pledged to repay outstanding revenue bonds, can be issued only if certain financial or other conditions are met.

## advance refunding

An advance refunding is a refinancing of a bond issue that will remain outstanding for more than 90 days after the sale of the refunding bonds, and is most often done to save money. Issuers are prohibited from doing more than one advance refunding per issue.

The issuer sells new bonds and uses the proceeds to buy either special State and Local Government Series securities from the U.S. Treasury or open-market Treasury or agency securities, and deposits them into an escrow account that will be used to pay off the refunded bonds at a call date or maturity. Tax law in general prohibits most municipalities from earning profits on the proceeds of bond issues, which is called arbitrage. In other words, the securities in escrow cannot spin off more in yield than the yield on the refunding bonds. If they do, the issuer must rebate the difference to the Treasury.

The refunded bonds are said to be prerefunded or escrowed to maturity. They usually rise in value because they are now secured not by an issuer's pledge but by a pot of top-rated Treasury securities. Most prerefunded bonds have maturities of five years or less, Bank of America Merrill Lynch Municipal Bond Strategist John Hallacy estimated in October 2010.

*See also* escrowed to maturity; prerefunded bonds; refunding; yield burning.

*Sources:*

MSRB online glossary at www.msrb.org.

"Waiting for Godot or QE2?" Bank of America Merrill Lynch Muni Commentary, October 29, 2010.

Wood, William H. "Municipal Bond Refundings." In *The Handbook of Municipal Bonds*, edited by Sylvan G. Feldstein and Frank Fabozzi. Hoboken, NJ: John Wiley & Sons, 2008.

## advertised sale

An advertised sale is also known as an auction sale or, most commonly, a competitive sale. So-called because the issuer places a notice in a newspaper that it intends to offer bonds for sale and invites bidders.

*See also* competitive sale; negotiated sale.

## "All bonds go to heaven"

This is an old market axiom describing how municipal bonds are bought and held, and rarely trade, after they are sold in the new-issue market. Trading is most active in the first 30 days of a bond's life, according to the Municipal Securities Rulemaking Board's transaction reports. This also helps explain why prices on outstanding municipal bonds rarely react to news in the way stock prices do.

The Securities and Exchange Commission's Office of Economic Analysis and Office of Municipal Securities studied municipal trading between December 12, 1999, and October 31, 2000, and found that about one-third of all bond issuers with outstanding debt had no trades in their securities during the period; about two-thirds had 25 or fewer trades; only 2 percent of issuers had 1,000 or more trades in their securities. In terms of the bonds themselves, about 70 percent did not trade at all during the period; another 15 percent traded five or fewer times; less than 1 percent traded more than 100 times.

*See also* issuer concentration; market activity.

*Sources:*

*Municipal Securities Rulemaking Board 2009 Fact Book.* Alexandria, VA: MSRB, 2010.

"Report on Transactions in Municipal Securities." Office of Economic Analysis and Office of Municipal Securities, Division of Market Regulation, Securities and Exchange Commission, July 1, 2004.

## Ambac

The nation's first municipal bond insurer, founded in 1971.

*See also* insurance.

## AMT

The Alternative Minimum Tax (AMT) was first introduced as part of the Tax Reform Act of 1986 to ensure that taxpayers pay some federal income tax. For taxpayers subject to the AMT, "certain tax preference items, including interest on some private activity bonds, otherwise not subject to taxation are added to the gross income of the taxpayer for calculating the federal income tax liability," says the MSRB. The American Recovery and Reinvestment Act of 2009 exempted these kinds of private-activity bonds from the tax during 2009 and 2010. About 3.9 million taxpayers were subject to the AMT in 2008. Onerous to calculate and unpopular with taxpayers, the AMT seemed a likely target for tax reform in 2011.

About 6 percent of new bonds are AMT bonds, Citigroup estimated in 2011, and over the years they have typically offered investors yield premiums of 30 to 50 basis points, although during the crisis year of 2008, this increased to almost 150 basis points. Most airport and other port bonds are subject to the AMT, as are industrial development bonds. Citigroup estimated that the AMT tends to be paid mainly by taxpayers making between $100,000 and $500,000 in adjusted gross income.

*See also* Mrs. Dodge; tax-exemption.

*Sources:*

Internal Revenue Service, *Statistics of Income Bulletin*, Winter 2010.
MSRB online glossary at www.msrb.org.
"Special Focus: Private Activity Bonds Subject to Alternative Minimum Tax May Be Extremely Attractive for the Right Investors." Municipal Market Comment, Citigroup Investment Research & Analysis, March 25, 2011.

## appropriation

The act of setting aside money to pay debt service on bonds or certificates of participation. Issuers of appropriation-backed securities usually state that their lawmakers may make such appropriations, but usually caution that they are not legally obligated to do so. Securities that rely solely on a government's promise to set aside money are marginally more risky than credits where the money is automatically budgeted.

Certificates of participation are backed by appropriations, while general obligation bonds are secured, with certain exceptions, by a municipality's full faith and credit pledge of taxes.

*See also* risk factors.

## arbitrage

In municipal finance, arbitrage refers to making a profit by borrowing at tax-exempt rates and investing in higher-yielding securities. This is forbidden by tax law, and the excess earnings must be rebated to the government. So-called arbitrage bonds are securities deemed by the Internal Revenue Service to have been issued not to make loans, but purely to make profits through an investment in guaranteed investment agreements. During the 1980s, various securities firms designed different securities structures to earn arbitrage, which were then investigated and often prohibited by the Internal Revenue Service. The Tax Reform Act of 1986 and subsequent amendments to tax law more sharply defined arbitrage and prescribed rebate requirements.

## Arkansas Default of 1933

Arkansas is the most recent state to default on its general obligation bonds, and it did so in 1933, during the Great Depression. The default was remedied within months, but it took eight years and the federal government's help to solve the underlying problem.

In 1927, Governor John S. Martineau proposed that the state assume the $54.8 million debt of hundreds of troubled road improvement districts and embark on the construction of a highway system. Combined with the state's own $84 million in highway bonds and $7.2 million in toll-bridge securities, the assumption of district bonds pushed Arkansas's debt to $146 million. Coupons on the bonds were as much as 5 percent.

"We have a state ranking 46th in per-capita wealth in 1929, ranking first in per-capita indebtedness" was how state Senator Lee Reaves summed up the matter in a 1943 article for the *Arkansas Historical Quarterly*. "Under the best of circumstances it would have been difficult to meet payments on the mounting debt."

The state tried refunding the bonds through an exchange program in 1932. This failed. In 1933, the General Assembly passed the Ellis Refunding

Act, which sought to exchange all outstanding highway debt for state bonds carrying a 3 percent coupon, maturing in 25 years.

"Interest on highway and toll-bridge bonds, amounting to $770,500, due March 1, is in default, and this fact spurred the Governor in his demand for a refunding program that would yield revenue sufficient to meet any emergency and insure stability to outstanding obligations," the *New York Times* reported.

Bondholders were having none of it. They went to Governor J. M. Futrell (who took office in January 1933), and protested that the new refunding violated the state's contract with bondholders, in that it replaced their first lien on automobile and gasoline taxes with the state's own full faith and credit pledge. Bondholders preferred their portion of a specific, dedicated revenue stream rather than the state's promise.

The bondholders—mainly northern and eastern banks and insurance companies—also said that reducing the interest rate amounted to partial "repudiation."

That was a loaded word in those days. Bond investors were still smarting from the repudiation of bonds used to finance railroads, the Confederacy, and various carpetbagger governments.

"There is a vast difference between repudiation and inability to pay," Governor Futrell told the *New York Times*. "Repudiation is refusal to pay when you are able to do so." The governor then took a shot at bond underwriters: "Arkansas has been oversold through a wrecking crew with the assistance of the bond buyers, despite their knowledge that the State highway issues were excessive. Although Arkansas has not received full benefit from its highway bonds, the state owes the debt, and will pay in time, but our peoples are struggling for existence and cannot pay additional taxes, nor meet present requirements."

The bondholders headed to Little Rock to negotiate. The state failed to make $10.5 million in bond payments on August 1.

In January 1934, the bondholders got a permanent injunction against the state, blocking the use of automobile and gasoline taxes for anything other than highway maintenance and debt service. Now "at the mercy of the bondholders," in the words of Senator Reaves's article, the state in 1934 agreed to a refunding that extended some maturities and required an increase in both those automobile and gasoline taxes.

That cured the 1933 default.

But the story does not end there. State officials said default would be again possible in 1944 when $12 million in principal and interest had to be repaid, and probable in 1949 when $41.3 million would come due. So in 1937, and again in 1939, the state tried to refund its $140 million in highway bonds. The effort was rebuffed by bondholders both times.

On April 1, 1941, $90.8 million worth of the outstanding highway bonds was callable; an additional $45 million was callable on July 1. The state made plans for another (this time uncontested) refunding.

A syndicate of 250 banks said it would bid on the new Arkansas refunding bonds, in conjunction with the Reconstruction Finance Corporation (RFC), a creation of Herbert Hoover's administration and a decidedly new entrant into the municipal bond market.

On February 27, 1941, to Wall Street's shock, the RFC bought the entire issue single-handedly. "In our several conferences with the bankers, they indicated to us they would not bid for as much as $90 million and that the interest rate would have to be 3.5 percent," RFC Chairman Jesse Jones said. "We thought this rate too high for a tax-exempt bond of a sovereign state," he told the *New York Times*.

The RFC bid, which averaged 3.2 percent, saved Arkansas $28 million over the life of the bonds. The corporation later sold the securities to Wall Street banks at a profit of $4 million. Arkansas never looked back. Today, the state ranks 46th in tax-supported debt per capita, at $312, according to Moody's Investors Service.

*See also* Chapter 9; default; refunding; repudiation.

*Sources:*

New York Times. "Arkansas Bonds Taken by the RFC." February 28, 1941.

New York Times. "Arkansas to Float $136,330,557 Issue." February 18, 1941.

New York Times. "Attack Refunding Voted in Arkansas." March 28, 1933.

New York Times. "Bondholders Move Against Arkansas." September 16, 1933.

New York Times. "Highway Revenues Tied Up in Arkansas." January 6, 1934.

New York Times. "New Bond Terms in Arkansas Seen." July 17, 1933.

Parke, A. W. "Arkansas Avoids Default on Bonds." *New York Times*, March 1, 1933.

Reaves, Lee. "Highway Bond Refunding in Arkansas." *Arkansas Historical Quarterly*, December 1943.

2010 State Debt Medians Report. Moody's Investors Service, May 2010.

## auction-rate securities

Auction-rate securities (ARSs) are bonds with interest rates that are typically reset by bidding every 7, 14, 28, or 35 days. The market for these kinds of securities froze in February 2008, when the Wall Street firms running the sales stopped bidding on the deals, leaving investors with billions of dollars of bonds they could not sell. States and localities have not sold any new issues of auction-rate securities since then.

American Express Company sold the first issue of auction-rate securities in 1984, with a $350 million sale of money-market preferred shares with dividends reset every 49 days. The first tax-exempt auction-rate security was sold by Tucson Electric Power Company in 1988.

"From the beginning, banks were manipulating the market," wrote Bloomberg News in May 2008, after the market froze. The story continued, "In 1995, investors learned that Lehman settled allegations by the Securities and Exchange Commission that it improperly bid at some American Express auctions," manipulating the process 13 times to prevent auctions from failing, and paying a fine of $850,000.

There were a lot of reasons for issuers to like this bond structure, which is why the market eventually grew to $330 billion, about half of which was municipal. It allowed them to borrow for long terms, sometimes as much as 40 years or more, at very short-term rates. Unlike variable-rate demand obligations, auction-rate securities were sold without a put option, so the issuers did not have to pay for a liquidity provider. ARSs were rated as long-term debt, so the issuers did not have to pay for a short-term rating. The securities were usually callable at par at any time, and convertible to variable- or fixed-rate debt. Issuers sometimes hedged their floating-rate risk with swaps, and often also insured the transactions against default. In 2001, municipal issuers sold $11 billion in auction-rate debt; in 2004, they sold a record $42 billion, and in 2007, $38.7 billion.

Investors, chiefly corporate cash managers and high-net-worth individuals, liked auction-rate paper because the securities paid them a little more in yield than they could earn in Treasury securities and money-market funds. And in the case of failed auctions, where there were more sellers than buyers, holders of some securities received a penalty rate, sometimes in the double digits. Not that auctions ever seemed to fail. From the market's origins in 1984 to 2006, there were only 13 failed auctions, according to Moody's Investors Service, out of the thousands held.

Issuers got to borrow at very low rates. Investors got a little more yield. The securities firms liked the market because it provided a regular stream of fee income after the initial bonds were sold; the underwriters also ran the regularly scheduled auctions.

In 2004, the SEC shook the market when it began an investigation into "deceptive, dishonest or unfair market practices" by auction-rate securities dealers. "There's too much risk to both the investor and issuer for it to be a blind auction on such a frequent schedule," Joseph Fichera of Saber Partners LLC, a financial advisory firm, an early critic of the process, commented at the time.

In May 2006, the commission fined 15 securities firms $13 million for sharing information about auctions and managing the process behind the scenes. Instead of prohibiting the practices, the SEC told the dealers they could continue managing the auctions in the way they always had, provided they told investors what they were doing. The Bond Market Association, a dealer organization, said it would put together "best practices" guidelines.

Underwriters began disclosing how these auctions worked. In August 2006, for example, the Culinary Institute of America sold $15 million in auction-rate revenue bonds to finance renovation and expansion at its Hyde Park, New York, campus.

On page 11 of the official statement, or offering document to the bonds, under "Bidding by Initial Broker-Dealer," underwriter RBC Capital Markets spelled it all out. A broker-dealer was "permitted, but not obligated" to submit orders for its own account as a bidder or a seller, "and routinely does so in the auction rate securities market in its sole discretion." The broker-dealer may place bids to prevent an auction from failing, or from clearing at a rate the dealer does not believe reflects the market, "even after obtaining knowledge of some or all of the other Orders submitted through it." The broker-dealer may also "routinely encourage bidding by others in Auctions," so that the auctions do not fail, or to prevent an auction from clearing at a rate that does not accurately reflect the market.

The head of the SEC's Office of Municipal Securities expressed reservations about the process in September 2006, well after the settlement, saying it still was not being made clear to all investors that the sales were manipulated behind the scenes. Speaking at a conference in Chicago, the SEC's Martha Haines observed that "it may not be accurate to call this an auction. I fear that investor and issuer confidence in the legitimacy of the market may be undermined unless market participants take active steps to address these issues."

"The concern about the current auction process is that municipalities and companies that sell the bonds can't know whether they're getting the lowest borrowing costs and investors can't know whether they're over-paying," wrote Bloomberg's Darrell Preston.

Nothing much came of this intriguing pause. The auction-rate market hummed along until late 2007, when investors spooked by the subprime crisis and its impact on bond insurers forced yields higher; some auctions failed. In the week of February 13, 2008, the major dealers stopped bidding for the paper entirely, and then thousands of auctions failed.

The proximate cause of the death of the auction-rate securities market was the subprime crisis. Perhaps just as important, though, was a little-noticed March 2007 accounting rule change. When the Financial Accounting Standards Board started to require that auction-rate securities be listed on balance sheets as short-term investments rather than cash equivalents, the paper became less attractive to corporate and institutional investors. They began to sell. The Wall Street firms running the auctions took the paper off their hands—and sold it to individual investors.

This group, at the time estimated to number around 200,000, learned all about what happened when the nearly unthinkable occurred, and auctions failed, not once but again and again and again. They could see their money, they could collect yield, but they could not lay their hands on the principal. In some cases, usually those involving municipal securities, they got a higher penalty rate. This in turn spurred state and local issuers to convert the debt to variable or fixed rates, and so offered the holders redemption. Corporate issuers, including many closed-end funds that had sold auction-rate preferred shares, often had no such incentive. Even if they paid a penalty rate, it was usually capped. Investors found that these issuers were under no obligation to buy back debt that might not mature for 30 or 40 years or that even, in some cases, was perpetual. The dealers who orig-inally sold them the investments no longer wanted to bid, although they were still paid to run the auctions.

It soon became apparent that most individual investors had not quite appreciated what they were getting themselves into, and that many of the brokers who sold the securities to them did not quite understand what they were selling, in many cases marketing auction-rate paper as a sort of cash equivalent that was very safe and very liquid. Unsurprisingly, few buyers bothered to read prospectuses or offering documents detailing what they were purchasing, even if they were readily available. There were a lot of angry investors.

The states got involved soon after the freeze, with New York Attorney General Andrew Cuomo and Massachusetts Secretary of State William Galvin leading the effort to reunite investors with their money.

"One of the developments from the ARS episode is that securities regulators at the state level, organized through the North American Securities Administrators Association, as well as certain state Attorneys General, undertook a large number of coordinated actions, in cooperation with the SEC and FINRA, to achieve dealer repurchases of ARS sold to their customers," wrote financial adviser and lawyer Robert Doty in his 2010 book, *From Turmoil to Tomorrow.*

"This broad nationally coordinated effort . . . raises questions about whether there may be more state involvement in the municipal securities market in the future," wrote Doty. "State securities laws generally contain antifraud and anti-negligence provisions, often with longer statutes of limitation than under federal law and an easier reach toward secondary parties."

Municipal issuers rushed to convert their auction-rate paper, often using the same underwriters that had put together the auction deals in the first place; fund companies with national reputations to protect, such as Nuveen Investments Inc. and Eaton Vance Corporation, as early as March announced they were working on ways to offer stuck customers their money back, or "liquidity at par," as it was called.

The gridlock among the dealers was not really remedied until that summer. Massachusetts Secretary of State Galvin filed administrative complaints against UBS Securities on June 26 and then against Merrill Lynch & Company on July 31. The complaints spelled out in excruciating detail how the market collapsed, and were punctuated by embarrassing e-mails from bankers demanding that analysts produce more helpful reports about what an "opportunity" auction-rate securities represented, and in some cases exulting at the wave of new business from issuers desperate to convert their auction-rate bonds to fixed-rate instruments.

UBS, Merrill, and Citigroup announced plans to buy back individual investors' auction paper in early August. They were not the only entities affected by the freeze; institutions also owned auction-rate securities, as did states and municipalities. In November 2010, Citigroup agreed to buy back $869 million of auction-rate securities backed by federally guaranteed student loans it had sold the state, as well as repay Massachusetts for losses on $200 million it had sold. The state made its first investments in student-loan ARSs in 1998.

*See also* variable-rate demand obligations; window bonds.

*Sources:*

Commonwealth of Massachusetts, Office of the Secretary of the Commonwealth, Securities Division, Administrative Complaint in the Matter of Merrill, Lynch, Pierce, Fenner & Smith, Inc., July 31, 2008.

Commonwealth of Massachusetts, Office of the Secretary of the Commonwealth, Securities Division, Administrative Complaint in the Matter of UBS Securities LLC and UBS Financial Services Inc., June 26, 2008.

Doty, Robert. *From Turmoil to Tomorrow.* Sacramento, CA: American Governmental Financial Services Co. e-book, 2010.

"15 Broker-Dealer Firms Settle SEC Charges Involving Violative Practices in the Auction Rate Securities Market." Securities and Exchange Commission, May 31, 2006.

Mysak, Joe. "Culinary Institute Sells Muni Bonds to House Chefs." Bloomberg News, September 15, 2006.

Preston, Darrell. "SEC's Haines Says Rigged Bids May Undermine Auction-Rate Market." Bloomberg News, September 29, 2006.

"Prolonged Disruption of Auction Rate Market Could Impact Some U.S. Public Finance Ratings." Moody's Investors Service Special Report, March 2008.

Quint, Michael. "Rigged Bids, SEC Help Dealers as Auction Bonds Fail." Bloomberg News, November 21, 2007.

Quint, Michael. "Wall Street's Customer's Man Unmasked Auction-Rate." Bloomberg News, May 30, 2008.

Wong, Douglas. "Citigroup and Hawaii Settle $1.1 Billion Auction-Rate Dispute." Bloomberg News, November 24, 2010.

## auction sale

*See* advertised sale; negotiated sale.

## authorities

The proliferation of bond-issuing authorities is a periodically contentious issue in public finance. These creations, responsible only to the state and sometimes not even then, have been called unaccountable, a shadow government, and worse. Critics say their establishment and use subverts democracy and defies the will of the people. Proponents say authorities are indispensable and allow governments to finance much-needed, long-term projects that might otherwise never see the light of day. What is inarguable is their proliferation. Of the 89,476 governmental entities in the Census Bureau's Census of Governments of 2007, 37,381 were "special districts," a number that includes authorities but excludes school districts.

The first authority in the United States was established by compact between the states of New York and New Jersey in 1921. The Port of New York Authority, as it was then called, was modeled after the Port of London Authority, founded in 1908. The London entity got its name from the legislation setting it up: almost every paragraph began with "Authority is hereby given." A key feature of the Port of New York Authority was that it be self-supporting, despite not having any taxing power of its own.

This is still a feature of many of the authorities established today. They are created to finance projects off-budget and without the use of taxes or the approval of voters. The bonds they sell are secured by user fees, such as tolls, although sometimes municipalities may pledge to make up shortfalls in debt service.

Not all authorities are alike. Authorities are often set up to finance single ventures, such as convention centers or stadiums. Some authorities are set up to help finance job creation in the private sector, such as the Arkansas Development Finance Authority, which acts as a conduit, selling tax-exempt industrial development bonds on behalf of corporate issuers. And there are authorities set up specifically to help finance campus housing, like the New York Dormitory Authority, or college and hospital expansion, like the New Hampshire Health and Education Facilities Finance Authority.

*Sources:*

Mysak, Joe, and Judith Schiffer. *Perpetual Motion: The Illustrated History of the Port Authority of New York and New Jersey.* General Publishing Group, Santa Monica, CA, 1997.

U.S. Census Bureau, Census of Governments, 2007.

# B

## bank-qualified

The Tax Reform Act of 1986 eliminated the cost-of-carry deduction for banks buying municipal bonds, with the exception of small issuers, those municipalities that reasonably expected not to sell more than $10 million worth in a given year. Banks could deduct 80 percent of the interest cost for carrying those bonds. Such bonds have typically comprised almost half of the number of issues sold annually, but less than 10 percent of the total dollar volume.

Under terms of the American Recovery and Reinvestment Act of 2009, the small-issue exemption was increased to $30 million. There were calls for its extension, but this provision expired as scheduled, at the end of 2010.

Bank-qualified issues typically make up around 50 percent of the number of issues sold in a year. In 2009, for example, bank-qualified bonds accounted for 6,014 issues totaling $33 billion, out of the 11,731 bond issues totaling $409.9 billion sold, according to Thomson Reuters.

*See also* issuer concentration; tax-exemption.

*Sources:*
*The Bond Buyer/Thomson Reuters 2010 Yearbook.* New York: Sourcemedia, 2010.
MSRB online glossary at www.msrb.org.

## basis points

A basis point is 0.01 or 1/100 of a percentage point and is used to set yields.

14

## Baum pools

In April 2000, 12 underwriting firms agreed to pay $140 million to settle federal charges that they defrauded states and localities through an obscure process called "yield burning," defined as systematically overcharging issuers for the Treasury securities they use to construct bond refunding escrows. A five-year ordeal was at an end.

Or was it? Yield burning, it turned out, and as Internal Revenue Service (IRS) officials later ruefully admitted, never ended. Even as securities industry officials were negotiating a "global settlement" with federal regulators, including the Securities and Exchange Commission, the U.S. Justice Department, the Internal Revenue Service, and the Treasury, some firms were putting together transactions that produced hefty profits by "burning down" or otherwise diverting the yield on a variety of instruments used in the reinvestment of bond proceeds, often also subverting the bidding process for such instruments.

IRS officials started talking about the situation in early 2003, and shortly thereafter bond issuers began receiving letters from the IRS advising them that the interest on their bonds might no longer be deemed tax-exempt. Some of the issuers disclosed such adverse opinions from the IRS in material-event notices, so the market learned about the next generation of yield burning, which this time apparently featured bid rigging and price-fixing in connection with guaranteed investment contracts.

As the Capital Projects Finance Authority put it in a disclosure notice in 2003, "The IRS has taken the position that certain aspects of the bidding process for the guaranteed investment contract in which the proceeds of the Bonds were invested appeared to facilitate the issuance of arbitrage bonds. Specifically, the IRS has informed the Authority that it believes that actions by the persons involved in the bidding (excluding the Authority) served to divert arbitrage normally rebated to the government to the underwriter to be used in part to fund issuance costs."

The issuer continued, "The IRS has informed the Authority that it believes that the bidding was structured to allow the winning bidder to underpay for the Agreement and simultaneously overpay for other investment agreements which were treated as outside of the bond transaction." The authority said it reached a closing agreement with the IRS "utilizing funds provided by third parties" to keep the interest on its securities tax-exempt.

Among the deals caught up in this new IRS sweep were 19 transactions totaling more than $2 billion underwritten by the George K. Baum & Co.

firm in Kansas City, Missouri, including the $300 million Capital Projects Finance Authority bonds sold in 2000. The so-called blind pool deals, sold by municipalities to raise money for unspecified projects, were originally marketed between 1997 and 2001. The firm settled with the IRS in November 2006 for an undisclosed sum, without admitting the charges.

*See also* arbitrage; bid rigging; guaranteed investment contracts; yield burning.

*Sources:*

Barnett, Susanna Duff. "IRS Grills Firms about Pooled Bonds: Structure Puts Baum under Microscope." *Bond Buyer*, August 8, 2003.

Braun, Martin Z. "George K. Baum & Co. Settles Municipal Bond Cases with IRS." Bloomberg News, November 10, 2006.

Davis, Mark. "IRS Adds to Complaints about Kansas City, Mo.–Based Investment Firm." *Kansas City Star*, January 19, 2005.

Davis, Mark. "Three Issuers Pay IRS over Baum Bonds." *Kansas City Star*, May 13, 2005.

Hume, Lynn, and Craig T. Ferris. "Issuer Settles with IRS over Suspect Deal: Investment Provider Payment at Issue." *Bond Buyer*, July 2, 2003.

## Bell, California, pay scandal

The news that the city manager of Bell, California, a city of 38,000 (most of whose residents lived in poverty), about 10 miles from Los Angeles, made almost $800,000 a year in salary, and almost $1.5 million annually once additional perks and benefits were added in, spurred a statewide rush to reform transparency in public-sector compensation in the summer of 2010. The story resonated with taxpayers across the nation concerned about the strain that high salaries and generous public pension plans and other postemployment benefits were putting on state and local budgets.

The Bell story began after reporters Jeff Gottlieb and Ruben Vives of the *Los Angeles Times* wrote about the nearby town of Maywood firing its own workforce and outsourcing the jobs to Bell. "Gottlieb and Vives wrote the story, and soon learned that the Los Angeles County District Attorney was investigating Bell for high salaries," reported PublicCEO.com, a website specializing in California local government news. After filing a Public Records Act request, the reporters were able to write "Is a City Manager Worth $800,000?" in the July 15, 2010, *Times*.

Nobody, not even fellow city managers—who rushed to distance themselves from the situation—thought so.

The story revealed that Chief Administrative Officer Robert Rizzo was paid $787,637, Police Chief Randy Adams $457,000, and Assistant City Manager Angela Spaccia $376,288 in annual salaries.

"If that's a number people choke on, maybe I'm in the wrong business," Rizzo told the *Times.* "I could go into private business and make that money."

"There are darned few $787,000 salaried positions anywhere in the private sector for managers who run an organization of similar size," observed Girard Miller, a public-pension expert and consultant at financial adviser PFM Group in Los Angeles. Bell had 80 full-time employees. "What would make for an interesting law would be a statute prohibiting excessive compensation in the public sector, with a clawback provision," Miller said at the time. "That could apply to excessive-pay union contracts as well."

There were no apologists for the $800,000 city manager, although Mayor Oscar Hernandez of Bell put out a press release after the offending officials resigned, saying the salaries were "in line with similar positions over the period of their tenure," and calling the *Los Angeles Times* coverage "unfair and unwarranted." A few days later, the mayor backpedaled, calling the salaries "indefensible."

The story prompted a citizen revolt, with Bell taxpayers demanding that the offending civil servants, as well as the city council members (most of whom paid themselves $100,000 a year for admittedly part-time labors) who had approved the pay packages, resign. They did so days after the story broke.

The Bell scandal erupted at a time when Californians were reeling from stories about bloated public-sector salaries and the "$100,000-a-year pension club" whose ranks numbered more than 12,000 in the state. Bell seemed to epitomize an out-of-control and tone-deaf public sector that was operating out of the public's view and entirely on its own terms. At the same time, it seemed that nothing could be done about the exorbitant—and city-council-approved—compensation. It was widely reported that the city manager could expect to collect as much as $30 million in retirement pay.

It didn't turn out that way. The city manager, mayor, and most of the city council were later indicted on official corruption charges. Governor Arnold Schwarzenegger called for all civil servants' salaries to be posted online. The League of California Cities released a "Manager Compensation

Survey" in September 2010, and California Controller John Chiang posted a "Local Government Salaries and Compensation" database online. None of the city managers listed made anywhere near $800,000.

The *Los Angeles Times* won a Pulitzer Prize in 2011 for its Bell coverage.

*Sources:*

Allen, Sam, Abbey Sewell, and Patrick McGreevy. "California's City Officials Scramble to Limit Damage from Bell Scandal." www.latimes.com, July 29, 2010.

Gottlieb, Jeff, and Ruben Vives. "Is a City Manager Worth $800,000?" *Los Angeles Times*, July 15, 2010.

Hernandez, Oscar. "City of Bell City Council Takes Action, Puts City Safety, Services and Children First." Mayor's statement, July 23, 2010.

Lopez, Steve. "The Bleeding Bell Blues." www.latimes.com, July 21, 2010.

Rainey, James. "On the Media: How Many More Bells Are Out There?" www.latimes.com, July 21, 2010.

Search of "Local Government Salaries and Compensation" database at www .sco.ca.gov.

Spencer, James. "The Story of How the Bell Scandal Broke." PublicCEO .com, August 11, 2010.

Vives, Ruben, and Jeff Gottlieb. "3 Bell Leaders to Quit in Pay Scandal." www.latimes.com, July 23, 2010.

## bid rigging

In November 2006, the Federal Bureau of Investigation raided the offices of brokers who specialized in the reinvestment of bond proceeds business. The Department of Justice said it was conducting an "investigation of anticompetitive practices in the municipal bond industry." A criminal grand jury handed out subpoenas to brokers and securities firms. Thus a multiyear probe into what happens after municipal bond issuers borrow money and have to reinvest the proceeds was revealed.

This investigation had been going on for some time. It was sparked by a series of IRS audits conducted in the early 2000s that showed the bidding process for such things as guaranteed investment contracts and forward purchase agreements was being compromised by the brokers running the sales and the banks bidding for the business. The audits turned up certain extra payments made among various parties to the transactions, as well as audio evidence of collusion. IRS officials as early as 2003 described evidence of price-fixing, bid rigging, and the paying of kickbacks in return for business. This gaming of the system, according to the IRS, was another version of yield burning, a diversion of arbitrage profits that may result in tax-exempt bonds being declared taxable. Reporters learned about what was going on in the disclosure notices filed by issuers, which sometimes included IRS correspondence. Some bond issuers initiated lawsuits claiming financial harm, many based on little more than the necessarily vague stories that had run in the press.

The raids were conducted in November 2006. In February 2007, Bank of America announced that it had entered into a leniency agreement with the Department of Justice in return for its cooperation. By late 2009, the Department of Justice was passing out criminal indictments and collecting guilty pleas from bankers and brokers. In December 2010, Bank of America settled with the Department of Justice, the SEC, the IRS, the Office of the Comptroller of the Currency, and 20 state attorneys general for $137 million. The inquiry and prosecutions are ongoing.

A handful of lawsuits provided a glimpse into the investigation. Two in particular, one filed by the City of Los Angeles and the other by the Sacramento Municipal Utility District (SMUD), were like the Rosetta Stone to understanding what was happening, because they were based on oral and documentary evidence from Bank of America and the bank's cooperating witness.

One of the more interesting passages described how the investigation began: "According to a proffer provided by Bank of America to SMUD, Bank of America's outside counsel had discovered evidence suggesting the existence of violations of antitrust laws by members of Bank of America's municipal derivative desk in 2004, which they brought to the attention of the Department of Justice. The DOJ explicitly instructed Bank of America's counsel to keep this information confidential and not to take any actions that would alert other persons at Bank of America or outside Bank of America that this evidence had been discovered. The DOJ's investigation has apparently been conducted in cooperation with investigations by the IRS and SEC of certain municipal derivative transactions for violations of tax and securities laws. In the course of these investigations, the IRS and SEC has apparently discovered evidence that strongly suggested that participants in such transactions had also violated the criminal antitrust laws, which was brought to the DOJ's attention."

*See also* yield burning.

*Sources:*

Braun, Martin Z., and Jeff Bliss. "Bank of America Deal in Muni Case May Be 'Tip of the Iceberg.'" Bloomberg News, December 8, 2010.

Hume, Lynn. "Bank Pays $137 Million to Globally Settle Probe." *Bond Buyer*, December 7, 2010.

"In the Matter of Bank of America Securities." Order Instituting Administrative and Cease-and-Desist Proceedings, December 7, 2010.

Mysak, Joe. "Bank of America Tattles on Municipal Bond Dealers." Bloomberg News, February 14, 2007.

Mysak, Joe. "Feds Finally Examine the Muni Reinvestment Business." Bloomberg News, November 22, 2006.

*Sacramento Municipal Utility District v. Bank of America, et al.*, United States District Court, Eastern District of California, November 12, 2009.

Selway, William, and Martin Z. Braun. "Bankers Rigging Municipal Contract Bids Admit to Cover-Up Lies." Bloomberg News, November 24, 2010.

## black-box deals

This is a term generally used to describe a series of transactions sold during the 1980s by a boutique firm called Matthews & Wright but also by certain major Wall Street firms, and designed solely to earn arbitrage profits. The proceeds of a bond issue were invested in a guaranteed investment contract. As a question at the time had it: Where did the proceeds go? They went into a black box.

*See also* arbitrage.

## blind pools

These are large bond issues sold to fund unspecified projects. They were suspected by IRS and Treasury officials to be designed to earn arbitrage profits, and tax-law writers have made them more difficult to sell. The latest amendments in 2006 state that there must be commitments when the bonds are issued to borrow at least 30 percent of the proceeds; the issuer must expect to lend at least 30 percent of the proceeds within a year and 95 percent within three years; and the issuer must apply net proceeds that are not lent at that pace to redeem bonds within 90 days.

*See also* arbitrage.

*Source:*

Fredric Weber, Fulbright & Jaworski LLP, Houston, Texas.

## Blue List

Published between 1935 and 2001, the Blue List was a daily listing of municipal bonds being offered by dealers, and a barometer of activity in the secondary market. The publication was founded in 1935 by Henry T. Dunn, a banker at Chase National Bank, and was so-called because it was printed on tissue-thin blue paper. The first issue contained 188 offerings from 27 dealers totaling $15.7 million; the last issue contained bonds totaling $461 million. Its all-time high was $3.2 billion, posted in 1987. Traders would turn to it first thing in the morning to gauge activity, some saying it was "like a municipal bond novel," but filled with facts, like names, dollar volumes, prices, and yields. This was at a time when the reports of market activity were largely a fiction, painted in broad strokes with dealer anecdotes as well as details of new-issue pricings. The publication grew obsolete with the advent of Internet-based trading platforms and other means of delivering inventory listings electronically. Standard & Poor's purchased the publication in 1963. The last issue appeared on August 17, 2001.

*See also* EMMA; market activity.

*Sources:*

Fine, Jacob. "S&P to Bid Adieu to Blue List." *Bond Buyer*, June 19, 2001.
Resnick, Amy B. "After Six Decades, the Blue List Calls It Quits." *Bond Buyer*, August 20, 2001.

## BOCES

A New York State creation, BOCES stands for Board of Cooperative Education Services, which are formed by two or more school districts and an advisory district to provide services on a shared basis that would not be feasible in an individual school district.

## bond anticipation notes

A short-term borrowing done in advance of a longer-term bond offering.
*See also* tax anticipation notes.

## bond banks

Vermont established the first state bond bank in 1970, with, as it says on its website, "a mandate to provide municipalities with access to capital markets at the lowest possible cost." In simplest terms, bond banks offer access to the municipal market for small issuers that might not otherwise be able to do so efficiently or economically. Bond banks buy bonds and loans from various entities of from $20,000 right on up to several millions of dollars, and bundle them into a single issue for sale in the municipal market, thus affording even the smallest localities some economies of scale, as well as access to tax-exempt interest rates. The Vermont Municipal Bond Bank has issued $1.1 billion in tax-exempt bonds for more than 700 projects and refinancings. Historically, bond banks were established in small-population or rural states, including Maine, New Hampshire, North Dakota, and Alaska. Most states today have found ways to offer their smallest municipalities the means to borrow money at tax-exempt rates, even if not through something called a state bond bank. The Virginia Resources Authority, for example, operates as a bond bank.

*Sources:*

$73,870,000 Vermont Municipal Bond Bank tax-exempt and taxable bonds, 2010 series 1, 2, 3, and 4 official statement, June 30, 2010.
Vermont Municipal Bond Bank website at www.vmbb.org.

## The Bond Buyer

*The Bond Buyer*, the daily newspaper that reports on the municipal bond market, was founded in 1891 by William F.G. Shanks, a journalist and former Civil War correspondent who discovered that the most requests his news-clipping service received were for stories about bonds. The newspaper carries news stories and features; data, including proposed bond sales and results of bond sales; bond elections; volume statistics; and legal advertising. The newspaper also publishes a statistical yearbook and a quarterly directory of names and telephone numbers known as the Municipal Marketplace or, more popularly, the Red Book, and runs a series of conferences. For most of the twentieth century, the newspaper also produced a weekly edition.
    *See also* William F. G. Shanks.

### *Bond Buyer* indexes

The oldest gauge of yields, *The Bond Buyer*'s 20-Bond General Obligation Index was established in 1917. The newspaper surveys underwriters on how much 20 issuers, including New York City, would have to pay to borrow money for 20 years, and publishes the average every Thursday afternoon. The index has a rating roughly equivalent to AA. Eleven of the same bonds are also used to calculate a high-grade index with a rating of AA+.

The 20- and 11-bond indexes were calculated on a monthly basis until 1946, when they became weekly. The record high for the 20-bond index was 13.44 percent, which it hit on January 14, 1982. The record low was 1.29 percent, which it posted on February 14, 1946.

A weekly revenue bond index was added in 1979, comprising 25 revenue bonds maturing in 30 years, with an average rating of A+. Its high was 14.32 percent, also reached in January 1982. The newspaper introduced a one-year note index in 1989.

The issuers used in the calculation of all of the indexes change from time to time, as their fortunes and credit ratings rise and fall.

*Source:*
*Bond Buyer.*

### bond counsel

Lawyers who are paid to verify that a bond is validly binding as well as whether it is tax-exempt. The business is divided between national firms that work in multiple states and regional firms that transact business in a single state.

*See also* legal opinion.

### "Bond Daddies"

"Bond Daddies are a nomadic Southern strain of telephone securities salesmen known for their tenacity on the job and ostentation off," wrote Constance Mitchell in the *Wall Street Journal* in 1989. "From offices lined with banks of phones, they cast for business with ceaseless cold calls, treating the customers they sign up to huge markups, repeated short-term buying and selling, and an array of other trading ploys rewarding chiefly for the broker. The species first appeared in Memphis in the 1960s, selling tax-exempts to senior citizens across the country."

*Source:*

Mitchell, Constance. "The Bond Daddies: Fast-Talking Brokers in Little Rock Target Small-City Treasuries—Cold Calling to Town Officers, They Arrange to Trade Often at High Markup—Big Bucks and Braggadocio." *Wall Street Journal,* April 12, 1989.

## bond purchase agreement

The contract between the underwriter and the issuer "setting forth the final terms, prices, and conditions upon which the underwriter purchases a new issue of municipal securities in a negotiated sale."

*Source:*

MSRB online glossary at www.msrb.org.

## bond year

A bond year is $1,000 of debt outstanding for one year. The number of bond years in an issue is the number of bonds times the number of years from the dated date to maturity. The number of bond years is used to calculate the average life of an issue and its net interest cost.

## book-entry-only system

Until 1983, municipal bonds were sold in bearer format, that is, with physical certificates. They are now sold in this registered, electronic format, usually described at length in the official statement to the issue.

## Bradford zeroes

A series of 14 nursing home and housing bond transactions designed by J.C. Bradford & Company of Nashville, Tennessee, and sold between 1988 and

1992 was deemed an artifice and device by the Internal Revenue Service. A typical transaction worked in this way: A knowledgeable investor would buy a bond issue sold for a marginal project, usually through a private placement; purchase an escrow account of government securities to defease the bonds; and have the underwriter, in this case J.C. Bradford, remarket the issue as triple-A-rated zero-coupon bonds; they would then split the profit.

"The device used consisted of three steps," the IRS said in a Preliminary Adverse Determination letter sent to the Colorado Health Facilities Authority, one of the issuers of the bonds, in April 2001: "(1) the purchase of the bonds by an insider, (2) the immediate creation of a defeasance escrow account, and (3) the resale of the bonds to investors in the secondary market after security had been enhanced."

The IRS continued, "There was no reasonable expectation that the debt service on the bonds would ever be repaid from project revenues. . . . Without the resale of the bonds, there was no reasonable or feasible way to provide escrow funding for the future payment of principal and interest on the Series 1991 bonds."

In other words, when side deals involving a bondholder and an underwriter provide the only source of repayment on a bond issue, and the responsibility of the issuer and borrower for the bonds is eliminated, then the "governmental purpose" that allows for tax-exemption goes out the window, said the IRS. Because of the zero-coupon nature of the transactions, the 14 deals, sold in California, Colorado, Georgia, Illinois, New York, and Tennessee, had an ultimate maturity value of $3.8 billion.

In May 1999, an IRS official told the *Wall Street Journal* that the agency had sent out six "adverse letters" in connection with zero-coupon bond remarketing transactions, without identifying the transactions in question. Several of the issuers involved later disclosed that they had received such letters. Well before any of that, the Bradford zeroes traded in the market as if they had already been declared taxable.

In May 2001, UBS PaineWebber Group Inc., which had acquired Bradford the year before, said it was seeking to settle the matter with the IRS. In 2002, the company and seven law firms paid $30 million to the IRS so that the collection of bonds could retain their tax-exempt status.

*See also* tax-exemption.

*Sources:*

Connor, John. "IRS Investigates Municipal Zeroes for Tax Violations." *Wall Street Journal*, June 4, 1999.

Internal Revenue Service, Tax Exempt and Governmental Entities Division, Preliminary Adverse Determination Re: Colorado Health Facilities Authority Retirement Housing Revenue Bonds, Liberty Heights Project, Series 1991A, Series 1991B, April 4, 2001.

Mysak, Joe. "When Tax-Exempt Bonds Trade Like Treasuries." Bloomberg News column, July 15, 1999.

Preston, Darrell. "UBS PaineWebber Seeks Settlement on Bradford Zero-Coupon Bonds." Bloomberg News, May 1, 2001.

UBS PaineWebber. "J.C. Bradford Affiliate of UBS PaineWebber Settles Bond Audits." Press release, July 24, 2002.

## Build America Bonds

A feature of the American Recovery and Reinvestment Act of 2009, the Build America Bonds (BABs) program paid municipal bond issuers a 35 percent subsidy on the interest rate they paid to investors, provided the issuer sold the bonds as fully taxable. The bonds proved very popular with issuers, who found that, with the subsidy, the taxable yield they paid investors was even lower than the rate they could get selling tax-exempt bonds. Issuers ultimately sold $187 billion worth of BABs. The theory was that BABs would be revenue-neutral, and the amount of federal income tax investors paid would more or less match the subsidy. Their popularity with overseas investors and other investors who do not pay U.S. income tax seemed to explode this theory. Tax-exempt purists, meanwhile, saw in the creation of the BABs program a not-so-veiled attempt by the Treasury to replace the tax-exempt market entirely, as it had attempted to do many times in the past. Despite calls to extend the program, even at a lower subsidy rate, BABs expired at the end of 2010, on schedule. In early 2011, there was talk of resurrecting the program.

The Build America Bonds experiment did not proceed without glitches. Trading in the first few issues sold showed widespread flipping of the securities, indicating that they were undervalued at the initial pricing and produced windfall profits for a few large buyers who then resold them. Professionals said such mispricing was common enough on new structures, and was the result of underwriter price discovery. Issuers rarely expressed anything but delight with how the deals were sold.

Some critics pointed out the obvious—that the biggest states, which sold the most bonds, also got most of the federal subsidy—while others observed that most BABs were underwritten by the same relative handful of dealers that dominated the tax-exempt market, and that they were extremely profitable for the underwriters. Some issuers, too, bowed out of the program after the Internal Revenue Service said it might deduct taxes owed from the subsidy paid out on the bonds, reinforcing some issuers' innate fears that the subsidy might be tinkered with in the years ahead, even as the debt service remained the same.

The BABs program did result in bringing new investors into the municipal bond market, and because it lowered the amount of tax-exempts sold, it helped decrease tax-free yields.

*See also* tax-exemption.

*Sources:*

Cooke, Jeremy. "Build America Bond Issuers Pay $100 Million Extra in Bank Fees." Bloomberg News, November 27, 2009.

Keogh, Bryan, and Joe Mysak. "Build America Bonds Give 'Wholesalers' $347 Million." Bloomberg News, April 24, 2009.

McDonald, Michael. "Building America with Obama Bonds Signals Munis' Fall." Bloomberg News, June 25, 2009.

# C

## CAFR

The Comprehensive Annual Financial Report (CAFR) is, in other words, a bond issuer's annual audited financial statements. Securities and Exchange Commission (SEC) Rule 15c2-12 prohibits underwriters from buying municipal bonds unless issuers promise to provide continuing disclosure. Most large, frequent issuers will do so by sending these annual reports to the MSRB's Electronic Municipal Market Access (EMMA) system for posting.

While the SEC requires corporate borrowers to file their annual audited financials within 60 to 90 days after the ends of their business years, no such time constraints are placed on municipal bond issuers. "The range in reporting time is huge among the slowest and fastest municipal bond borrowers when it comes to closing the books and providing the information to the public," wrote Richard Ciccarone, president and chief executive officer of Merritt Research Services LLC, in 2010. "The average time it takes for an audit document to be signed after the close of the fiscal year is about five months," he wrote, adding that it can take another month before the document is approved by the governmental body and sent out. Large, single-purpose wholesale electric agencies were the quickest to file, with a median time of just over three months from the end of a fiscal year, whereas states were the slowest, with a median time of just under six months. "No state would have passed the SEC corporate requirement of 60 to 90 days," he wrote.

*See also* Rule 15c2-12; Tower Amendment.

*Sources:*

Ciccarone, Richard A. "Just How Slowly Do Municipal Bond Annual Audit Reports Waddle In after the Close of the Fiscal Year?" Merritt Research Services, 2010.

Pope, Robert Dean. *Making Good Disclosure: The Role and Responsibilities of State and Local Officials under Federal Securities Laws.* Chicago: Government Finance Officers Association, 2001.

## calls

A call is an issuer's right to redeem its bonds prior to maturity. The most common call is in 10 years at a price of 100 percent or par. An issuer may also make use of premium calls, in which it pays the bondholder more than 100 percent to call its bonds, various optional and emergency calls, and mandatory sinking-fund redemptions to pay off debt early. Not all issuers choose to exercise 10-year calls, and some bonds are sold as noncallable. Housing bonds are notorious for the number and variety of calls available to the issuers. Calls are more of a risk than is default in the municipal bond market.

*See also* escrowed to maturity.

## Canadian interest cost

*See* true interest cost.

## capital appreciation bond

A capital appreciation bond (CAB) is a bond purchased at a deep discount to face value, which pays principal, and "investment return is considered to be in the form of compounded interest rather than accreted original issue discount," according to the Municipal Securities Rulemaking Board. "For this reason only the initial principal amount of a CAB would be counted against a municipal issuer's statutory debt limit, rather than the total par value, as in the case of a traditional zero-coupon bond."

*See also* zero-coupon bonds.

*Source:*

MSRB online glossary at www.msrb.org.

## capital gains

Investors are subject to capital gains taxes in a variety of situations: if they buy a bond and sell it later at a higher price (for example, if a bond is prerefunded, the price will jump, and some investors choose to sell and record a profit); if they buy a bond at a discount and it gets called or it matures at par; if they sell a zero-coupon bond before maturity and its price is above the accreted value; or if they buy a bond at par and it gets called at a premium.

*Sources:*

MSRB online glossary at www.msrb.org.
Wilen, John. E-mail with investor John Wilen, April 4, 2011.

## certificates of participation

Certificates of participation represent an interest in payments that the issuer has promised to make, and are subject to annual appropriation. The issuers of these kinds of securities usually state that their city councils or legislatures are under no obligation to make such appropriations.

*See also* lease financings; risk factors.

## Chapter 9

Chapter 9, the section of U.S. bankruptcy law pertaining to municipalities, is widely misunderstood. For one thing, states cannot enter bankruptcy. For another, Chapter 9 is strictly voluntary; creditors cannot petition for a municipality to be declared bankrupt. For a third, municipalities have to prove that they are, in fact, insolvent, and can no longer pay their bills. They also have to show that they have attempted to avoid bankruptcy. Finally, localities have to be specifically authorized to enter Chapter 9; 26 states forbid their municipalities to do so, and most others discourage it. In 2011, for example, Michigan assembled SWAT teams of financial managers designed to take over municipalities that could no longer make the hard decisions needed to avoid insolvency. There is a reason bankruptcy is rare in the municipal market.

Chapter 9 is no panacea for all financial ills, and despite the enthusiasm among some commentators in calling for more municipalities to seek its protection in the wake of the Great Recession (primarily in order to reject collective bargaining agreements, including union salary and other benefits), most municipalities seek to avoid bankruptcy if at all possible. It is costly, time-consuming, and unpredictable, and even the lawyers who specialize in the practice call it a last resort. Well before a municipality files for Chapter 9, a state government usually finds it in its interest to enter the fray, fearing that the bankruptcy of a large, full-service municipality within its borders would harm the borrowing ability of all its other municipalities. In 1975, for example, New York State took an active role when New York City lost access to the credit markets, setting up a financial control board to provide oversight and the Municipal Assistance Corporation to supply cash for the city, which had a bankruptcy filing drawn up.

In January 2010, Fitch Ratings cautioned governmental entities against even thinking about it. "Bankruptcy compromises bondholder security," the company said in a Special Comment. "Therefore, the consideration of bankruptcy as a viable option for relief in itself calls into question the issuer's willingness to pay commitment."

Until the Great Depression, there were no specific laws governing municipal bankruptcy. In 1934, Congress amended the Bankruptcy Act of 1898 to include municipalities. The new law was ruled unconstitutional by the Supreme Court in 1936 because it impinged on state sovereignty, and legislation was recast in 1937. In 1938, according to George Hempel's *The Postwar Quality of State and Local Debt*, 35 municipal bankruptcies were filed, a number that rose to 71 in 1939 and a record 104 in 1940. In 1946, Chapter 9 became a formal part of the Bankruptcy Act.

Chapter 9 is relatively narrow in scope. "The limited but vital role of the Bankruptcy Court is to supervise the effective and appropriate adjustment of municipal debt," wrote James E. Spiotto, a partner in the law firm of Chapman & Cutler in Chicago and an expert in Chapter 9, in *The Handbook of Municipal Bonds*. This includes collective bargaining agreements with public employee labor unions.

"The court cannot take over operation of the municipality, remove governing board members, direct the actions of the governing board or appoint a receiver or trustee to run the affairs of the municipality," wrote John Knox and Marc Levinson, attorneys at Orrick, Herrington & Sutcliffe LLP in "Municipal Bankruptcy: Avoiding and Using Chapter 9 in Times of Fiscal Stress." The firm worked on the 2009 bankruptcy of Vallejo, California, which both rejected some collective bargaining agreements and impaired certain classes of bondholder. Some lawyers believe that general obligation debt could be compromised in bankruptcy, while debt that relies on special revenues would be spared; however, there is no unanimity on this point among lawyers.

There is no guarantee of success with Chapter 9. If a plan of adjustment cannot be produced, the case can be dismissed, "and the municipality continues to exist with all of its problems and claims as it did before the bankruptcy, with whatever remedies are available to the municipality and its creditors under state law," wrote Knox and Levinson.

"It's not a strategy," Knox later said in an interview. "All it does is give you some breathing space to rearrange your affairs."

For all these reasons, Chapter 9 is rare. The record year for municipal bankruptcy filings since 1980 was 1991, when 18 Chapter 9 cases were filed (this was also a record year for municipal bond defaults, eclipsed only in 2008), according to the American Bankruptcy Institute. In 2010, Chapter 9 filings fell to six from 10 the previous year, and included two sanitary and improvement districts in Nebraska, an Idaho hospital, a municipal utility district in Texas, a community improvement district in Missouri, and a South Carolina toll road.

*See also* default; New York City financial crisis of 1975; Orange County, California.

*Sources:*

Applegate, Austin. "Municipals and Chapter 9: An Overview." Barclays Capital Municipal Credit Research, February 23, 2010.

Hempel, George H. *The Postwar Quality of State and Local Debt.* Cambridge, MA: National Bureau of Economic Research, 1971.

Knox, John. Interview with John Knox, Orrick, Herrington & Sutcliffe, January 3, 2011.

Knox, John, and Marc Levinson. "Municipal Bankruptcy: Avoiding and Using Chapter 9 in Times of Fiscal Stress." Orrick, Herrington & Sutcliffe LLP, 2009.

Newland, Misty, and James Wiemken. "What Credit Concerns Does Talk of Municipal Bankruptcy Raise?" Standard & Poor's, December 15, 2009.

Raphael, Richard, et al. "The Perils of Considering Municipal Bankruptcy," Fitch Ratings, January 27, 2010.

Skeel, David. "Give States a Way to Go Bankrupt." *Weekly Standard,* November 29, 2010.

Spiotto, James E. "Chapter 9: The Last Resort for Financially Distressed Municipalities," in Feldstein, Sylvan G., and Frank J. Fabozzi. *The Handbook of Municipal Bonds.* Hoboken, NJ: John Wiley & Sons, 2008.

Vekshin, Alison, and Martin Z. Braun. "Vallejo's Bankruptcy 'Failure' Scares Cities into Cutting Costs." Bloomberg News, December 14, 2010.

## charter schools

Charter schools are independent public institutions founded by parents and teachers dissatisfied with the traditional public school system. A charter school is funded by tax dollars, but sets its own curriculum, budget, and hiring practices. The school operates under a short-term contract, or charter, from a school district. The money a school gets funds operations, not capital needs; the schools themselves have no taxing power. In recent years, several charter schools have tapped the municipal bond market for money to build. They usually pay high yields, because the schools typically have almost no track records, are small in size, and enjoy limited demand, and because of the nature of the charters themselves, which typically must be renewed every three to five years. Since 1999, about $2.5 billion in rated tax-exempt debt has been sold for charter schools; more often than not, the schools sell unrated debt. Standard & Poor's in 2011 said it has ratings on $1.8 billion in bonds issued by 123 charter schools in 18 states and the District of Columbia, the top three states being Colorado, Michigan, and Texas. Most of the debt (59 percent) was rated BBB–. Colorado is the only state that backs charter schools through a moral obligation program. Texas was considering allowing the state Permanent School Fund to back qualified charter school debt in 2011.

*Sources:*

Hitchcock, David G. "U.S. Charter Schools Hit Their Stride." Standard & Poor's, April 28, 2011.

Mildenberg, David. "Texas May Provide Guarantees for Charter School Debt Offerings." Bloomberg News, March 3, 2011.

Mysak, Joe. "A Colorado Charter School's Bond Makes the Grade." Bloomberg News, September 23, 1999.

## closed-end funds

*See* mutual funds.

## cogeneration projects

*See* garbage.

## colleges and universities

Nonprofit colleges and universities routinely sell both taxable and tax-exempt debt to finance construction and development, and in recent years certain secondary schools have done so, too. These require more research than the typical school district, whose bonds are generally secured by taxes and streams of state money and often also may be backed by state intercept programs should the district run into financial distress. For investors, the usual rules apply: the safest securities are those sold by large, selective, well-known, and well-endowed schools.

## community development districts

A community development district (CDD) bond is a variety of bond sold in Florida to encourage real estate development, hence a version of what are nationally termed *dirt bonds*.

CDDs were authorized by the Florida Uniform Community Development District Act of 1980, which provided for the establishment of independent districts to manage and finance community development. The districts have the power to sell general obligation, revenue, and special assessment bonds to pay for things like roads, sewers, and utility lines. The bonds are repaid from taxes and special assessments levied on the property. Until the property is improved and houses are sold, these fees are paid by the developer. If the developer is unable to sell houses or home sites, the bonds default.

Florida has more than 600 such districts, and the real estate bust resulted in widespread CDD defaults. Of the 183 municipal bond issuers that defaulted in 2009, 97 were Florida CDDs. In 2008, 43 of the 162 bonds that went bust were CDDs. The carnage surpassed similar dirt-district meltdowns in Colorado in the 1980s, Texas in the late 1980s and early 1990s, and California in the 1990s.

*See also* dirt bonds.

*Sources:*

"Florida Bust Propels Muni Default Spike: Chart of the Day." Bloomberg News, September 1, 2009.

"Florida CDD Update." *Distressed Debt Securities Newsletter,* December 2009.

Hart, Jerry. "Eaton Vance Dumps Dirt Bonds as Florida Land Districts Default." Bloomberg News, March 9, 2010.

## competitive sale

Also known as advertised sale or auction sale, competitive sale is where an issuer offers its bonds for sale and underwriters bid against each other to purchase the bonds. Once the dominant method of sale, the competitive route is now used to sell roughly 20 percent of the dollar volume of municipal bonds that are sold each year.

Proponents of competitive sale say it results in the best prices and removes politics from the process, because the winners of the bonds are determined strictly by the numbers. The underwriter bidding the best price wins. There have been several studies done on both sides of the issue, but none so comprehensive as to be conclusive.

The underwriter bidding the best price wins. With a negotiated sale, the issuer chooses the winning underwriter and discusses terms of the issue's pricing. Several studies have been done on both methods and which is best for issuers to use, but none so comprehensive as to be conclusive.

*See also* negotiated sale.

## computers

The first use of a computer to calculate a bid for municipal bonds took place on August 17, 1961, when the State Street Securities Corp., a subsidiary of William Morris & Co., submitted a bid for $100 million in California school bonds. Bidding alone against a 400-member syndicate headed by Bank of America, the Morris firm won, with a bid producing a net interests cost of 3.7544 percent compared to 3.860 percent for the syndicate. "A Brilliant Coup," wrote *The Daily Bond Buyer.* "California Bond Gamble Pays Off," headlined the *New York Times,* which reported that the firm made a profit of $1 million after this experiment with "the complexities of electronic 'thinking' machinery." The newspaper observed that the firm had been known primarily for its computer-driven portfolio evaluation services, and marveled, "Only a week or so ago, the device turned out for a big bank in fifteen minutes what had taken six persons two weeks to do last year."

Morris won another California bond issue a month later, and the firm was on its way. Over the next 20 months, the firm won more, and smaller, bond deals. On May 8, 1963, the firm won a $122 million Washington Public Power Supply System revenue bond issue. The bid proved too aggressive, and the firm lost $3 million. The Morris firm closed in September of that year, but the point had been made. Computers were here to stay.

*Sources:*

Doran, John J. "Back in Prehistory, 400 Firms Lost to One with a Computer. They Got the Idea." *Bond Buyer*, October 7, 1991.

Heffernan, Paul. "California Bond Gamble Pays Off." *New York Times*, August 20, 1961.


## constitutional protection of tax-exemption

*See* tax-exemption.


## convention centers

Stop the madness!

There are "some doubts that the meeting/convention business is active enough to absorb an ever increasing amount of additional floor space. One must question whether many of these erstwhile host cities, now actively borrowing, will be left with underutilized convention halls and, in some cases, convention hotels. However, there is no question that some cities will be left with heavy debt burdens extending many years into the future."

These words of caution were written not in 2011, or in 2010, but by two analysts for the company then known as John Nuveen & Co. in Chicago, in October 1994, in a report entitled "An Investor's Guide to Municipal Convention Center Bonds." The authors noted that in 1993, U.S. convention centers operated at an average of 41 percent of capacity.

That was tens of millions of square feet ago, and still cities and towns across the United States are building or planning to build new convention centers, expanding existing ones, and either building or expanding adjoining convention center headquarters hotels, because, as all paid consultants know, convention centers just won't work as well as they ought to unless there is a 500-room, 1,000-room, or 2,000-room hotel right next door.

What fueled the ongoing convention center space race? The promise was that putting up these buildings would translate into trade shows and conventions and thousands of visitors, all of whom would spend millions of dollars in a city's theaters, restaurants, museums, stadiums, and hotels. Despite mounting evidence that the actual results are much more modest, and perhaps may even disappoint, and after almost two decades of analytical skepticism and dissent, mayors and city councils across the land seem as enthusiastic as ever to undertake such multimillion-dollar projects. Small cities dreamed of becoming larger, larger ones dreamed of becoming destination locations for event planners, and the largest hoped still to challenge the two cities that seemed to be the clear winners of the so-called space race: Las Vegas, Nevada, and Orlando, Florida.

Convention centers were never expected to pay their way, but to create new jobs, stimulate local economies, and boost sales tax and other revenue. Cities and towns financed their construction with bond issues, usually secured by an array of taxes and fees but sometimes also with their general obligation pledges. In 1998, tax law changed to allow municipalities to finance convention center hotels. "The change allowed cities to set up nonprofit corporations to borrow money by selling revenue bonds," Standard & Poor's noted in 2003. "Publicly financed and owned convention center hotels allow cities to borrow at lower interest rates by accessing the tax-exempt market, and at the same time give them more control over how the hotels are built and run. The convention center hotels also produce income for the cities. However, the cities have to back up the hotel projects with tax dollars and don't collect the property taxes that a private hotel would generate. In these types of situations the cities are investing in the hotel as an 'insurance policy' for its convention center and urban renewal efforts." In undertaking the construction of those attached or adjacent hotels designed to provide conventioneers with walkable rooms, cities in the waning years of the twentieth century quickly found themselves going where private companies and developers feared to tread. And so they got into the hotel business themselves, financing and building the structures on their own, often securing the bond issues sold to build them with taxes on rooms in other hotels in the same city. The cities then paid professionals to manage the businesses.

Are cities chasing the past? Certainly today such events as conferences and conventions seem like expensive and time-consuming luxuries. Attendance at the *TradeShow Week* top 200 events has been unpromising at best. In 1988, 3.68 million people attended the top 200 shows. This rose to a peak of 5.08 million in 1996 and declined after that. In 2009, attendance was 3.84 million. (*TradeShow Week* went out of business in 2010.)

Definitive aggregate statistics are hard to come by, and the consulting firms that provide feasibility studies for convention centers and headquarters hotels refuse to elaborate on their findings. One feasibility study in 2009 showed that spending in the meetings business had increased 14 percent between 1989 and 2007. Exhibit space, meanwhile, grew more than 83 percent during the same period. Recent attendance figures for various individual convention centers showed steep declines during the Great Recession.

Heywood Sanders, a professor of public policy at the University of Texas at San Antonio, perhaps the foremost critic of convention centers as economic engines, observed in an interview in 2011 that the big question was why cities continue to pursue the business: "Part of the answer is fiscal— the use of revenue bonds tied to visitor taxes that don't require voter approval has changed the local political landscape. But the larger answer is that in city after city, local business leaders see a new or expanded convention center as a means of changing the landscape of development. A big new center represents a public commitment to downtown renewal, or an anchor for new investment. In other words, it is only rarely about visitor activity or economic impact. It's about land."

*See also* tourist attractions.

*Sources:*

Cohen, David I., and John W. Illyes. "An Investor's Guide to Municipal Convention Center Bonds." John Nuveen & Co., October 1994.

$506,300,000 Dallas, Texas, Convention Center Authority, official statement, August 20, 2009.

Macdonald, Laura A. "U.S. Cities Seek Funding Alternatives for Convention Center Headquarter Hotels." Standard & Poor's, June 18, 2003.

Mysak, Joe. "Vegas Raises Cash, Taunts Rivals in Show Business." Bloomberg News, November 16, 2007.

"Q&A: Heywood Sanders," Bloomberg Brief Municipal Market, February 25, 2011.

Sanders, Heywood. "Space Available: The Realities of Convention Centers as Economic Development Strategy." Research Brief, Brookings Institution, January 2005.

Sanders, Heywood. Testimony on Convention Centers and Local Economic Development, House of Representatives, Domestic Policy Subcommittee, March 2007.

## CPI-linked municipals

Inflation is the scourge of fixed-income investors. As inflation rises, their income remains the same, and their purchasing power erodes. To counter the effect of inflation for bond investors, the U.S. Treasury in January 1997 sold the first issue of Treasury inflation-protected securities (TIPS), tied to changes in the consumer price index (CPI). Bankers immediately looked for ways to copy the so-called TIPS approach to the tax-exempt market. In March 1997, Goldman, Sachs & Company priced the first issue of CPI-linked municipals, $40 million of water and sewer revenue bonds for the city of Orlando, Florida.

Here's how it worked: The semiannual coupon pays investors the percentage change in the CPI over the previous six-month period, plus a fixed spread. As Goldman Sachs explained it at the time in a marketing memorandum, "If CPI inflation continued at 3.66%, the annualized rate for February, 1997, and if the spreads were 1.00%, the coupon on the Muni CPIs would be 4.66% for the year."

The underlying spread on such issues has ranged from as little as 20 basis points to as much as 210. Only about three dozen issuers—including New York City; Miami-Dade County, Florida; the Southern Minnesota Municipal Power Agency; and the state of Connecticut—have sold $2 billion in CPI-linked municipals since the instrument was created, usually as part of larger bond deals. They normally enter into swaps to hedge their floating-rate risk.

With the CPI currently hovering around 1 percent, the market for CPI-linked munis has remained almost nonexistent: nobody is very worried about inflation. Expect issuance to pick up when the inflation number tops 4 percent.

*Sources:*

"City of Orlando, Florida, Offers the First Issue of Inflation-Protected Tax-Exempt Bonds; Goldman Sachs, as Sole Manager, to Price Today Approximately $40 Million Muni CPIs." Press release, March 27, 1997.

Crosby, Chris. "Understanding Municipal CPI Bonds." Raymond James & Associates, April 10, 1997.

Lamp, Evan. "Why Consider CPI-Based Municipals?" Merrill Lynch & Co., June 18, 1997.

## cram-down

Issuers experiencing financial distress are sometimes able to seek accommodation from investors by delaying repayment of interest and principal. In extreme cram-down cases, issuers may seek to replace their bonds with a smaller amount of securities, and with lower or even sometimes no coupon interest.

*See also* tourist attractions.

## credit default swaps

Common in the corporate market, credit default swaps (CDSs) have been used in the municipal market only since 2004, in part because insurance against default had been readily available.

Credit default swaps allow investors to buy protection against an issuer failing to make debt-service payments. Their cost is measured in basis points. A basis point on a CDS protecting $10 million of debt for five years is equivalent to $1,000. So, for example, if a CDS was quoted on an issuer at 100 basis points, it would cost $100,000 to insure $10 million of that particular issuer's bonds for five years. Buyers of CDSs need not own the underlying bonds.

There are CDSs available on major U.S. municipal issuers like California, Illinois, Texas, New York State, and New York City. In May 2008, Markit Group Ltd., a London-based financial data firm that also offers corporate and mortgage credit default swaps, introduced a municipal credit default swap index, the Markit MCDX index, composed of 50 municipal issuers and designed by seven securities firms, including Merrill Lynch & Company, Goldman Sachs Group Inc., and UBS AG. The index allows investors to take a point of view on the market as a whole. In other words, for the first time investors could short the entire municipal market if they felt issuers' credits were deteriorating.

Stories about the index, and about how a number of banks and securities firms were recommending it to customers at the same time they also underwrote state and municipal bonds, got the attention of a number of elected officials. These officials suggested that widening credit default swap spreads and the accompanying publicity this would garner might drive up their cost of borrowing. For example, California treasurer Bill Lockyer in early 2010 asked a number of firms that had underwritten the state's bonds to detail their participation in the CDS market. "Data reported in the news media and other sources show that the prices, or spreads, on California CDS wrongly brand our bonds as a greater risk than those issued by such nations as Kazakhstan, Croatia, Bulgaria and Thailand," he wrote. "The perception of risk could adversely affect the price of our bonds when we go to market." He posted their replies on the state treasury website.

Not everyone thought municipal credit default swaps were evil. "Issuers benefit when investors have access to low-cost information that complements traditional credit ratings, even if that information suggests higher default risk," Justin Marlowe, an assistant professor at the Daniel J. Evans School of Public Affairs at the University of Washington in Seattle, wrote in a study in 2010. "My sense is this happens because high credit default swap spreads reassure investors that a low-management-quality issuer's 'dirty laundry' has been aired in full," he explained. "It's counterintuitive, I know."

*See also* insurance.

*Sources:*

Dugan, Ianthe Jeanne. "Scrutiny for Bets on Municipal Debt." *Wall Street Journal*, May 14, 2010.

Marlowe, Justin. "Municipal Credit Default Swaps: Implications for Issuers." Study by Justin Marlowe, Assistant Professor of Public Affairs, Daniel J. Evans School of Public Affairs, University of Washington, August 11, 2010.

McDonald, Michael, and Shannon D. Harrington. "Merrill, Goldman among Firms Starting Muni Credit Default Index." Bloomberg News, April 29, 2008.

"MCDX: Municipal CDX Index." High Grade Strategy and Credit Derivatives Research, J.P. Morgan Securities, May 1, 2008.

McNichol, Dunstan, and Sharona Coutts. "Goldman Sachs Sells New Jersey Bonds, Then Warns of Default." *Newark Star-Ledger*, November 24, 2008.

"Municipal Strategy Note." J.P. Morgan Securities, February 25, 2010.

Mysak, Joe. "California Declares War on State Bond Short-Sellers." Bloomberg News, April 27, 2010.

Mysak, Joe. "Goldman Draws Ire for Advising Default Swaps against New Jersey." Bloomberg News, December 10, 2008.

*New York Times.* "Short-Selling on States Can Pay Off." DealBook, October 3, 2008.
"State of the Markets: Best Long and Short Risk Strategies." Goldman, Sachs & Co., September 2008.

## credit enhancement

Credit enhancement is using a third-party guarantee to lower risk and costs when borrowing money. Municipal bond insurance is a good example of credit enhancement; using a bank letter of credit or state intercept program is another.

*See also* insurance; Texas Permanent School Fund.

## current refunding

*See* refunding.

## CUSIP

Standard & Poor's Corporation runs the American Bankers Association's Committee on Uniform Securities Identification Procedures (CUSIP) number program assigned by CUSIP Global Services to government and municipal securities and to stocks of registered U.S. companies. The CUSIP number consists of nine characters. The first six identify the issuer, the following two identify the issue, and the final character is a check digit. S&P collects licensing fees for the numbers, which range from thousands to hundreds of thousands of dollars.

*Sources:*

Ackerman, Andrew. "Fight over CUSIP Fees Heats Up." *Bond Buyer*, November 11, 2010.
Preston, Darrell. "SEC Asked to End S&P's 'Chilling' Fees for Security ID Numbers." Bloomberg News, November 11, 2010.

# D

## "Deadly Sins"

In amending Rule 15c2-12 in 1994, the Securities and Exchange Commission (SEC) said there were 11 material events that must be disclosed to investors as soon as possible. They rapidly took on the name of the 11 Deadly Sins. They are:

1. Principal and interest payment delinquencies.
2. Nonpayment-related defaults.
3. Unscheduled draws on reserves.
4. Unscheduled draws on credit enhancements.
5. Substitution of credit or liquidity providers, or their failure to perform.
6. Adverse tax opinions or events affecting the tax-exempt status of the security.
7. Modifications to rights of security holders.
8. Bond calls.
9. Defeasances.
10. Matters affecting collateral.
11. Rating changes.

In July 2009, the SEC proposed amendments to Rule 15c2-12 to include tender offers, bankruptcies, and mergers.

The material events notices are sent to the MSRB's Electronic Municipal Market Access (EMMA) system to be disseminated.

*See also* disclosure; EMMA; MSRB; Rule 15c2-12; Tower Amendment.

## debt per capita

Net tax-supported debt per capita is one measure of how much money states and municipalities have borrowed. Moody's Investors Service defines it as "debt secured by state operating resources which could otherwise be used for state operations. Any debt to which state resources are pledged for repayment is considered to be net tax-supported debt." Moody's publishes an annual "State Debt Medians Report" survey in the spring, summarizing the previous year's data. In 2009, according to the 2010 report, state net tax-supported debt increased 10.3 percent, to $460 billion from $417 billion, reflecting increased issuance to meet demand, the need for budget relief, a low interest-rate environment, and the introduction of the Build America Bonds and Qualified School Construction Bonds programs. The report also noted that Connecticut ranked first in net tax-supported debt per capita, at $4,859, and was followed by Massachusetts at $4,606; Hawaii, $3,996; New Jersey, $3,669; and New York, $3,135. At No. 50 on the list was Nebraska, with $15; at No. 49 was Iowa, with $73. The median for the states was $936. As a percentage of personal income, the median for the United States was 2.5 percent.

*Source:*

2010 State Debt Medians Report. Moody's Investors Service, May 2010.

## default

A rare occurrence in the modern municipal bond market, default is the failure to make timely payment of principal and interest, or to comply otherwise with features of a bond's indenture.

Investors in modern times had to look hard to find bonds likely to default. They usually found them by chasing yield in the unrated portion of the market. Moody's Investors Service, in a Special Comment on U.S. municipal bond defaults and recoveries, found that of the thousands of bonds it had rated annually from 1970 to 2009, only 54 had defaulted, with 78 percent of those in health care or housing. This in itself is important to remember in terms of default. When ratings companies discuss default, they usually refer only to the bonds they have rated, not to the market at large.

Buyers of munis that go bad tend to get back more on average than investors in corporate bonds. The average municipal bond recovery is 66 percent of par value compared with 42 percent for corporate securities, according to Moody's.

In a study of defaults published in 2003, Fitch Ratings explained why holders of governmental bonds fared best: "If a payment is missed on a tax-backed or essential service (e.g., water/sewer) revenue bond, there is generally a full recovery, because the municipality is an ongoing entity, and the debt remains in force (very few municipalities have become 'ghost towns' in the 20th century)."

The first U.S. issuer to default on its bonds was the city of Mobile, Alabama, in 1839, on $513,000 in debt. The proximate causes were two fires, a yellow fever epidemic, and the depression of 1837, according to A.M. Hillhouse in his landmark 1936 work, *Municipal Bonds: A Century of Experience*. The default was cured in 1843.

The Great Depression produced the most defaults. From 1929 to 1937, 4,771 issuers defaulted on $2.85 billion in bonds, or about 15 percent of the total amount of state and local debt outstanding, according to George Hempel's *The Postwar Quality of State and Local Debt* (1971). Most of these were general obligation bonds, revenue bonds having been sold only since 1885. Only 12 revenue bonds defaulted during this period, totaling $18.7 million.

Almost 30 percent of the bonds that defaulted during the Depression were sold by reclamation, levee, irrigation, and drainage districts. And the defaults were concentrated: Issuers in 14 states accounted for about 80 percent of the bonds that failed to pay. Total losses to investors amounted to $100 million, or one-half of 1 percent of the average amount of municipal debt outstanding.

To put this into perspective, the total volume of bonds sold annually during this period was usually a little more than $1 billion, a mark that was breached only in 1921. Annual bond sales did not break the $2 billion mark until 1947, and broke the $10 billion mark in 1963.

In the modern era, it has been claimed that municipal bonds have a default rate of less than 1 percent. That's true, but not all municipal bonds are alike. General obligation bonds—that is, those backed by the full faith and credit taxing power of a municipality—have a default rate of one-quarter of 1 percent, Fitch said in a 2003 study; industrial development bonds (IDBs), those sold on behalf of corporate issuers and "municipal" in name only, have a default rate closer to 15 percent. In a 2000 study of defaults, Standard & Poor's J. J. Kenny estimated that it took an average of 42 months to settle an IDB default, with the average recovery being 50 cents on the dollar.

Since 1980, the most bonds defaulted in 1991 (259 defaults), with a dollar total that year of $4.95 billion. In 2008, the record was broken in terms of dollar volume, $8.53 billion, although the actual number of deals was smaller, at 168.

In the wake of the Great Recession, and in particular after the sovereign debt crises in Greece and Ireland, there was intense media scrutiny of U.S. states and municipalities, both in the mainstream media and in the blogosphere. A number of observers—some culturally or politically biased against state and local borrowing, others unappreciative of the breadth of governmental resources—made headlines predicting widespread defaults, bankruptcies, and even the entire collapse of the municipal market. The most prominent example was that of Meredith Whitney, the banking analyst, who on December 19, 2010, in a CBS *60 Minutes* segment entitled "Day of Reckoning" predicted that there would be 50 to 100 significant defaults in 2011 totaling "hundreds of billions" of dollars. In March 2011, Roubini Global Economics, the consulting firm owned by economist Nouriel Roubini, predicted that there would be $100 billion in municipal bond defaults over the next five years, although confined to the usual sectors.

The governments that have defaulted on their obligations generally remedy them within months—Cleveland, New York City, and Orange County, California, for example, all defaulted on their debt, and all cured the defaults in relatively short order. The biggest default in the history of the municipal market, $2.25 billion, was that of the Washington Public Power Supply System in 1983.

*See also* Chapter 9; dirt bonds; Heartland fund implosion; issuer concentration; New York City financial crisis of 1975; Orange County, California; tourist attractions; Washington Public Power Supply System.

*Sources:*

"A Complete Look at Monetary Defaults during the 1990s." Standard & Poor's J. J. Kenny, 2000.

Hempel, George. *The Postwar Quality of State and Local Debt.* Cambridge, MA: National Bureau of Economic Research, 1971.

Hillhouse, A. M. *Municipal Bonds: A Century of Experience.* Englewood Cliffs, NJ: Prentice-Hall, 1936.

Litvack, David. "Municipal Default Risk." FitchIBCA, September 15, 1999.

Litvack, David. "Municipal Default Risk Revisited." Fitch Ratings, June 23, 2003.

"A Look at Payment Defaults in the 90s." Standard & Poor's J. J. Kenny, 1999.
"Municipal Bond Defaults." FitchIBCA, August 25, 1999.
"U.S. Municipal Bond Defaults and Recoveries, 1970–2009." Moody's
Investors Service, February 2010.

## Denver International Airport

It was a big white elephant on the High Plains, too expensive for airlines to use and too far away from downtown—24 miles—for passengers to patronize. It was "Federico's Folly," after the mayor of Denver, Federico Peña, who proposed and championed its construction. It was destined to be one of the biggest public works disasters of all time.

And yet, in the end, it was none of those things, instead proving to be an ambitious, visionary, if at its creation ill-starred, public works project of a kind perhaps no longer possible. Announced in 1985 and advanced as a vast improvement over Stapleton, the existing airport serving Denver, it was approved by voters at referendum in 1987. The new airport's October 1993 opening was delayed, not once but four times, because of a recalcitrant automated baggage system. Originally projected at $1.7 billion, the airport's cost eventually ballooned to $4.9 billion. Critics, and there were many, wondered if the thing was economically viable at all and talked darkly of "the next WPPSS," referring to the $2.25 billion default by the Washington Public Power Supply System.

There was a lot for naysayers to be skeptical about. Even analysts at one of the firms underwriting some of the airport's bonds were dubious, as early as the fall of 1990, suggesting that the airport's escalating costs and optimistic traffic projections, coupled with rising fuel prices and the perilous financial condition of some of the airlines, might lead more cautious investors intent on holding only investment-grade securities to reconsider their positions in the new airport bonds. In 1991, there was even talk of mothballing the project, if only on a temporary basis. The drumbeat of bad news only got worse as the years went on, Standard & Poor's finally downgrading Denver International Airport bonds to BB, or junk, by May 1994. Prices on the bonds fell from over par to the 80s.

Betting against the airport—a needful thing in a strategic location—turned out to be a big mistake. The airport opened in February 1995 and proved an almost immediate success, although the baggage system never worked and was abandoned for a more conventional one. In 2011, the airport embarked upon a new $1 billion capital plan featuring expanded rail service to Denver's Union Station and a 500-room airport hotel.

*Sources:*

Brooke, James. "Denver Airport Nestles into Its Lair." *New York Times*, March 6, 1996.
Fumento, Michael. "Federico's Folly." *American Spectator*, December 1993.
Leib, Jeffrey. "Denver Airport Flying High Despite Challenges." *Denver Post*, February 20, 2005.
"Plane Tales from the Hills." *Grant's Municipal Bond Observer*, November 25, 1994.

## Dillon's rule

*See* legal opinion.

## dirt bonds

Fast-growing states like Colorado, Texas, and Florida have authorized real estate developers to sell tax-exempt bonds to help finance construction of roads, sewers, and utility lines. The bonds are secured by taxes and special assessments on the property, first paid by the developer and then by the new residents who move in. When real estate booms go bust and people stop buying houses, the bonds default. New-issue dirt bonds are often sold without credit ratings, and often carry speculative yield premiums to entice buyers.

The entities set up to sell these kinds of bonds are called metropolitan districts in Colorado, municipal utility districts in Texas, and community development districts in Florida, for example.

Developers can cure the defaults in a number of ways. They can resume regular payments after making up those they missed. They can give investors bonds that carry lower interest rates and longer maturities in exchange for the defaulted bonds. In the worst case, trustees can foreclose on the property and distribute the proceeds.

Dirt-bond defaults take time to work out. Settlements have taken an average of 58 months to reach, and resulted in payments of about 70 cents on the dollar, according to a 2000 study of municipal defaults by Standard & Poor's J. J. Kenny. Some California defaults took almost a decade to resolve.

Specialists in this kind of paper are usually located in-state, and familiarize themselves with the property that acts as collateral for the loans.

*See also* community development districts.

## disclosure

The word *disclosure* refers both to the information an issuer puts in the offering documents to its bonds as well as to the information that it sends to the Municipal Securities Rulemaking Board's Electronic Municipal Market Access (EMMA) system for promulgation to investors. New York City's financial crisis of 1975 and the Washington Public Power Supply System's record $2.25 billion default in 1983 were the grandparents of the modern push for disclosure, while the debate over call features and the escrowed-to-maturity bond flap of the late 1980s were its actual parents. Those two eruptions led the MSRB to ask the SEC, in a December 1987 letter concerning "the adequacy of information in the municipal securities market," for the creation of "a mandatory repository of official statements and certain refunding documents." The MSRB said that the requirement to supply such documents to a repository should be placed on issuers. The letter noted that while the Tower Amendment prohibited the board from directly or indirectly requiring issuers to supply such documentation to the board or to customers, "no similar restrictions apply to the Commission."

The SEC put the onus squarely on dealers, proposing Exchange Act Rule 15c2-12 on September 22, 1988. In June 1989, the SEC adopted Rule 15c2-12, which said that underwriters could not sell any bond over $1 million unless the issuer agreed to deliver an official statement within seven business days of the sale. The MSRB then adopted Rule G-36, which required underwriters to send official statements to the board, and then announced the creation of an information repository, which later became the Municipal Securities Information Library (MSIL) system. Thus the era of modern municipal market disclosure was codified. In 1994, the rule was amended to prohibit underwriters from buying bonds unless an issuer agreed to provide continuing disclosure on its financial condition.

"Rule 15c2-12, a rule regulating broker/dealers rather than issuers, does not technically require an issuer to produce an official statement. It simply means that an issuer cannot practically sell bonds in a public offering without an official statement, since no underwriter could buy them," wrote Robert Dean Pope in 2001.

Paul Maco, the first head of the SEC's Office of Municipal Securities, used to give a speech to elected and appointed finance officers whose message was: "You are responsible for your bond issues." The SEC has cited inaccurate or inadequate disclosure in bond documents in proceedings against Orange County, California, the city of San Diego, the city of Miami, and the state of New Jersey, among others.

*See also* EMMA; escrowed to maturity; New York City financial crisis of 1975; Tower Amendment; Washington Public Power Supply System.

*Sources:*

"Letter to the SEC on Information in the Municipal Securities Markets," December 17, 1987. *MSRB Reports,* January 1988.

Pope, Robert Dean. *Making Good Disclosure: The Role and Responsibilities of State and Local Officials under the Federal Securities Laws.* Chicago: Government Finance Officers Association, 2001.

"Report of the Municipal Securities Rulemaking Board on the Regulation of the Municipal Securities Market." Materials presented before the Hearing on Regulation of the Municipal Securities Market, House Subcommittee on Telecommunications and Finance, September 9, 1993.

Taylor, Christopher. "Milestones in Municipal Securities Regulation." Municipal Securities Rulemaking Board, Alexandria, VA, 2006.

## Dodd-Frank Wall Street Reform and Consumer Protection Act

This act, passed in 2010 in the wake of the financial crisis, gave the Municipal Securities Rulemaking Board responsibility for protecting state and local issuers and public pension plans as well as investors. Dodd-Frank also specifically gave the board oversight of the financial advisers and consultants who help states and localities with their financings and investments, a group that had been largely unregulated, some of whom, it was found, had behaved in predatory fashion.

In response, the MSRB embarked upon a series of rulemaking initiatives. These included requiring advisers to register with the board, prohibiting such advisers from making most campaign contributions, requiring that they disclose conflicts of interest, prohibiting their splitting fees with banks and earning "excessive compensation." In addition, the board asked underwriters to disclose material risks associated with transactions, to disclose conflicts of interest, including payments made to the underwriters by third parties, and to ensure that they paid fair and reasonable prices for bonds, among other things.

The MSRB's website, www.msrb.org, contains numerous descriptions, interpretations, and updates on its Dodd-Frank rulemaking.

*See also* bid rigging; Jefferson County, Alabama; swaps.

*Sources:*

Selway, William. "Wall Street Banks Face Muni Disclosure Rules to Protect Issuer." Bloomberg News, August 3, 2011.

Selway, William. "U.S. Municipal Advisers Face Fee Limits in Dodd-Frank Rules." Bloomberg News, August 23, 2011.

## Mrs. Dodge

Mrs. Anna Thompson Dodge was often cited during the twentieth century by critics of the municipal bond market who wanted to end the tax-exemption on state and local bonds, which they viewed solely as a tax shelter for the rich. According to the obituary published in the *New York Times*, after her husband, automotive pioneer Horace E. Dodge, died in 1920, "the $59 million Mrs. Dodge inherited was put into tax-free municipal bonds. The money was said to have earned on the average of $1.5 million a year, and Mrs. Dodge never had to pay a federal income tax."

*Source:*

*New York Times.* "Mrs. Horace Dodge Dies at 103; Among World's Richest Women." June 4, 1970.

# E

## elections

Voters are asked to approve tax initiatives, bond issues backed by their taxes, and various other initiatives and referenda year-round, although the majority of such proposals are voted on in November elections. The record year for bond proposals was 2006, when the country was in the midst of a boom and the suburbs of suburbs needed infrastructure. Voters were asked to approve $109 billion in bonds, and passed $90 billion of them, or 82.5 percent. That was also the record year for bonds on the November general election ballot; voters approved $69.6 billion of the $78.6 billion they were asked to consider.

The record year for bond approvals was 2004, when voters passed 90.7 percent of the issues they were asked about. The record year for approvals in a general election was 1947, when voters passed 96.4 percent of the $1.1 billion in bonds on the ballot. The worst year for bond approvals was 1975, when voters passed only 29.3 percent of the bonds they were polled on. The worst general election for bonds was also 1975, when voters approved 9.5 percent of the $6.5 billion of bonds on the ballot.

The worst decade for bonds at the November election was the 1970s; voters approved 49.15 percent of the bonds they were asked to consider. The best decade for bonds on November ballots was the 1980s, when voters approved almost 83 percent of the bonds; the first decade of the 2000s came in second, with 80.93 percent, a number that seems bound to decline as a result of the recession that began in late 2007.

The approval ratio on bonds has been declining for years now, perhaps a little more slowly than most people thought it would. In 2006, voters approved 88.6 percent of the record $78.6 billion in new borrowing they were asked about. That fell to 83.7 percent in 2007, to 82.1 percent in 2008, to 77.5 percent in 2009, and to 72 percent in 2010, according to New York–based Ipreo Holdings LLC. The lowest approval ratio in the past two decades was 40.6 percent in 1990.

Far more important to credit quality are the numerous initiatives and referenda that are put on ballots every year to cap or roll back taxes or otherwise limit local governments' access to their tax base or ability to borrow.

*See also* initiative and referendum; risk factors.

*Source:*

*The Bond Buyer/Thomson Reuters 2010 Yearbook.* New York: Sourcemedia, 2010.


# EMMA

Launched in March 2008, the Municipal Securities Rulemaking Board's Electronic Municipal Market Access (EMMA) website is the free source for official statements dating from 1990, continuing disclosure documents (such as notices of default and other material events), advance refunding documents, and real-time trade price information.

The idea for this resource dates from the 1984–1986 debate over the mandatory disclosure of call features, which culminated in the MSRB's August 1986 request for comments on an amendment to Rule G-15, which would require dealers to deliver to customers, upon request, written information about the call features of a purchased security. "Ten years ago, an issue may have had only an optional refunding call and a schedule of sinking fund call," said the request for comments. "Today, most issues include those redemption features as well as a number of extraordinary calls. These developments heighten the necessity of a dealer meeting its obligation to explain all material features of a municipal security, including call features, to a customer at or before executing a transaction in the security, and to ensure that any recommended transaction is suitable for the customer in light of the particular features of the security and information known about the customer."

Dealers rebuffed the proposal, saying it would be impossible to comply with this new amendment because there was no central repository of the official statements that contained this information, and it was unrealistic to expect them to maintain libraries of the offering documents for all the bonds they might buy and sell in the secondary market. Several suggested that it might be a good idea for the MSRB to champion the establishment of such a repository. The debate escalated in December 1986, when the Kansas Highway Department announced it wanted to exercise a call on bonds it had previously escrowed to maturity.

In December 1987, the MSRB sent SEC Chairman David Ruder a letter concerning "the adequacy of information in the municipal securities market." The letter called for the creation of "a mandatory repository of official statements and certain refunding documents," and said that, ideally, the requirement to supply such documents to a repository should be placed on issuers. The letter noted that while the Tower Amendment prohibited the MSRB from directly or indirectly requiring issuers to supply such documentation to the Board or to customers, "no similar restrictions apply to the Commission."

In June 1989, the SEC adopted Exchange Act Rule 15c2-12, which said that underwriters could not sell any bond over $1 million unless the issuer agreed to deliver an official statement within seven business days of the sale. The MSRB adopted Rule G-36, which required underwriters to send official statements to the Board, and then announced the creation of an information repository, which later became the Municipal Securities Information Library (MSIL) system.

*See also* disclosure; escrowed to maturity; Rule 15c2-12; Tower Amendment.

*Sources:*

"Disclosure of Call Features to Customers: Rule G-15." Request for Comment, August 19, 1986. *MSRB Reports* 6, no. 4, September 1986.

"Letter to the SEC on Information in the Municipal Securities Markets," December 17, 1987. *MSRB Reports*, January 1988.

"Report of the Municipal Securities Rulemaking Board on the Regulation of the Municipal Securities Market." Materials presented before the Hearing on Regulation of the Municipal Securities Market, House Subcommittee on Telecommunications and Finance, September 9, 1993.

Taylor, Christopher. "Milestones in Municipal Securities Regulation." Municipal Securities Rulemaking Board, Alexandria, VA, 2006.

## escrow churning

First described by Michael Lissack in 1995, when he turned the industry in for yield burning, escrow churning refers to the repeated replacement and sale of the securities used in open-market escrow accounts between the time a refunding bond issue is priced and when the deal is closed, typically a period of three weeks. The underwriter then presents the profit to the issuer as "present value savings." Lawyers defended the practice, said Lissack, contending the trades, also known as escrow rollouts, were not taking place with actual bond proceeds, which they said did not exist until the sale closed. Critics of the transactions said municipalities had no business engaging in speculative trading with bond proceeds or, if they were not bond proceeds, with money lent to them by underwriters.

*See also* yield burning.

*Source:*

"Escrow-Churning." *Grant's Municipal Bond Observer*, September 8, 1995.


## escrowed to maturity

All escrowed-to-maturity bonds are prerefunded, but not all prerefunded bonds are escrowed to maturity. Not even all escrowed-to-maturity bonds are escrowed "to maturity."

This was the lesson of one of the most contentious episodes of the 1980s, one that bridges the almost impossible to fathom gap between the old municipal market and the new, comparatively transparent one.

When interest rates fall, municipalities consider refunding their out-standing high-coupon debt, in the same way a homeowner might weigh refinancing the mortgage. This opportunity usually occurs well before the first time an issuer has the opportunity to call its bonds, which is typically in 10 years, so the issuer engages in what is termed an advance refunding. The issuer sells new bonds, and uses the proceeds to buy a portfolio of Treasury or agency securities, which is then used to pay debt service on the original high-interest bonds. Depending on the needs of the issuer, those original bonds will be redeemed at their call date or upon their maturity. The results are called prerefunded or escrowed-to-maturity bonds (pre-re's or ETMs).

Investors love this kind of paper. The bonds typically carry relatively high coupons, for one thing, and are backed by Treasury securities (or in some cases some other triple-A-rated collateral), so they no longer rely on the fiscal fortunes of an issuer for their repayment. Finally, they presumably have some time to run, so the buyer gets to enjoy high-quality, tax-exempt income for years to come. When the bonds trade, naturally, they do so at premium prices.

In late 1986, investors' security and serenity were both shattered when some issuers decided to call bonds that they had previously escrowed "to maturity." The story broke on December 5, 1986, when some dealers expressed outrage over a negotiated $46 million Kansas City, Kansas, Board of Public Utilities deal that had been priced two days before, and that would have resulted in some securities the board had sold in 1982 and escrowed to maturity in 1984 being called in 1994 instead of from 1997 through 2001. Bond counsel said that escrowing the bonds to maturity did not extinguish the call provisions on the original bonds. At the time, nobody had ever heard of such a thing.

The argument that was to flare up well into a new century was framed on the very first day the bickering broke out in public. On the one hand, there were dealers who had sold investors ETM bonds as risk-free and long-term, relying on the convention that when a bond was escrowed "to maturity," it meant to maturity. On the other hand, there were issuers eager to take advantage of a plunge in interest rates—by December 1986, tax-exempt yields as measured by *The Bond Buyer*'s 20-Bond General Obligation Index had fallen 670 basis points from their all-time high of 13.44 percent reached in January 1982—and bankers, underwriters, lawyers, and financial advisers were only too happy to help such clients.

Market participants predicted that if the Kansas City deal went through, no escrowed-to-maturity bond was safe, and that there was a good chance investors might sue dealers for misrepresentation.

It is not overstating things to say that the escrowed-to-maturity episode was the catalyst that helped produce the modern, more transparent municipal market.

This was not the first time that dealers' knowledge about calls had come into question. That summer, the Municipal Securities Rulemaking Board had proposed an amendment to its Rule G-15 that would require dealers to deliver to customers written information about the call provisions on bonds they purchase within five days, upon request. "The delivery of a copy of the portion of the issue's official statement that describes the call features would be sufficient," the August Request for Comment said.

Dealers denied this request. "In some cases, official statements for some secondary issues may not be available," wrote Margaret Curvin of Manufacturers Hanover Trust Company on October 30, 1986. "Since the official statements are not readily available shortly after the original offering of any given issue a dealer would have to obtain a copy of every official statement for every municipal issue on the market," wrote Mark Moore of Continental Bank in Chicago in an October 28 letter. "The recordkeeping requirements for any one dealer would be a logistical nightmare and most probably cost prohibitive."

Merrill Lynch & Company vice president and counsel Valentina Stum wrote in a November 12 letter that no centralized source of call data existed, and that even official statements rarely outlined call provisions in summary fashion: "This scenario suggests that a firm's marketing, sales and/or trading personnel typically possess sufficient expertise to scrutinize what is essentially a legal document, in order to arrive at a comfortable conclusion that all call, as well as contingent call, information has been appropriately and accurately disclosed." The letter suggested that the MSRB establish a clearinghouse for such data.

On December 9, 1986, the Kansas Highway Department planned to sell competitively $93 million in bonds in order to call an issue that it had sold in January 1985 and escrowed to maturity in November 1985. The transaction would have resulted in the call of the refunded bonds in 1994, instead of from 1995 through 1999. In a rare display of unity, Wall Street refused to bid on the bonds, many dealers saying that while the plan might be legal, it was objectionable, even unethical. The issuer canceled the sale, citing "market conditions."

There may have been unity, but there was not unanimity, even within firms. The executive director of the MSRB at the time, Christopher Taylor, said that the existence of calls on escrowed-to-maturity bonds seemed to be "a material fact. It looks like underwriters assumed that escrowed-to-maturity bonds were not callable, and that's a big mistake. Somebody did not do their homework," he said. "The industry is supposed to disclose material facts at the time of sale, and it seems it is being faced with a tremendous information problem." And even some dealers at the time said it looked as if brokerage houses might be guilty of gross negligence in not knowing precisely what they were selling.

One municipal analyst, Kendrick D. Anderson of Harris Trust and Savings Bank in Chicago (which said it would not bid on the Kansas highway bonds), said the refusal was "like King Canute commanding the tide not to come in. Virtually every old bond—certainly nine out of 10—has this kind of call provision in it, and if it saves money for issuers, this is the kind of financing we'll see over the next several weeks."

Texas Attorney General Jim Mattox was the next to weigh in on the matter, sending a letter on December 18 "to all bond counsel," advising them that Texas bonds that were escrowed to maturity were also not callable to maturity. In Texas, the attorney general rules on the legality of bond issues. Local bond counsels were unlikely to proceed against his wishes.

The letter, written by Susan Lee Voss, chief of the public finance section, cited 1948 case law and said that when bonds are refunded, the refunded bonds are no longer outstanding "for any purpose other than payment of principal at maturity when due. Obviously that means that the provisions of the order/resolution/ordinance which authorized the refunded bonds are defeased, and their security is replaced by the escrow agreement and securities therein pledged to payment of principal and interest on the refunded bonds."

This was the kind of straightforward opinion the market was looking for. The problem was that not everyone was seeking it. The dealer organization then known as the Public Securities Association (PSA) said it was assessing the situation, one dealer calling it "potentially explosive."

Just how explosive? As usual in MuniLand, nobody could actually say just how big the problem might be. Very few refundings had been done in 1981 and 1982, when interest rates were at historic highs, but rates were plummeting. In 1983, $10.7 billion in bonds had been sold purely for refunding (that is, not combined with new-money sales), and in 1984, another $11 billion worth were sold. In 1985, as rates fell, $54 billion in bonds were sold for refunding; in 1986, $52 billion. Observers estimated the amount of bonds that may have been escrowed "to maturity" at between $20 billion and $50 billion, but this was no more than an educated guess.

The bond issue that had started it all, the $46 million Kansas City Board of Public Utilities deal, was canceled as the year closed after the bond counsel failed to deliver documents. There were rumors that other issuers were interested in such transactions because of the obvious savings to be had, but only one, Bristol Township, Pennsylvania, actually managed to close a deal.

In February 1987, the Public Securities Association adopted a resolution urging issuers "not exercise any possible perceived rights to call by optional redemption escrowed-to-maturity bonds, and not cause such redemptions in the future, unless the official statements for such escrowed-to-maturity bonds and the bonds issued to refund such escrowed-to-maturity bonds and the published notice of defeasance, read together, clearly and specifically describe the issuer's legal ability to call by optional redemption such escrowed-to-maturity bonds after defeasance." The PSA began its resolution by stating that, after all, issuers, investors, underwriters, and other market participants "universally have treated escrowed-to-maturity bonds as noncallable."

In March, the MSRB sent letters to the PSA, the Government Finance Officers Association, and the National Association of Bond Lawyers saying it was essential for them to note in official statements for refunding issues and in defeasance notices whether they were also reserving the right to call escrowed-to-maturity issues. In May, the board asked for comment on a new amendment to Rule G-15, this time requiring dealers to send customers official statements to a transaction, if requested. The board also asked for comment on whether the escrow agreements involved in escrowed-to-maturity issues were accessible by dealers, and if those, too, ought to be made available to customers, along with official statements (this would be adopted as Rule G-36 by the MSRB in 1990).

At its July 1987 meeting, the board interpreted its G-17 rule on fair dealing to require that dealers assisting issuers in preparing disclosure documents relating to escrowed-to-maturity securities alert them of the need to disclose whether they had reserved a call on those securities. And it put out an interpretation of its confirmation rules saying that bonds could be described as escrowed to maturity only when no optional call features had been reserved.

Still, the topic did not go away. Investors were angry that ETM bond prices were still battered. In September, the MSRB sent a letter to the SEC saying that its efforts and the PSA's resolution "do not appear to be sufficient to allay confusion whether outstanding escrowed-to-maturity issues of municipal securities are subject to early redemption." The board said it was "concerned that this issue is having a deleterious effect on investor confidence in the municipal securities market and believes that Commission intervention is necessary."

The SEC responded in June 1988, saying that before a security was sold as escrowed to maturity or prerefunded to the first call, the dealer involved "should have conducted a reasonable investigation to satisfy itself that the documents relating to the prior bond issue and the refunding bond issue, including the official statement and escrow trust agreement, support such characterization." The SEC also said that when bonds had been advance refunded, and the proceeds placed in an escrow account sufficient to make scheduled interest payments and to redeem the prior bonds at maturity, "it would be misleading for the issuer to reserve optional redemption rights without disclosing this fact."

The escrowed-to-maturity stew would simmer along for years. In December 1987, the MSRB sent the SEC another letter, this time concerning "adequacy of information" in the municipal securities market. "In the secondary market, dealers often do not retain official statements and may not have quick access to official statements to review complete descriptive information for issues they are trading," said the letter. "Since summary sources do not contain complete descriptive information, some dealers trade municipal securities to customers without knowledge of important features of the securities. This has resulted in pricing and trading inefficiencies and customer protection concerns. One of the most common issues raised in customer arbitrations brought under the Board's rules is whether call features adequately were disclosed to a customer at the time of trade."

And then the board came up with a solution: "The Board believes that the problems discussed above could be resolved within the current statutory framework by the creation of a mandatory repository of official statements and certain refunding documents," with the requirement to supply the documents placed on issuers. Thus was born the idea for a central electronic repository, the Municipal Securities Information Library, which would eventually become the MSRB's EMMA. This would be the key to the modern, transparent municipal bond market, where prices, data, disclosure notices, and documents are available at the click of a mouse. The SEC adopted Rule 15c2-12 in 1989, which prohibited underwriters from selling any bond greater than $1 million unless the issuer agreed to prepare an official statement to the transaction and produce it in a timely manner after the date of sale. The SEC also required underwriters to review the official statement to ensure that all key facts about an issue had been disclosed. The Municipal Securities Rulemaking Board then published its concept for a Municipal Securities Information Library as a repository for such documents, and adopted Rule G-36, requiring underwriters to send the documents to the repository. In 1994, the rule was amended to prohibit underwriters from buying bonds unless an issuer agreed to provide continuing disclosure.

How big was the escrowed-to-maturity bond imbroglio? In 1992, Kenny S&P information services estimated that of the 60,386 separate escrowed-to-maturity bonds it had on file, issuers specifically reserved the right to call 577 of them, those 577 maturities representing perhaps 79 transactions. In 1997, one dealer estimated that perhaps three dozen issuers with about $1 billion in bonds represented the threat.

In the end, a relative handful of issuers called bonds they had escrowed to maturity. Perhaps the last gasp came in December 2004, when the National Association of Securities Dealers fined Morgan Stanley $100,000 and ordered the firm to pay restitution of $211,510 to customers for failing to tell them that bonds they had been sold as escrowed to maturity were also callable. The firm blamed a software glitch.

*See also* advance refunding; EMMA; market activity; Rule 15c2-12; Tower Amendment.

*Sources:*

"All the King's Horses." *Grant's Municipal Bond Observer*, May 15, 1998.

American Banker–*Bond Buyer*. *The Bond Buyer 1990 Yearbook*. New York: Thomson Publishing Corp., 1990.

"And Then There Were None." *Grant's Municipal Finance*, February 25, 1999.

*The Bond Buyer 2010 Yearbook*. New York: Sourcemedia, 2010.

Cahill, Tom. "Gainesville's Plan to Call Municipal Bonds Prompting Suit." Bloomberg News, May 5, 1998.

"Delivery of Final Official Statements to the Board: Rules G-36 and G-8." Request for Comment, August 9, 1989. *MSRB Reports* 9, no. 2, August 1989.

"Delivery of Official Statements in Secondary Market Transactions: Rule G-15." Request for Comment, May 13, 1987. *MSRB Reports* 7, no. 3, June 1987.

"Disclosure of Call Features to Customers: Rule G-15." Comment letters from Manufacturers Hanover Trust Co., October 30, 1986; Continental Bank, October 28, 1986; and Merrill Lynch & Co., November 12, 1986.

"Disclosure of Call Features to Customers: Rule G-15." Request for Comment, August 19, 1986. *MSRB Reports* 6, no. 4, September 1986.

Emmet, Christopher. Telephone interview with Christopher Emmet, Emmet & Co., November 10, 2010.

"$46 Mil Kansas City Public Utilities Sale Canceled." Munifacts 192, December 30, 1986.

"Guiding Principles for a Central Electronic Repository." *MSRB Reports* 9, no. 2, August 1989.

"Letters on Escrowed-to-Maturity Securities." *MSRB Reports* 8, no. 4, August 1988.

"Letter to SEC on Information in the Municipal Securities Markets." December 17, 1987. *MSRB Reports* 8, no. 1, January 1988.

Mysak, Joe. "Escrow Agreement Change on Kansas Bonds Generates Outrage, Interest." *Bond Buyer*, December 8, 1986.

Mysak, Joe. "PSA Advises Issuers to Avoid ETM Bond Calls." *Bond Buyer*, February 6, 1987.

Mysak, Joe. "The PSA Tackles a Thorny Ethical Question." Credit Markets, *Bond Buyer*, December 29, 1986.

"Re: Optional Redemption of Escrowed-to-Maturity Securities." Letter from Robert L.D. Colby, deputy director of the SEC, to Christopher Taylor, executive director of the MSRB, May 4, 1998.

Taylor, Christopher. E-mail, November 9, 2010.

Voss, Susan Lee. "To All Bond Counsel." Letter from Jim Mattox, Attorney General of Texas, December 18, 1986.

"The War's Over." *Grant's Municipal Bond Observer*, December 12, 1997.

Yacoe, Donald, and Joe Mysak. "Market Outrage Forces Kansas to Cancel Sale of Bond Issue." *Bond Buyer*, December 9, 1986.

# F

## feasibility studies

Feasibility studies are reports, prepared by consulting firms, that are appended to certain bond issues. They describe the market for a project or product and offer revenue estimates based on a number of scenarios. Most tobacco bond issues, for example, carried an updated, 40-page "Forecast of U.S. Cigarette Consumption" by Global Insight USA.

Feasibility studies are stuffed with useful information and data, especially about comparable enterprises located elsewhere, and generally unavailable anywhere else. For example, bond issues for convention centers and convention center hotels often contain information on the convention business nationally, and carry data on how other similarly situated hotels are faring. Still, investors should keep in mind that the purpose of the reports is to show why a project like a paper de-inking mill or a convention center hotel will succeed. Often the most readable and accessible portion of an official statement, they are not known as "infeasibility" studies for a reason.

*See also* Chapter 9; default; tourist attractions.

## Fed Flow of Funds report

Formally known as Federal Reserve Statistical Release Z1, the "Flow of Funds Accounts of the United States" is published quarterly by the Board of Governors of the Federal Reserve System. It is chiefly used by analysts to track municipal securities ownership by sector, including households, banks,

63

insurance companies, and mutual funds. In the modern era, households are the largest owners of municipal securities, with $1 trillion of the $2.8 trillion outstanding. Mutual funds come in second, with $532 billion, and property and casualty insurers third, with $371 billion. The Fed Flow of Funds report is also useful in tracking holdings of state and local government employee retirement funds.

*See also* Who owns municipal bonds?

*Source:*

"Flow of Funds Accounts of the United States: Flows and Outstandings, Third Quarter 2010." Board of Governors of the Federal Reserve System, Washington, DC, December 9, 2010.

## Ferber trial

Mark Ferber was a smart, politically savvy banker for Lazard, Freres & Company with a very loyal stable of issuer clients. What he did not tell them was that when he was acting as their financial adviser and recommending that they hedge their bets with an interest-rate swap from Merrill Lynch & Company, then one of the few firms specializing in municipal swaps, he and Lazard were also being paid by Merrill. That cut of the action eventually amounted to millions of dollars. The secret contract between Ferber and Lazard and Merrill was uncovered by the office of the Massachusetts inspector general. The U.S. Attorney's trial against Ferber began in May 1996 and lasted three months. The case provided a rare glimpse at the world of public finance, and transfixed the municipal market, because Ferber was a high-ranking, high-profile figure. Convicted in August, Ferber was sentenced in December to 33 months in prison and fined $1 million. In October 1995, Merrill Lynch, which was then the dominant firm in the municipal swaps business, and Lazard, where Ferber had been a partner, paid $24 million to settle fraud charges in connection with their arrangement.

Noteworthy were U.S. District Court Judge William Young's comments made at Ferber's sentencing. The essence of the case was that Ferber as a financial adviser acted as a fiduciary agent and should have told his clients, which included the District of Columbia, the Massachusetts Water Resources Authority, and the Michigan Department of Transportation, about his side deal with Merrill Lynch. Judge Young said he was "appalled" by the municipal bond lawyers in the case. "If there had been appropriate legal advice to the municipal bond industry here," he said, "you would not be going to prison and there would not be the need for government regulation that is so evident here." The judge called Ferber a "faithless agent," and said, "There must be no question of the duty of disclosure. And if this sorry lot of municipal bond attorneys do not understand it, let me spell it out. It is required that every potentially conflicting engagement of a fiduciary agent be disclosed to the principal in writing in detail before that conflict is undertaken." Judge Young faulted the "communal conduct" of the municipal bond market's participants. He said, "Graft, kickbacks, corruption do not occur in isolation. They occur out of people or groups of people and their approach to doing business, even the quotidian business of day-to-day transactions."

He continued, "If anyone, any one of these groups of people had held themselves to the ethical standards that society expects of them, I am fully satisfied that you would have been warned off, that you would have gone on with your otherwise distinguished career." That is not what happened, and Judge Young faulted the culture of a market that countenanced side deals, secret agreements, and finders' fees. He called it a whole way of doing business. A decade later, in November 2006, the Federal Bureau of Investigation raided the offices of brokers who specialized in the reinvestment of bond proceeds business, and the Department of Justice said it was conducting an "investigation of anticompetitive practices in the municipal bond industry" that included side deals, secret arrangements, and finders' fees.

*See also* bid rigging; New Jersey Turnpike scandal of 1993; pay-to-play.

*Sources:*

Kurkjian, Stephen. "Papers Show Links between Ferber, Firm." *Boston Globe*, December 17, 1993.

Mysak, Joe. "Lessons of Ferber's Trial Ignored 10 Years Later." Bloomberg News, January 4, 2006.

Wayne, Leslie. "A Side Deal and a Wizard's Undoing." *New York Times*, May 15, 1994.

## 50 percent coupon

In the 1970s, bankers began using so-called trick coupons at auction in order, as *Bond Buyer* columnist William J. Ryan wrote at the time, "to make the offerings as attractive as possible to the ultimate buyer."

In September 1972, for example, the state of Minnesota took bids on $25 million of general obligation bonds maturing in 20 years. Dillon, Read & Company (which departed the municipal bond business in 1997) submitted the winning bid, with the first four maturities carrying 50 percent coupons, and the last seven carrying 0.10 percent coupons. The net interest cost (NIC) was 4.557 percent.

State Treasurer Val Bjornson said he was satisfied with the results of the sale. He also said he was going to recommend that a maximum rate differential be included next time out to avoid things like 50 percent coupons.

The 50 percent coupons sparked a debate on the merits of using net interest cost, which does not take into account the time value of money, compared with true interest cost (TIC), to evaluate bids.

At the University of Oregon, scholars Michael H. Hopewell, George G. Kaufman, and Richard R. West figured that had Minnesota used true interest cost to calculate the bids, the Dillon, Read TIC would have been 5.50 percent, almost a full point higher than the NIC. The difference, they said, cost the state about a million dollars.

Hopewell and Kaufman later elaborated on their analysis in the *Journal of Financial and Quantitative Analysis*, in a March 1974 article entitled "The Cost of Inefficient Coupons on Municipal Bonds," which said that the NIC method of calculating bids encouraged underwriters to submit weird high-low patterns of coupons, which they deemed "inefficient" and costly.

Issuers, they said, "may accept a 'wrong' bid, that is, a bid other than the lowest TIC bid."

At the time, only two issuers in the country used TIC.

Underwriters working on negotiated transactions have also used 50 percent coupons in recent years. The underwriter then known as Salomon Smith Barney used 50 percent coupons on certain maturities of the Metropolitan Pier and Exposition Authority in Chicago's bond issues in both 1992 and 1998. The underwriter stripped the coupons from the bonds, and sold both zero-coupon and current-coupon bonds.

The price on the 50 percent coupon bonds was not 100 cents on the dollar but 479.029, making the yield to their 2009 maturity a reasonable 4.728 percent. As the underwriter explained back then, you get more "production" with premium-price bonds—the issuer gets more proceeds, more cash. The $7.58 million in 50 percent coupon bonds it sold translated to $36.3 million at those super-premium prices.

In October 2006, South Carolina rejected a bid from Goldman, Sachs Group Inc. that included bonds priced with 50 percent coupons, as well as coupons of 5 percent, 1 percent, and 0.05 percent. "While the apparent winning bid conformed to the bid parameters prescribed by the notice of sale, all bids were rejected because the proposed coupon structure did not yield the results necessary to maintain compliance with the state's constitutional debt limitation," debt manager Rick Harmon said in a statement.

*Sources:*

Braun, Martin Z. "South Carolina Scraps Auction After Rejecting Goldman Bid." Bloomberg News, October 10, 2006.
"Premium Bonds." *Grant's Municipal Bond Observer*, September 4, 1998.

## financial advisers

A financial adviser (often spelled "advisor" by the FAs themselves) is an agent of the issuer who assists in the structuring and sale of bonds, who may be independent or who may work for a bank or securities firm. "Unless the issuer has sufficient in-house expertise and access to market information, it should hire an outside financial adviser prior to undertaking a debt financing," says the Government Finance Officers Association (GFOA) Best Practice. "A financial adviser represents the issuer, and only the issuer, in the sale of bonds. Issuers should assure themselves that the selected financial adviser has the necessary expertise to assist the issuer in selecting other financial professionals, planning the bond sale, and successfully selling and closing the bonds." The financial adviser can be chosen for single or multiple sales, and can help with both competitive and negotiated transactions. The MSRB gained oversight over financial advisers in 2010.

*Source:*

GFOA Best Practice. "Selecting Financial Advisors." October 17, 2008.

## fiscal year

A fiscal year is a 12-month period used for accounting purposes by most governmental entities, usually beginning in June or July, rarely the same as a calendar year. States and municipalities typically file audited financials from three to six months, or longer, after the ends of their fiscal years.

*See also* CAFR; Rule 15c2-12; Tower Amendment.

## 501(c)(3) issuers

These are organizations recognized by the Internal Revenue Service as not-for-profit entities. A 501(c)(3) organization can borrow money to finance projects on a tax-exempt basis through a conduit issuer. Examples include not-for-profit colleges and universities, hospitals, museums, and retirement homes.

*See also* house museums.

*Source:*
MSRB online glossary at www.msrb.org.

## flipping

Flipping is what happens after an underwriter sells big blocks of bonds to a handful of favored large investors, such as mutual fund managers, who then resell, or flip, the bonds in smaller pieces to banks and other securities firms at a higher price, essentially acting as wholesalers, thus helping convert the bonds into a retail product. In the stock market, of course, flipping occurs after investors favored with initial public offerings (IPOs) sell their shares to take advantage of the price run-up common after the IPO. That flipping also occurred in municipal securities became apparent only after the MSRB began its transaction reporting program, which started in 1995 and which finally covered all transactions in 2000. Observers noticed wide spreads in price, as well as how certain bonds, especially those initially offered at a discount, jumped in price. The primary concern with the flipping of municipal bonds was that the issuers of the bonds did not get the optimal price in the first place. For their part, issuers usually seemed unaware of the practice, and did not care very much about it even when it was brought to their attention. They accepted the presence of wholesalers who helped parcel out their bond issues as a matter of fact. Flipping struck some critics as refuting the rationale for choosing negotiated underwriting, which was supposed to result in the best price on bond issues because of the sales effort used to get the bonds into the hands of final investors. Flipping was most often, but not exclusively, seen in negotiated transactions. In recent years, certain of the more sophisticated issuers have tracked how their bonds trade to ensure the best pricing and execution.

*See also* Build America Bonds; issue price.

*Source:*

Taylor, Christopher. "Milestones in Municipal Securities Regulation 1975–2005." Municipal Securities Rulemaking Board, Alexandria, VA, 2006.

## floaters/inverse floaters

This structure divides an issuer's debt-service payment into two pieces: one bears a variable rate set periodically at a Dutch auction, at which investors stipulate the lowest rate they will accept. The holder of this piece, the floater or tender-option note, usually has the right to tender the notes back at par. The notes are usually backed by a top-rated letter-of-credit bank, and are purchased by tax-exempt money-market mutual funds. The other part of the interest payment goes toward the inverse floater, also known as a residual, which bears the coupon rate on the whole bond minus the auction rate. If short-term rates move higher, holders of the inverse floaters see their return diminish, and eventually may receive none at all. If short-term rates decline, the inverse floater holders make more.

The floater/inverse floater structure was first introduced to the municipal new-issue market by Shearson Lehman Hutton Inc. in March 1990, with a product called RIBs/SAVRs. SAVRs stood for Select Auction Variable Rate Securities, whose interest rate was set at Dutch auction every 35 days. The inverse floater, RIBs, stood for Residual Interest Bonds. The first issuer to use the structure was the Nebraska Investment Finance Authority on a $120 million Government National Mortgage Association–backed single-family mortgage revenue bond deal featuring $50 million in SAVRs, $50 million in RIBs, and $20 million in plain-vanilla serial refunding bonds. There was no put.

The first few deals usually featured an equal number of floaters and inverse floaters, but gradually the portion of inverse floaters shrank. Some buyers purchased both parts of a deal, essentially buying a fixed-rate security. The Shearson Lehman Hutton structure was swiftly copied by other major firms.

This structure, and others like it, essentially segregating and cutting up cash flows, was first used in structuring new municipal issues in the 1990s.

Floaters/inverse floaters are also sold by tender-option bond (TOB) programs, under which a bank or other institutional investor buys bonds, deposits them into a trust, and sells floating-rate securities to other investors; these date from the 1980s. At the height of the mania for TOB programs from around 2002 to 2007, it was estimated that they held as much as $180 billion in bonds.

*See also* tender-option bond programs.

*Sources:*

Dickson, Steven. "New Breed of Derivatives from Lehman: Inverse Floaters Spawn 'Bulls' and 'Bears.'" *Bond Buyer*, February 19, 1992.

Hampton, Ted. "Shearson Unveils Investment Device That Uses Short- and Long-Term Debt." *Bond Buyer*, March 9, 1990.

Quint, Michael. "Hedge Funds Help 'Stodgy' Municipals Beat Treasuries." Bloomberg News, December 18, 2006.

## flow control

*See* garbage.

# G

## garbage

In the spring of 1987, the fully loaded Mobro 4000 barge wandered up and down the East Coast of the United States and into the Caribbean looking for somewhere to dump its load of Long Islanders' garbage. "Its journey had a strange effect on America," wrote John Tierney in the *New York Times* almost a decade later. "The citizens of the richest society in the history of the planet suddenly became obsessed with personally handling their own waste."

Television stations covered the barge's sad voyage, the result of a deal with North Carolina landfill owners falling through, and newsmagazines rushed to write stories whose message was all the same: we're drowning in our own garbage (*Newsweek*'s cover story was called "Buried Alive").

The story line satisfied a peculiarly American lust for self-flagellation. This was a crisis that people's own profligate, wasteful, uncaring behavior had caused.

And so the nation embraced a number of ideas. One was that it was running out of landfill space. Another was that even burying garbage in landfills was unsafe and that what really ought to be done was burn the stuff in efficient, clean, environmentally friendly incinerators—and that burning stuff in those incinerators could provide yet another source of energy. A variation on the theme was that special mills could take one form of waste and transform it into something else useful and maybe even salable.

It took more than a decade to disprove the notion that the country was running out of landfills, but that made no difference. The story was too good. The municipal market played a key role in financing these incinerators and mills. Tens of billions of dollars in bonds were sold to build incinerators designed to burn garbage and produce electricity and steam, and mills designed to transform old tires into crumb rubber, the waste from sugar refining into power, wood scraps into synthetic wood, old paper into fresh new reams, dead chickens (or "broiler mortality," as the industry called it) into chicken feed. In the 1980s, it was mainly garbage incinerators. The 1990s seemed to specialize in mills that recycled stuff. And in the early 2000s, the market saw millions of dollars raised for refineries designed to turn animal waste into fuel.

Some of these things worked. Others worked, but only after the bonds that had been sold to build them had defaulted and more time and money were spent to get them right. And still others never really worked at all, and were sold for—what else?—scrap.

There were a number of lessons to be learned from these various episodes, besides the first one, that the country was not running out of landfills at all, and perhaps that environmentally tinged hysteria was not really a good way to formulate public policy. That was the lesson that should have been learned by taxpayers, so often called upon to foot the bill.

For investors, the first lesson, as always, was to check precisely what and who secures a bond's repayment. To the extent a municipality is either fully or even partly behind the repayment of the bonds, they are safer. There are always well-publicized exceptions that prove the rule—the incinerator that Harrisburg, Pennsylvania, guaranteed, for example.

It is impossible to generalize about such financings, yet it may be good to keep a few points in mind.

- It's not as easy as you might think. Sometimes it's the technology. Sometimes it's the people who run the equipment or manage the operation. Time is rarely on the investor's side, and time is what incinerators or mills require to get up and running and in production.
- Politics does not trump the law of supply and demand. The government may like the idea of encouraging and subsidizing production of recycled paper or ethanol right now, but it may not always. What will happen if the price supports are knocked away? Is a project economically viable on its own?
- Price matters. Plants that burn or recycle stuff depend on a steady supply of it, at a certain price. And if the plant actually is meant to produce something of value, it also depends on people paying a certain price for that product. Even the nuttiest feasibility study contains price projections. It

does not take much analytical skill to figure out that prices go up and down, and that the base-case scenario is not the only one.

• All the king's horses. Don't be fooled by big names. The leading engineering firms may put together very reasonable-sounding feasibility studies saying why a project should work, and the bonds may be underwritten by the biggest and best securities firms, and they will have legal opinions from the top bond lawyers. They can run into trouble all the same.

Finally, consider the judicial wild card. In 1994, the Supreme Court decided *C & A Carbone, Inc. v. Clarkstown*, striking down a flow-control ordinance that forced garbage haulers to deliver waste to a particular private processing facility. Owners of the tax-exempt bonds sold to build hundreds of waste-to-energy plants worried that flow control had been outlawed, and that haulers were thereby free to take garbage wherever they could dump it most cheaply. Incinerators reduced prices, or tipping fees, and otherwise scrambled to assure their own economic viability. Prices of bonds fell, and certain incinerators were put on watch by the rating companies.

In 2007, the Supreme Court decided *United Haulers Association, Inc. v. Oneida-Herkimer Solid Waste Management Authority*. "The only salient difference is that the laws at issue here require haulers to bring waste to facilities owned and operated by a state-created public benefit corporation," said the Opinion of the Court. "We find this difference to be constitutionally significant. Disposing of trash had been a traditional government activity for years, and laws that favor the government in such areas—but treat every private business, whether in-state or out-of-state, exactly the same—do not discriminate against interstate commerce for purposes of the Commerce Clause."

Flow control, it seemed, was back. At least it was if the municipal government was directing garbage to a municipal facility. Or was it?

*Sources:*

Lamar, Jacob V., Jr., Joseph J. Kane, and Susan Kinsley. "Don't Be a Litterbarge." *Time*, May 4, 1987.

Tierney, John. "Recycling Is Garbage." *New York Times Magazine*, June 30, 1996.

*United Haulers Association, Inc., et al., Petitioners v. Oneida-Herkimer Solid Waste Management Authority et al.* Opinion of the Court, U.S. Supreme Court, April 30, 2007.

## gas prepayment bonds

Municipal gas and electric utilities sell these kinds of tax-exempt bonds through a conduit agency to finance their purchases of long-term (20- to 30-year) supplies of natural gas at a discounted price, typically figured off an index on a monthly basis. Perhaps the most notorious example of one of these transactions going wrong was the September 2008 Main Street Natural Gas Inc. default on $709 million of gas-project revenue bonds, sparked by the bankruptcy of Lehman Brothers Holdings Inc. and its subsidiary, Lehman Brothers Commodities Services. After the bankruptcy, Lehman stopped delivering gas, and the issuer terminated the transaction. The guarantor on the obligation was Lehman Brothers Holdings, which in bankruptcy could not make a termination payment that would have resulted in the redemption of the bonds. Bondholders joined unsecured creditors in bankruptcy court.

*Sources:*

Cooke, Jeremy. "Lehman-Backed Muni Gas Bonds Trade for Cents; Deliveries Halted." Bloomberg News, September 26, 2008.
"Gas Prepayment Bonds." Rating Methodology, Moody's Investors Service, December 2008.

## GASB

Based in South Norwalk, Connecticut, the Governmental Accounting Standards Board (GASB) sets guidelines for state and local government financial reporting. Adherence to the standards is optional.
   *See also* pensions.

## general obligation

General obligation (GO) bonds are the good, old-fashioned municipal bonds that people think of when they think about the municipal bond market. Usually voter-approved, they are backed by the taxing power of state or local governments, on either a limited or an unlimited basis. In 2009, GO bonds accounted for 38 percent of the $410 billion in municipal bonds sold, according to *The Bond Buyer*; in 2008, they composed 28 percent of new-issue volume. Revenue bonds account for the majority of bonds sold every year, and have since the 1970s.

*See also* revenue bonds.

*Source:*

*The Bond Buyer/Thomson Reuters 2010 Yearbook.* New York: Sourcemedia, 2010.

## GFOA

The Government Finance Officers Association (GFOA) of the United States and Canada, based in Chicago, was founded in 1906, and is the primary professional organization for state and local government finance officials. With 17,500 members, the GFOA's mission statement says its purpose "is to enhance and promote the professional management of governments for the public benefit by identifying and developing financial policies and best practices and promoting their use through education, training, facilitation of member networking, and leadership." The organization runs conferences and training programs throughout the year, publishes a magazine, offers consulting services, and maintains an office in Washington, DC. Base membership fees range from $160 for officials from cities and counties with populations of less than 5,000 up to $4,620 for those from cities and counties of more than one million.

Other organizations for state government officials involved in municipal finance include the National Association of State Auditors, Controllers and Treasurers; the National Association of State Treasurers; the National Association of State Budget Officers; and the National Conference of State Legislatures.

*Source:*

Jeffrey Esser, GFOA executive director.

## golf courses

Golf courses are financed both as stand-alone municipal projects with varying levels of governmental involvement and as parts of real estate developments. Although perfectly legitimate as public finance projects, and often successful, golf courses have figured into some of the market's more notorious foibles. During the 1990s, for example, a California firm called Pacific Genesis Group underwrote a series of roughly $250 million in high-yield transactions designed to fund real estate developments almost invariably featuring golf courses. In 1996, state treasurer Matt Fong took the unusual step of asking the Securities and Exchange Commission (SEC) to examine the bond issues, which he said threatened the integrity of the bond market. All the bonds defaulted after regulators shut the firm down in 2001. In 2006, the SEC accused a Pennsylvania underwriter, Robert J. Bradbury, of fraud after he invested his four client school districts' money in unrated golf course notes his firm had also underwritten. The banker pleaded guilty, was fined, and went to prison. And in 2010, Buena Vista, Virginia, attracted attention after it failed to appropriate money to pay debt service for a $9.2 million lease revenue bond issue it sold in 2005 to build a municipal golf course. "Failure to appropriate demonstrates uncertainty about the city's willingness to meet its obligations," Moody's Investors Service said in withdrawing the city's rating. The incident was especially noteworthy because Buena Vista pledged its City Hall and police department building as collateral for the bonds.

*Sources:*

Braun, Martin Z. "Pennsylvania Underwriter Sued by SEC for Defrauding Schools." Bloomberg News, August 3, 2006.

"Moody's Downgrades to Ba1 and Withdraws Buena Vista, Va.'s Rating," *Bond Buyer*, June 11, 2010.

Mysak, Joe. "NASD Action Shows the Folly of Chasing Muni Yield." Bloomberg News, March 4, 2005.

$9,205,000 Public Recreational Facilities Authority of Buena Vista, Virginia, Series 2005A, Official Statement, April 7, 2005.

Pearson, Sophia. "Philadelphia Banker Gets 366-Day Sentence for Fraud." Bloomberg News, December 14, 2009.

## government census

Conducted every five years, the government census determines the number of governmental entities in the United States. In 2007, there were 89,476 general and special purpose governments, including 37,381 so-called special districts, which category covers authorities, and 14,561 public school systems.

*Source:*

U.S. Census Bureau.

## guaranteed investment contracts

Municipalities rarely use the money they borrow immediately. Instead, they invest the money and draw it down as needed. Tax law prohibits them from earning profits on the invested money. The guaranteed investment contract (GIC) provides them with a yield-restricted vehicle that can be tailored to a municipality's schedule. GICs were at the center of the federal government's investigation into anticompetitive practices in the municipal bond market. "Issuers deposit funds into GICs in return for a guaranteed fixed or variable rate of return as well as the repayment of the principal in accordance with the terms of the investment agreement," Moody's wrote in 2008. "In some cases the interest earnings and the principal repayment are factored into the calculation of funds available to pay bondholders."

*See also* bid rigging; last looks; swaps; yield burning.

*Source:*

Lipitz, Gregory. "Methodology Update: Ratings That Rely on Guaranteed Investment Contracts." Moody's Investors Service, December 2008.

# H

## *Hammersmith*

*Hazell v. Hammersmith and Fulham Borough Council,* a 1991 decision by the House of Lords, found that swaps in the United Kingdom were ultra vires—in other words, that the localities involved did not have the legal power to enter into swaps transactions with banks. In light of the decision, most U.S. bankers have ascertained that issuer clients did have the authority to engage in interest-rate swaps.

## Heartland fund implosion

On September 28, 2000, Milwaukee-based Heartland Advisors, Inc. reduced the net asset value of its High-Yield Municipal Bond Fund by 8.2 percent, to $8.03 from $8.75 per share. It also reduced the net asset value (NAV) on its High Yield Short Duration Muni Fund by 2.1 percent, to $8.91 from $9.10 per share. The firm announced that Thomas Conlin, manager of the two funds, had resigned, and warned, "No one can say for sure that there's not going to be a further net asset value decline" in the funds. Then on October 13, Heartland did it again, this time lowering the NAV on the bond fund to $2.45 per share, on the short-duration fund to $4.87, and on its Taxable Short Duration High Yield Municipal Fund to $9.14 from $9.77. The evaporation of shareholder value in a municipal bond fund was unprecedented.

And so the Golden Age of Public Finance, when everything, it seemed, could be financed in the municipal bond market, came to an end.

The backstory to the Heartland disaster was the boom in the high-yield market during the 1990s, as municipalities from coast to coast sold more and more bonds designed to boost their local economies. They sold bonds for nursing homes, for-profit prisons, housing developments in the desert, aquariums, racetracks, golf courses, theme parks, tourist attractions, and mills created to take one thing (usually garbage or waste of some sort) and turn it into something else (usually steam or electric power). In most cases, the bonds were not backed by municipal taxing power, but by the money to be generated by the new projects. In other cases, municipalities overcame whatever inhibitions they may have had about getting into the hotel or hospitality or waste-to-energy business, and borrowed the money and built the projects themselves, backing them with their own general obligation pledges.

Everything, it seemed, could be financed in some corner of the municipal bond market, and, usually, at low, tax-exempt interest rates. Between 1982, when tax-exempt rates peaked at 13.44 percent, and the beginning of the new century, the cost of borrowing money fell more than seven full points.

At the same time, the municipal bond market, like the rest of the financial world, saw the rise of the professional money manager, and that had consequences of its own. More money managers competed to buy municipal bonds, even the sketchier varieties. After all, if one or two credits in an individual investor's portfolio, which might contain only four names, go bust, that's a catastrophe. If three or four credits in a fund manager's portfolio of 200 names go bust, it's a footnote. More risky and speculative transactions made their way into the market, and were snapped up.

At the beginning of the 1980s, only 10 percent of the muni bonds outstanding were under the control of bank trust officers or mutual fund managers. By the end of the 1990s, about half was. In 1984, there were 48 municipal bond mutual funds; in 2000, there were more than 250. In 1982, there were three municipal bond funds that termed themselves "high yield"; in 2000, there were more than 50. More and more buyers vied for high-yield bonds, and spreads contracted. By the end of the 1990s, "high yield" in MuniLand meant 6 percent or 7 percent, not 10 percent or more. The Heartland high-yield fund advertised a 6.85 percent yield on August 31, 2000.

What happened at Heartland? The managers buying the bonds made some spectacularly bad choices of nursing home, theme park, and multi-family housing bonds. Of the 54 bonds contained in the high-yield fund, 27 ran into some kind of trouble; of the 71 bonds held in the short-duration fund, 14 were showing signs of difficulty. In a market as illiquid as the one for high-yield municipals, this was disastrous, because it meant that the fund could not easily sell bonds to cover redemptions. As well, the Heartland fiasco illuminated one of the fund industry's dirty little secrets, which is that managers, in consultation with pricing services, determine what the bonds they own are worth.

The Securities and Exchange Commission froze the assets of the Heartland high-yield municipal funds in March 2001 and placed them into receivership. The SEC sued Heartland and several of its officers in December 2003, beginning the summary of its complaint: "In slightly over two weeks, investors in municipal bond mutual funds managed by Heartland Advisors, Inc. lost approximately $93 million—losses that are directly attributable to the Defendants' fraudulent behavior." Chief among the SEC's allegations was that Heartland failed to price the bonds in its funds accurately, "with the result that the funds' shares were sold at incorrect per-share Net Asset Values."

In January 2008, Heartland settled with the SEC for $3.5 million, after the government withdrew the fraud claims and instead said the defendants' conduct was negligent.

The Heartland implosion knocked something out of the municipal bond market. Bonds for nursing homes and development projects are still sold, of course, but the weird is no longer on consistent offer as it was for a brief moment in the 1990s.

*See also* tourist attractions.

*Sources:*

Damato, Karen. "Heartland's Bond Prices Face Spotlight." *Wall Street Journal*, October 25, 2000.

In the Matter of Heartland Advisors, Inc. et al., Cease and Desist Order, Administrative Proceeding, Securities and Exchange Commission, January 25, 2008.

Mysak, Joe. "My Cat Could Have Chosen a Better Batch of Bonds." Bloomberg News, November 30, 2000.

Scheer, David. "Heartland Advisors Settles SEC Bond-Pricing Complaint." Bloomberg News, January 28, 2008.

*Securities and Exchange Commission, Plaintiff, v. Heartland Advisors Inc. et al.*, U.S. District Court for the Eastern District of Wisconsin, December 11, 2003.

Whalen, Robert. "Heartland Muni Funds Serve as Reminder: High Yield = High Risk." Bloomberg News, September 29, 2000.

Whalen, Robert. "SEC Freezes Assets of Three Heartland Muni Funds." Bloomberg News, March 22, 2001.

## house museums

The former homes of authors, statesmen, financiers, and other notables are often turned into museums by their heirs, adoring fans, museum curators, and historians. They sometimes tap the municipal bond market as 501(c)(3) not-for-profit organizations for low-cost, tax-exempt financing instead of using their endowments or waiting for pledges to come in. The Isabella Stewart Gardner Museum in Boston, George Washington's Mount Vernon and Thomas Jefferson's Monticello in Virginia, the J.P. Morgan Library in New York, and the Henry Flagler house in Palm Beach, Florida, have all successfully sold municipal bonds to pay for renovation and expansion in recent years. House museum visits can be intriguing, transporting, or melancholy, depending on the condition of the house and its contents.

There are a lot of things to look for in house museum obligations. Where is the house museum? How long has it been open? What is the annual attendance? Does it have cultural or historical relevance? What is the physical state? What is the financial condition? Is there any way to gauge the management? Are there interested, committed descendants of the famous person on the governing board? These things can usually be gauged with a look through the offering documents and financials, preferably combined with a visit.

Those are all good questions, but one of the biggest things for investors to look for with house museums—of the 20,000 museums in the country, there are an estimated 16,000 house museums, and new ones are being created at a rate of two a week—is cash. Look for investments that are going to spin off income. Look for an endowment.

Consider, for example, the Henry Morrison Flagler Museum in Palm Beach, Florida. Flagler, born in 1830, was one of the founders of the Standard Oil Company with John D. Rockefeller, and an early developer of the state of Florida. His 55-room house, named Whitehall, was built in 1902 as a wedding present for his second wife. The magnificent Beaux Arts pile was lived in by the Flaglers for the season, about six weeks from New Year's through George Washington's birthday.

Flagler died in 1913. His heir did not want to live in Whitehall. It was sold and much of the contents dispersed. It was turned into a hotel, which was tacked onto the rear of the house with a 10-story, 300-room tower. By 1959, the hotel was failing and the whole place in danger of being razed. Flagler's granddaughter bought the property and turned it into a museum, which opened in 1960. The tower was torn down in 1963.

Open year-round, the museum attracts about 100,000 visitors annually. That's a good turnout for a house museum, but buyers of the $9 million in bonds sold by Palm Beach County in 2003 (to finance the construction of a pavilion to house Flagler's private railroad car along with a café) could have noticed one thing about the bonds: the Flagler had investments on hand worth almost $52 million. Case closed.

The bonds, general obligations of the museum, were rated AA– by Standard & Poor's, and were structured as variable-rate demand obligations, whose interest rate was reset weekly, affording the Flagler financing at around 1 percent.

As for that 100,000 attendance, in 2003 John Blades, executive director of the Flagler, estimated that it cost the museum about $62 per person to host visitors; at the time, adult tickets were $8 apiece. In the grand scheme, attendance is a relatively small portion of the revenue pie.

Or take Henry Flagler's fellow Gilded Age grandee, J.P. Morgan. In 2004, the New York City Trust for Cultural Resources sold $50 million in revenue bonds for expansion and renovation of the Pierpont Morgan Library, located on Madison Avenue and 36th Street in Manhattan. Morgan did not live at the library, but he did conduct business there. The library was built in 1906; an annex was built in 1928. The Morgan House, an adjoining brownstone townhouse, built in 1853, was acquired by the trust in 1988.

The new bonds paid for a reading room, performance hall, and multilevel underground vault to house the library's holdings, all designed by noted museum architect Renzo Piano. They were structured precisely like the Flagler bonds, as variable-rate demand obligations with rates reset every seven days. Like the Flagler, the Morgan pays around 1 percent to borrow money. And like the Flagler, attendance was a minor consideration: "Attendance at the library has always been relatively modest, accounting for just 3% to 4% of total revenues, or about $400,000 each year," Standard & Poor's said in its analysis of the bond issue, which it rated A+. What the library did have was an endowment. When Jack Morgan, J. P. Morgan's son, donated the library to the city of New York in 1924, he included an endowment of $1.5 million. It has since grown to $115 million.

Finally, there is the Isabella Stewart Gardner Museum in Boston. Gardner (1840–1924), a wealthy society figure, art collector, and patron, decided to build the museum in 1898; ground was broken in 1899, and the structure was finished in 1900. The museum opened—for a few days each year—in 1903. It may be a stretch to include the Gardner in an entry on house museums, but unlike the Morgan library, Gardner actually lived there, on the top floor. In November 2009, the museum sold a $35 million revenue bond issue through the Massachusetts Health and Educational Facilities Authority to help finance a $115 million renovation and expansion, designed, like the Morgan's, by Renzo Piano. Annual attendance is around 200,000. Operating revenue in 2009 totaled just over $2 million, while contributed income was almost $16 million. The museum also has $106 million in investments. And, as Standard & Poor's noted in rating these bonds AA–, "another credit strength is the museum's renowned collection."

*See also* variable-rate demand obligations.

*Sources:*

Chernow, Ron. *Titan: The Life of John D. Rockefeller, Sr.* New York: Random House, 1998.

$50,000,000 Trust for Cultural Resources of the City of New York Revenue Bonds, Series 2004, January 16, 2004.

$9,000,000 Palm Beach County, Florida, Variable Rate Demand Revenue Bonds, Henry Morrison Flagler Museum Project, April 2003.

Strouse, Jean. *Morgan, American Financier.* New York: Random House, 1999.

$35,000,000 Massachusetts Health and Educational Facilities Authority Revenue Bonds, Isabella Stewart Gardner Museum Issues, Series A.

## "Ideas in public finance blow in from the West"

This market axiom reflects the explosion in the various revenue-supported securities that were created in California after voters in 1978 approved the Proposition 13 property tax cap, some of which structures were later adapted to use in other states. "Proposition 13 was one of the most significant events to affect the structure of the municipal securities market and the activities of the Municipal Securities Rulemaking Board," Christopher Taylor explained in 2006. "Prior to Proposition 13, bonds were typically backed by the ability of the political jurisdiction to raise property taxes. In California, many bonds had two sources of revenue to be used for debt service payments—a use tax or fee backed by an overall pledge to increase property taxes. Market participants viewed the property tax as the primary source of revenue for debt service. The limitation on the increases in property taxes forced investors and other market participants now to treat the streams of revenue from the use tax or fee as the primary source of revenue. Bonds that heretofore had been valued the same were now revalued based on the strength of the use tax or fee revenue streams. The limitation on the use of property taxes as a revenue source forced issuers and dealers to find creative ways to fund necessary infrastructure needs; for example, issuing bonds backed solely by part of a sales tax."

*Source:*

Taylor, Christopher. "Milestones in Municipal Securities Regulation 1975–2005." Municipal Securities Rulemaking Board, Alexandria, VA, 2006.

## indenture

An indenture is the legal document describing the terms and conditions of a bond offering, the rights of the bondholder, and the obligations of the issuer to the bondholder. The document is also referred to as a bond resolution or a deed of trust. It is not to be confused with the official statement of a bond issue.

## Indian tribes

Native American Indian tribes have been authorized to sell tax-exempt securities since 1982. They rarely do so, for a variety of reasons. For one, most tribes are very small, usually numbering between 150 and 3,000 members. For another, they are usually located in rural areas, and while land-rich, tribes are usually cash-poor.

Finally, and perhaps this is the biggest stumbling block, Indian tribes enjoy sovereign immunity. "If the tribe borrows money from a lender and agrees to repay the loan over time but does not waive its sovereign immunity, the lender has no assurance that the tribe will not claim sovereign immunity if a suit is brought by the lender for the repayment of the loan," says Jesse Smith, an investment banker with Seattle-Northwest Securities Corporation, in his 1995 book, *An Introduction to Tax-Exempt Financing for Indian Tribes*.

In order to tap the municipal bond market, tribes have to waive sovereign immunity, which many are reluctant to do. "A tribe which chooses not to waive immunity in any fashion restricts its ability to transact business," Smith says.

*Source:*

Smith, Jesse M. *An Introduction to Tax-Exempt Financing for Indian Tribes*. Seattle, WA: Seattle-Northwest Securities Corp., 1995.

## industrial development bonds

Also know as industrial development revenue bonds and industrial revenue bonds, industrial development bonds (IDBs) are securities sold by municipal entities to encourage corporate projects that will bring some form of benefit to a community, such as new jobs and more tax revenue. The issuers act as conduits so that the borrowers gain access to low-cost, tax-exempt financing rates; the bonds are entirely the responsibility of the corporate borrowers.

Issuance of such bonds was sharply restricted by the Tax Reform Act of 1986, which eliminated some purposes for which IDBs could be sold, and placed the remainder under a cap determined by population. IDBs typically pay more in yield than traditional, governmental municipal borrowers, because repayment of the bonds is dependent upon a private company's fortunes for repayment, rather than the taxing power of a municipality. Such bonds also have a higher rate of default. In 2003, Fitch Ratings found that IDBs had a default rate of around 15 percent, compared with the overall municipal default rate of well under 1 percent.

Buying opportunities in these kinds of bonds usually accompany any sharp sell-off in the municipal bond market, such as occurred in late 2010 and in 2011. The tax-exempt corporate debt of a company sometimes trades at cheaper prices than the same company's taxable debt, purely because mutual funds are selling all varieties of municipal bonds to satisfy shareholder redemptions. If investors are comfortable with the company as a credit, they can gain an extra 25 to 50 basis points or more for buying the municipal bond.

*See also* default; tax-exemption.

## initiative and referendum

The exemplars of what might be termed popular democracy, initiative and referendum allow citizens to bypass their legislatures to put statutory and constitutional measures for consideration on the ballot.

The first state to adopt the initiative was South Dakota in 1898; 23 other states have adopted it since then, the last being Mississippi in 1992, according to the National Conference of State Legislatures (NCSL). There are two types of initiative—direct, where qualifying proposals go straight to the ballot, and indirect, where the measure is submitted to the legislature first.

Referendum is similar to initiative. Legislative referenda—such as bond issues—are submitted to the voters for their approval in all 50 states. Popular referenda are measures that appear on the ballot after petition, and allow voters to approve or disapprove acts of the legislature, according to the NCSL. Popular referendum is allowed in 24 states.

Recall, a related activity, allows for the removal of public officials before the end of their term, and is permitted in 18 states.

Initiative and referendum are the products of boom and bust. "In the late 1800s, indebted farmers and frontiersmen who had moved out West felt that they were subjected to the special interests of industrialist bankers, railroad barons and land speculators," explained Natalie Cohen, senior municipal analyst at Wells Fargo Securities, in a piece of market commentary in 2010. "It was the farmers' belief that these greedy influences had corrupted legislatures and that they were being taxed to help those special interests." The initiative and referendum movement was born.

The pattern, wrote analyst Cohen, repeated in the 1970s, after a rapid run-up in real estate values and a recession. In 1978, California passed Proposition 13, which reduced property taxes by 57 percent. "High oil prices, the 1973 oil crisis and a stock market plunge in 1973–1974 strained household budgets and led to several other voter-initiated tax limitations during this time. Idaho voters, who passed Petition No. 1 in 1978, had seen residential taxes nearly double between 1969 and 1978. In Massachusetts, state and local taxes had grown from 103% of the national average to 124% of the national average in the 1970s. In 1980, voters in that state approved Proposition 2½, which limited tax increases to 2.5%. A similar boom/bust pattern in Colorado in the 1980s eventually led to the 'taxpayer bill of rights,' or TABOR, which sought to significantly limit government (1992)."

Tax caps may have unanticipated consequences. Voters in Saco, Maine, approved a tax cap in 1979 that led the town to default on its general obligation (GO) debt. California's Proposition 13 forced issuers to come up with new ways to borrow money in the municipal bond market that did not include the use of scarce general obligation bond authority. Subsequent limitations in the state further restricted various municipalities' access to their tax base, which is one reason Orange County, California, was forced to enter Chapter 9 bankruptcy in 1994. The wealthy county had no way to tap its vast tax base.

Investors think of general obligation bonds as being valid and legally binding obligations, payable from ad valorem taxes levied on all taxable real property "without limitation as to rate or amount." Tax caps change that equation, and can turn unlimited general obligations to limited general obligations.

So, for example, in the official statement to a Massachusetts town's GO bond today, one may read: "The bonds are valid general obligations and the principal of and interest on the bonds are payable from ad valorem taxes which may be levied upon all taxable property within the territorial limits of the town and taxable by it subject to the limitations imposed by Chapter 59, Section 21C of the general laws (Proposition 2½)," the tax cap approved by the state's voters in 1980.

These GO bonds have a limited call on the town's tax base, right? Except if you read on, you find out that voters in any municipality may vote to exclude from the tax cap any amounts needed to pay debt service on bonds issued before Proposition 2½ was approved, that local voters may exempt subsequent bond issues from the cap, and that bonds incurred before November 4, 1980, "may be constitutionally entitled to payment from taxes in excess of the statutory limit."

*See also* Chapter 9; general obligation; Orange County, California; Saco, Maine.

*Sources:*

Cohen, Natalie. "Election Follow-Up: Taxpayer Initiatives." Wells Fargo Securities Municipal Securities Research, November 5, 2010.

"Initiative, Referendum and Recall." National Conference of State Legislatures website at www.ncsl.org.

Mysak, Joe. "Bonds Aren't Safe When Governments Taxes Are Capped." Bloomberg News, May 5, 2010.

## insider trading

Insider trading in the stock market is trading by company officials and others on information not available to the general public. The same thing can be done in the municipal bond market. It's just not as easy. The potential is there, because millions of dollars are in question. The trouble is that it would be tricky to execute. The trader would need a lot of money, at least relative to the stock market, because municipal bonds are sold in denominations of $5,000. Most dealers do not want $5,000 or $10,000 or $15,000 pieces; they want to work in blocks of $100,000 or more. That's the first problem. The second is that trading on insider information in the muni bond market would not give the same bang for the buck, because bonds do not move as much or as fast as stocks.

Here's how it might work. You are a finance officer, and you know that your municipality is going to advance refund a bond issue. That means you are going to sell a new bond issue, and with some of the proceeds you are going to invest in a pot of special Treasury securities that will provide the funds needed to pay the debt service on the outstanding bonds to be refunded.

Say your old bonds are out there trading at a price of 98. When they are refunded, they are no longer dependent on your municipality's financial fortunes; they are now backed by that pot of Treasury securities, and so rated triple-A. They're gold. They go up in price, maybe to 104 or 105.

At least in theory, you could call up your wealthy mother-in-law and tell her to buy those old bonds, or you could buy them yourself.

In 1992, the Securities and Exchange Commission prosecuted just such a case. The Kentucky Infrastructure Authority solicited tender offers for a portion of a bond issue it had sold in 1973. The authority was required to redeem $760,000 of bonds. It received $650,000 worth. The SEC said that N. Donald Morse II, the secretary/treasurer of the authority, knew that the authority needed another $110,000 of bonds to complete the tender. He went out and bought $110,000 of the bonds from a bondholder for a price of 94 (it cost him $103,400). He registered the bonds in the name of a bank, not in his own name.

Morse then told the trustee running the tender the serial numbers of the $760,000 in bonds to be accepted for tender, including his $110,000 worth of bonds, according to the SEC. The tender price was 99 7/8. Morse made $6,462.50. Morse sold his bonds "without disclosing to the authority his ownership . . . and that he had obtained them at a lower price than he was tendering in breach of a fiduciary duty or other relationship of trust and confidence that Morse owed to the Authority," the SEC said in its complaint.

The gist of the insider trading case was that Morse bought the bonds for himself while in possession of material nonpublic information—that the authority needed another $110,000 in bonds to complete its tender. Morse settled with the SEC, and agreed to disgorge his profits.

*Source:*

*SEC v. N. Donald Morse II, U.S. District Court for the Eastern District of Kentucky*, Civil Action No. 92-64, June 23, 1992.

## insurance

A product dating from 1971, bond insurance for a brief time in the late 1990s and early 2000s managed to cover 50 percent or more of the new-issue market each year. Once enormously profitable, the major insurers were shut out of the business in 2008 after losing their triple-A-claims-paying ratings from Moody's, Standard & Poor's, and Fitch because of their losses on collateralized debt obligations (CDOs) and subprime mortgage securities.

Bond insurance guarantees the timely and regular—not accelerated—payment of principal and interest should an issuer fail to do so. The first mention of the concept of municipal bond insurance was contained in a front-page story in the Saturday, April 3, 1897, edition of *The Daily Bond Buyer* concerning the founding of the First Municipal Bond Assurance Company of America.

FMBACA, as it would have been known in the acronym-mad municipal bond insurance industry of the twentieth century, envisioned insuring timely debt-service payment of bonds both in the new issue and the secondary market (the latter not accomplished until the modern business was almost two decades old). *The Daily Bond Buyer* was skeptical: "The first class Cities which are selling low rate interest bearing bonds for long terms at a high basis just now are not likely to ask any insurance for which they will have to pay," the newspaper editorialized. "It is uncertain as yet if any large purchaser of original issues of bonds by large cities will be willing to pay any considerable percentage to have guaranteed the bonds which the cities themselves guarantee." The insurer disappeared without a trace, and evidently without insuring a single bond.

It was not until 1971 that the first municipal bond was insured, a $600,000 general obligation bond sold by Juneau, Alaska, and guaranteed by Ambac (originally the American Municipal Bond Assurance Corporation). The earliest hurdle for the concept of bond insurance was the tax treatment of any debt-service payment an insurer might make. Ambac said that it would be tax-exempt, because the company would be acting as a substitute for the municipality whose security it insured. The IRS accepted the argument.

The idea behind bond insurance was a simple one, the name perhaps confusing to some. The issuer of the bonds purchased credit enhancement in the form of an insurance company's triple-A rating. The so-called insurance was not an instrument like, say, fire or accident insurance, where the municipality could use it if it needed it. Insurers actively discouraged bond issuers from tapping their policies at all, and maintained large staffs to monitor the financial health of the municipalities whose bonds they covered and to assist them in times of financial distress (usually by helping to restructure their debt). Those occasions were rare, because the insurers said they underwrote to a zero-loss standard; that is, they insured only credits on which they never expected to pay a claim. As some critics claimed, the bond insurers never offered their product to a municipality that really needed it.

This is how bond insurance worked. Say a city wants to borrow $1 million for 10 years in the municipal bond market. The city's own rating would result in paying 6 percent to borrow that money. But if the city pays to use the insurance company's triple-A rating, that cost comes down to 5 percent. The difference between borrowing money at 6 percent and borrowing it at 5 percent is $100,000 over the 10 years.

The insurance lasts as long as the debt is outstanding. The premium is paid up front and is quoted in basis points of total principal and interest. In this case, let's say the insurance costs 25 basis points, or one-fourth of 1 percent. Principal and interest payments total $1,500,000, so the premium works out to $3,750. City taxpayers save $96,250 over the life of the loan by buying the insurance.

That savings is realized immediately at the pricing of the bond deal. Market convention dictated that issuers using negotiation to sell their bonds paid the premium from a portion of the bond proceeds, while winning underwriters paid for the insurance on bonds sold at auction.

Insurance for a product that had a default rate of less than 1 percent in the first place was a tough sell. A full decade after bond insurance debuted, it covered only 5 percent of the new-issue market—$2.3 billion of the $46 billion in total volume sold in 1981. And this was after New York City's well-publicized brush with bankruptcy; there was no surge in demand for municipal bond insurance.

The product's big break occurred in 1985, when a then-record $204 billion of municipal bonds were sold, as issuers rushed to market to beat tax-reform measures that threatened to curb their ability to sell certain kinds of debt. Salespeople deluged with supply found that insurance made for a simpler sell; rather than providing an extensive description of a bond's various security features, they found they could point to the insured, triple-A nature of the paper. The individual investors who were soon to dominate the market (after tax reform did away with cost-of-carry deductions for banks on all but the smallest issues) were a receptive audience, unprepared and reluctant to sift through the myriad details of a bond's underlying credit characteristics.

And so in 1985, insured penetration reached almost 22 percent, more than $44 billion of the $204 billion sold that year. This was to be remembered as the happy time for the industry, as bankers, underwriters, lawyers, and analysts, too, worked through a busy fall and a December that is still the record for a month of municipal bond sales: $54.7 billion.

Twenty years after the introduction of bond insurance, penetration reached 30 percent, $52 billion of the $173 billion sold. At the time, premium rates averaged in the 25- to 35-basis-point range. In 1992, another record year, when states and municipalities sold $235 billion in bonds, insurers guaranteed $80.6 billion, or 34 percent. The first time that insurance covered 50 percent of the market was 1998, when $145 billion of the $286.7 billion sold carried the insurers' triple-As. The high-water mark was reached in 2005, when issuers sold a record $408 billion in bonds, 57 percent of which was insured.

Not everyone was a cheerleader for bond insurance. Some mutual fund portfolio managers grumbled that credit enhancement sucked yield out of the market, and some issuers complained that it diluted the value of their own good ratings. Some critics said the insurers were overleveraged, and that an always-imminent wave of delinquencies could wipe them out. Others questioned the product's existence at all: why did issuers use it when it was clearly unneeded? The concept of bond insurance seemed to annoy a great many people. And yet it was inarguable that the idea of wrapping the multifarious and usually small and infrequent issuers that constitute the municipal market with some sort of homogenizing credit could help those issuers. Bond banks, the first of which opened for business in 1970, were a variety of enhancement; state intercept programs, which became more prevalent in the 1980s, were another.

The bond insurance business was relatively small, and dominated at its height by four major firms: Ambac, the Municipal Bond Insurance Association (MBIA), the Financial Guaranty Insurance Company (FGIC), and Financial Security Assurance (FSA), MBIA being the big dog in the pack. The aforementioned Ambac began in 1971, and at the time it insured its first issue conferred only a double-A rating on those who used it. MBIA was incorporated in 1971 and insured its first deal in 1974 (at a triple-A level). FGIC opened in 1983, and was followed by Bond Investors Guaranty and FSA (which began life as a corporate insurer) in 1985 (FSA insured its first municipal transaction in 1990). San Francisco–based Capital Guaranty started doing business in 1986. Bond Investors Guaranty was acquired by MBIA in 1989, Capital Guaranty by FSA in 1995.

In 1971, Standard & Poor's was the first rating company to take bond insurance into account when grading a municipal security. Moody's did so only in 1984, and Fitch in 1991. It soon became necessary for insurers to buy three triple-A ratings in order to remain competitive. It was surprising that it took so long for the rating agencies to accept the concept; the insurers and their rapidly growing books of business became a profitable line for the raters.

The bond insurance business was small, and it was competitive, despite a relatively high cost of entry in terms of capital and a smallish talent pool from which to draw the staffs of analysts needed to monitor existing business and assess new business. It was inevitable that premium levels would shrink as insurers cut prices to gain market share. The insurers said they underwrote to a zero-loss standard, but the original premium structure was set up to withstand defaults. In 1986, Gerald Friedman, one of the founders of Ambac and later of FGIC, said he calculated the premium levels that could accommodate between six and 12 defaults per 100 issues, a greater than Great Depression default scenario, and that level was 80 basis points. In 1990, participants estimated that premiums had shrunk to 50 basis points, and in 1991, to between 25 and 35 basis points. By the time the new century began, premiums had dwindled to as little as 5 or 10 basis points on the best credits.

The insurers had already started looking elsewhere for ways to enhance their profitability, and that was to prove their undoing. Their move into insuring riskier structured finance transactions, asset-backed securities (ABSs), and collateralized debt obligations was considered at the time, however—the mid- to late 1990s—to be a natural evolution. By this time, three of the big four, Ambac, MBIA, and FSA, were publicly held, and both the stockholders and the equity analysts who covered the companies demanded growth. In asset-backed securities, the insurers thought they had found a way to duplicate the free lunch they had for so long enjoyed in the municipal market.

The first to question what the insurers were doing was William Ackman, a hedge fund manager who in December 2002 produced a report, "Is MBIA Triple A?" subtitled "A Detailed Analysis of SPVs, CDOs, and Accounting and Reserving Policies at MBIA, Inc." Special purpose vehicles (SPVs) and collateralized debt obligations (CDOs), which collected subprime loans in packages, would become all too familiar to Americans in the years ahead. Ackman, who was shorting MBIA's stock, answered the question posed by his title in the negative.

"In MBIA's traditional business of guaranteeing municipal debt, the company had an informational advantage compared to Wall Street that enabled it to profit from the sale of insurance to municipalities which could not easily access capital without its guarantee," Ackman explained. "In contrast, MBIA's recent growth has been driven by the structured finance markets for which there are alternatives to monoline guarantees." And in this business, Ackman wrote, MBIA did not have an informational advantage. The company was taking on too much risk for too little reward.

Ackman even described precisely when MBIA began venturing into new frontiers: "At a board meeting in Bermuda in 1991, the board and management concluded that it would have to expand the company's charter—which had previously restricted MBIA's business to muni guarantees—in order to meet the company's earnings and growth targets in light of increasing competition and the limited size of the municipal market. In 1992, the company diversified its business to begin guaranteeing other financial obligations." And so the seeds of destruction were sown.

This move into insuring nonmunicipal transactions did not occur in secret. The other insurers followed suit, and it was widely discussed at industry conferences and events. The move was widely heralded by the analysts who covered the companies, both at securities firms and at the rating agencies. The analysts pointed out that the asset-backed securities market looked to be even safer than the municipal bond market.

In 2002, when Ackman originally made his case, the idea that any of the insurers might allow their triple-A ratings to fail was inconceivable. The stock prices of the publicly held insurers rose, and rose, and business never seemed better; indeed, in the municipal bond market, the group reached its collective peak in 2005, when they insured 57 percent of all municipals. That a fall would come only a few years later and that it would be almost absolute was as fantastic as—well, as imagining that Bear Stearns, Lehman Brothers, and Merrill Lynch would someday disappear from the scene as bankrupts or acquisitions. In those days, when analysts discussed "counterparty risk" in any transaction featuring municipalities and major Wall Street banks—such transactions usually concerned swaps—it was always quietly presumed that the ones at risk of failing to live up to their part of a bargain were the municipalities involved, certainly not the big banks or the bond insurers.

In May 2007, short seller Ackman struck again, this time with a piece on the impending collapse of the ABS market entitled "Who's Holding the Bag?" His answer: the bond insurers, but ultimately, all those who were relying on the insurers to make good on bond defaults. A credit event would overwhelm the insurers' available capital, he wrote.

This time, people were listening. By the fall of 2007, jitters about the insurers' exposure to the subprime losses that were now mounting roiled the auction-rate securities market (insurers often backed the issues), and a number of auctions failed. The rush to cash out was blamed on the insurers' exposure to the ABS and subprime market. In January 2008, Moody's put both Ambac and MBIA under review; Fitch cut FGIC and Ambac to AA. In February, the auction-rate market froze, as dealers stopped supporting the auctions altogether. In April, Fitch cut MBIA to AA. In early June, Standard & Poor's downgraded MBIA and Ambac; later that month, Moody's cut MBIA to A, and Ambac to Aa. In November 2008, Assured Guaranty bought FSA, and continued as the last bond insurer with an AAA Standard & Poor's rating.

In early 2008, Warren Buffett entered the bond insurance business with Berkshire Hathaway Assurance Corporation. The firm did a limited amount of business, and in February 2009, in his annual letter to shareholders, Buffett famously warned that governments with guaranteed debt might choose to default rather than raise the taxes necessary to pay debt service. "What mayor or city council is going to choose pain to local citizens in the form of major tax increases over pain to a faraway bond insurer?" he asked. He called bond insurance "a dangerous business." In April, Moody's downgraded Berkshire's parent company, and the bond insurer lost its Aaa rating, too.

If there was a punctuation mark to the meltdown of the bond insurers, it came on March 4, 2008, when California treasurer Bill Lockyer and 14 other government finance officers sent a five-page letter to Fitch, Moody's, and Standard & Poor's demanding justice. The letter was sort of a long-delayed follow-up to the March 2007 admission by Moody's that if rated on a single scale and compared with corporate securities, municipal bonds would be rated higher. Rating municipal bonds differently from corporates was responsible for the creation of the bond insurance industry, the officials wrote. "Municipal bond issuers have paid enormous sums to buy bond insurance that—at least in part—brought their ratings up to the level they would have been on a corporate, or global, rating scale," the letter said. Between 2003 and 2007, California alone had spent $102 million to get its general obligation bonds insured. Wasn't it time to treat all bonds equally?

It would take almost another two years for the Great Recalibration of ratings to take place, and when it was over, it turned out that no, not everyone was rated triple-A, even when considered on a global scale. The length and depth of the Great Recession, meanwhile, meant that a number of issuers were downgraded.

More insults to the insurance industry were to come. In November 2008, Moody's published a Special Comment on "The Changing Business of Financial Guaranty Insurance." By this time, with the exception of FSA and Assured Guaranty, its acquirer, the downgraded bond insurers were clinging to the notion that they might still remain in business if they could only ring-fence their municipal portfolios and form new entities. "Achieving a stand-alone Aaa rating for a muni-only guarantor would likely be difficult absent its ability to defend against product encroachment, secure reliable access to new funding in stress scenarios, and protect against the removal of capital and risk management resources in a run-off scenario."

In other words, a triple-A municipal bond insurer was an impossibility, according to Moody's.

More was to come. Assured Guaranty clung to its franchise throughout 2009 and much of 2010; even with a single AAA from Standard & Poor's, business remained for the company to capture, and it insured 1,697 issues in 2010 totaling $27 billion. On October 25, 2010, S&P lowered its rating on Assured to AA+, saying, "The current state of the financial guarantee market, with only one organization issuing new policies, is symptomatic of investors' and issuers' diminished demand for bond insurance." And in January, S&P requested comment on new bond insurance criteria that would, Assured said, likely result in a further (and, to Assured's thinking, unwarranted) downgrade. In August 2010, FGIC Corporation, the holding company for Financial Guaranty Insurance Company, declared bankruptcy.

In March 2011, Fitch Ratings, which had suspended all financial guaranty ratings and criteria in February 2010, asked if municipal bond insurance was still relevant, answered that it probably was (especially for "midsize and smaller" municipal credits), and said that it had received numerous inquiries from potential new start-ups. The firm observed that the natural rating range for an existing insurer was probably A, that for a start-up perhaps BBB. The firm concluded that "there are certain risks inherent to the industry that can not be fully mitigated," including the need for very high levels of operating leverage to achieve acceptable returns on capital, a narrow business focus, and sale of a product that is "nice to have" rather than "need to have."

The final chapter has yet to be written on municipal bond insurance. At AA+, Assured was still doing business in 2011, and MBIA was arguing that fraud had been committed in the creation of many of the bundled mortgage securities it had insured, especially those of the most recent vintage.

*See also* auction-rate securities; bond banks; market activity; Recalibration of 2010; Texas Permanent School Fund.

*Sources:*

Ackman, William. "Is MBIA Triple A? A Detailed Analysis of SPVs, CDOs, and Accounting and Reserving Policies at MBIA, Inc." Gotham Partners, New York, December 9, 2002.

Ackman, William. "Who's Holding the Bag?" Pershing Square Capital Management, May 2007.

*Bond Buyer* yearbooks for three decades.

Boyle, Nicholas. "Digging Up the Roots of Bond Insurance." *Bond Buyer* Centennial Edition, August 1991.

Buffett, Warren. Annual letter to Berkshire Hathaway shareholders, February 2009.

"The Changing Business of Financial Guaranty Insurance." Special Comment, Moody's Investors Service, November 2008.

"Financial Guaranty—Revisited." Fitch Ratings Special Report, March 29, 2011.

Lockyer, Bill, et al. Letter to the rating agencies, March 4, 2008.

"Municipal Bond Insurance." *Daily Bond Buyer*, April 3, 1897.

Mysak, Joe. "Gerald Friedman Blasts Muni Bond Insurers over Capital Adequacy." *Bond Buyer*, May 28, 1987.

"Request for Comment: Bond Insurance Criteria." Standard & Poor's, January 24, 2011.

Richard, Christine. *Confidence Game: How a Hedge Fund Manager Called Wall Street's Bluff.* Hoboken, NJ: John Wiley & Sons, 2010.

Richard, Christine, and Darrell Preston. "Bond Insurance Charade Costs U.S. Taxpayers $2.5 Billion a Year." Bloomberg News, October 5, 2006.

## interest

Most bond issuers pay interest, or, as the Municipal Securities Rulemaking Board puts it, compensation "generally calculated as an annual percentage of the principal amount" of a bond, on a semiannual basis. Issuers of zero-coupon bonds pay no interest, but the bonds are sold at a deep discount and paid at 100 percent upon maturity.

## inverse floaters

A type of bond structure used both in the new-issue market and in the secondary market, where banks buy bonds, deposit them into a trust, and cut up the payments into floaters, whose rates are reset periodically, and inverse floaters, which take the remainder.

*See also* floaters/inverse floaters; tender-option bond programs.

## investment pools

States and counties manage pools of money for governmental entities ranging in size from school districts to cities and towns, to afford them safety, ease of access, and savings due to economies of scale. There are about 100 such pools in the United States, and they operate much like money-market funds, offering municipalities a place to park cash like tax proceeds. More often than not, such pools invest in U.S. Treasury securities, certificates of deposit, and commercial paper.

Unfortunate examples of investment pools running into trouble include the Orange County, California, Investment Pool; Cuyahoga County, Ohio's Secured Assets Fund Earnings (SAFE) pool; and TexPool—all of which lost money in 1994 because of their investments in derivative securities (Orange County eventually declaring bankruptcy because of losses in the pool)—and the Florida Investment Pool, which in November 2007 froze the fund to stop withdrawals.

The Florida pool, which until that time had been the largest public money market fund in the United States, held $26 billion for about 1,000 school districts, towns, and local agencies in the state. Participants rushed to pull their money out of the fund after it revealed that it held close to $1 billion in subprime-tainted assets.

*See also* Orange County, California.

*Sources:*

Evans, David. "Florida Got Lehman Help Before Run on School's Funds." Bloomberg News, December 18, 2007.

Evans, David. "Public School Funds Hit by SEV Debts Hidden in Investment Pools." Bloomberg News, November 15, 2007.

## issue price

According to Section 148 of the Internal Revenue Code of 1986, the issue price of bonds that are publicly offered is the first price at which a substantial amount of bonds is sold to the public, a "substantial amount" being 10 percent. Underwriters provide bond issuers with a Tax Matters Certificate typically stating that not less than 10 percent of each maturity has been sold at the issue price, and that such price "is not unreasonably low." Underwriters also sign a Certificate of Purchaser stating, "A substantial amount (not less than 10 percent) of each maturity of the Bonds was sold to the public or final purchasers (not including bond houses, or brokers or similar persons or organizations acting in the capacity of Purchasers or wholesalers) at or below such initial reoffering price." The question of issue price was called into question in the early 2000s after observers discovered flipping in municipal securities, or sales to certain large investors who then resold the bonds in smaller lots at much higher prices.

*See also* flipping.

*Source:*

Mysak, Joe. "Bond Market Is Set to Debate If Issue Price Matters." Bloomberg News, September 1, 2006.


## issuer concentration

A relatively small number of issuers dominate the market. Of the $3.7 trillion in total outstanding municipal debt, the top 10 states and their municipalities accounted for $2.15 trillion, or 58 percent. The top five states—California, New York, Texas, Illinois, and Florida—accounted for $1.65 trillion, or almost 46 percent of the entire market, according to a Bloomberg estimate made in mid-2011.

"Only 7 percent of issuers had $100 million or more in securities outstanding," the Securities and Exchange Commission (SEC) said in a 2004 study of transactions in municipal securities. "However, this latter group was responsible for the vast majority of the principal amount of securities traded (84 percent)."

By comparison, two-thirds of municipal issuers had $10 million or less in securities outstanding, according to the SEC. At the time the SEC produced this study, it calculated that there were 51,000 issuers with bonds outstanding.

In terms of number of deals, the SEC said that about half of all issuers had 10 or fewer securities outstanding; only 3 percent had 100 or more separate securities. In a 2006 study, the Internal Revenue Service found that of the 14,419 long-term governmental bonds sold in 2004, three-quarters were for $5 million or less. All those small issues accounted for only 6.7 percent of the dollar amount of bonds sold.

The composition of the market has a direct impact on the ease with which investors can sell their bonds, if they must. The bonds of large issuers who are frequently in the market are more easily sold than the small transactions offered by municipalities once every few years, and whose bonds almost take on the characteristics of collectibles.

*See also* "All bonds go to heaven"; secondary market.

*Sources:*

Belmonte, Cynthia. "Tax-Exempt Bonds, 2003–2004." *Internal Revenue Service Statistics of Income Bulletin*, Fall 2006.

Fischer, Philip, and Yingchen Li. "Issuer Concentration in the Muni Market." Merrill Lynch & Co., August 28, 1998.

"Report on Transactions in Municipal Securities." Office of Economic Analysis and Office of Municipal Securities, Securities and Exchange Commission, July 1, 2004.

# J

## Jefferson County, Alabama

What began as a court-ordered water cleanup ended with a sewer district under receivership, a county on the brink of bankruptcy, and public officials, bankers, and building contractors serving prison terms. At the center of the municipal bond market's scandal of the (new) century was a potent mixture of auction-rate and variable-rate debt and interest-rate swaps whose costs skyrocketed as the subprime crisis claimed the top ratings of the financial guarantors backing the debt.

The Jefferson County disaster epitomized all that was wrong with public finance in the 1990s and early 2000s. And it was almost uniquely a municipal finance story, unlike many of the other governmental collapses that have dotted the market's history.

The New York City meltdown of 1975, for example, occurred primarily because banks (finally) refused to keep lending to the profligate government of a city that seemed intent on destroying its own industrial base. The Washington Public Power Supply System defaulted on $2.25 billion in bonds in 1983 after a court ruled invalid certain contracts putting participants in the project on the hook for its debt. Orange County, California, declared bankruptcy in 1994 because losses on leveraged investments led to insolvency. Municipal securities were collateral damage in each of these examples. In Jefferson County, Alabama, the financing process was directly implicated.

The story began with the county's 1996 agreement to stop dumping untreated sewage into the Cahaba River. The consent decree agreed to by the county was onerous; some say unreasonable. "I believe the County did not resist these terms vigorously because the tougher the decree the more the engineers, lawyers, and financiers benefited from the resulting engineering, construction, financing, and legal fees and costs," banker and one-time county adviser James H. White III declared at a 2010 symposium on the county's disaster.

"The Jefferson County sewer consent decree required that specified results be achieved but was not based on analysis of the facilities required to achieve those results, estimates of capital and operating costs, or the affordability and reasonableness of the sewer service charges implied by such cost estimates," said White. His firm participated in the December 2002 review of the program, whose cost estimates had increased from between $250 million and $1.2 billion in 1996 to $2.4 billion by 2002 (they would eventually amount to $3.2 billion).

The review (by BE&K Engineering Company; CH2M HILL; Porter, White & Company; and the Public Affairs Research Council of Alabama) was released in October 2003, and concluded that the county had embarked on the sewer program without a comprehensive strategy to prioritize improvements and track costs, and without even an engineering feasibility study. The result was that the program just grew, morphing from remediation to expansion. Incompetence and mismanagement swiftly combined with bribery, corruption, and massive cost overruns.

The stage, however, was set for the next phase of this disaster, the actual financing. And here the Jefferson County story has something for everyone concerned with public finance, good government, and the municipal bond market. All the transactions were done through negotiation. Interest-rate swaps featured prominently every step of the way. Most of the politicians involved seemed more intent on giving out business than in monitoring costs and risks. Pay-to-play, it later turned out, was rampant. There was enough blame to go around that bond insurers, rating companies, and the market's regulators all could be assigned a role in this bomb.

In an effort to stretch out the repayment of the project, not entirely an unjust motive in a jurisdiction that already charged some of the highest sewer fees in the region, the county turned all of its fixed-rate debt to a synthetic fixed rate with the help of variable-rate securities and billions of dollars in swaps. The final blow came when the subprime collapse claimed the bond insurers' top ratings, triggering a variable-rate explosion that could be remedied only by the payment of enormous termination fees and another round of financing.

At the heart of the Jefferson County story are the swaps, whose use Wall Street securities firms had embraced in the 1990s as a way to bolster the dwindling amounts they could earn on underwriting municipal bonds. Underwriting spreads, or the amounts the dealers could make from selling bonds, had dropped from $20 or more per $1,000 in the 1970s to $5 or so in the early 2000s. To make money, Wall Street turned to the reinvestment of proceeds business, pushing issuers to sell auction-rate and variable-rate debt (which also offered the opportunity to make regular fee income from running auctions and remarketing), and the sales of interest-rate swaps and derivatives.

Unlike most scandals in MuniLand, when transactions are examined only in retrospect, in Jefferson County one of the commissioners asked questions right up front. Commissioner Bettye Fine Collins in March 1997 held up the county's first swap transaction until the director of finance could return from the underwriter's office in St. Petersburg, Florida, and explain how the deal worked. She was ridiculed for doing so—the delay costing the county $900,000 due to a movement in the swaps market—in an editorial cartoon in the pages of the *Birmingham News*. Collins wanted some more detail on why the county was replacing its variable-rate debt with fixed-rate debt swapped back to variable rate. The transaction was featured as a "Deal in the Spotlight" in the *Bond Buyer* newspaper.

Between 1997 and 2003, the county financed its sewer cleanup, selling $3.6 billion in what are called sewer revenue warrants. From 2002 to 2004, the county converted its fixed-rate debt to variable and auction rate and then swapped back to fixed rate with the use of 23 various swap transactions totaling $6.7 billion.

The plan sounds worse than the actual logic behind it. In a hypothetical example, an issuer borrows money in the fixed-rate market at, say, 5 percent. In the auction- and variable-rate market, the same issuer pays short-term rates that are reset periodically, and these are usually in the 2 percent or 3 percent range. So the issuer can borrow long-term, for 30 or 40 years, and always pay short-term rates. By entering into a swap, the issuer gets a counterparty to pay it a rate that will reset periodically, and pays the counterparty a fixed rate—say, 3.25 percent. The issuer bets, or hopes, or trusts that the variable rate it receives from the counterparty matches the rate it has to pay on its debt. The fixed rate it pays the counterparty is even lower than it could possibly get in the regular fixed-rate market. That's the theory. There were all sorts of pitfalls for the unsophisticated, but there was nothing wrong with the theory. By restructuring the debt this way, county commissioners thought they could forestall higher sewer rates.

The county became adept at using swaps during this period, or thought it did, and in 2003 and 2004 even hosted what it called "Investor Relations Forums" in which it invited local government debt issuers and others to listen to presentations from its bankers and advisers about financial matters and how they, too, could use swaps. The September 2004 forum even featured a day entitled "Derivatives: Getting the Right Deal Done Right" that included a session on swap valuation and transparency. As the brochure to the event noted, "Contemplating a swap requires a higher level of analysis by issuers and more intensive post-deal monitoring." In retrospect, this was like Orange County, California, treasurer Robert Citron giving lessons on public fund risk management.

The forum was scheduled for September 2004. That also marked the return of the county and its deals to the national spotlight, which has not dimmed to this day. That was when the Securities and Exchange Commission asked the county finance director for all documents relating to the sewer financing, including that swap portfolio. County officials said they were surprised by the SEC inquiry. Some said it might have to do with the pay-to-play trial then going on in Philadelphia, which happened to include Jefferson County's former lead banker, Charles LeCroy of J.P. Morgan Securities (he would plead guilty to federal fraud charges in the Philadelphia trial and spend three months in prison). A little later, the Internal Revenue Service said it, too, was looking into the Jefferson County transactions.

People—academics, analysts, regulators, and the press—finally started asking questions about that restructuring; about why the county had used so many swaps; and about how much the bankers, brokers, and advisers had been paid. In March 2005, the Alabama Department of Examiners of Public Accounts said it looked like the county's swapping from 1997 to 2004 had actually cost it $85 million. That announcement further fueled stories in both the local and the national press. At this point, it was still second-guessing, and the county was growing sensitive about it. Finance director Steve Sayler told the *Wall Street Journal*, "It's easy to pick on us because we're supposedly a bunch of dumb country bumpkins and rednecks."

In an August 2005 analysis, Bloomberg News said it looked like the county had paid about twice as much as it should have on the bulk of the swap transactions.

In the nonfinancial world, meanwhile, the U.S. Attorney began prosecuting corruption and bribery among former officials, contractors, and the county's Environmental Services Department, which had overseen the sewer project's construction.

In November 2006, the U.S. Justice Department acknowledged that it was conducting an inquiry into "anti-competitive practices" in the municipal bond market, and the Federal Bureau of Investigation raided several brokers who specialized in the reinvestment of proceeds business. In December, the SEC subpoenaed county officials in connection with the sewer refinancing and swaps.

In January 2007, Porter, White & Company produced a report saying that the county had paid about $120 million to the banks with which it had engaged in swaps, when a fairer price would have been between $20 million and $40 million. The report, along with subsequent stories, confirmed that swaps could be very lucrative for the banks in the business of providing them, and that municipal issuers, including the county, were ill-equipped to determine whether the prices they were paying for the instruments were fair market value. It turned out that the county, like most issuers, had relied on the representations of the professionals it had hired.

Until the subprime crisis intervened, and absent any enforcement proceedings, the debate about municipalities' use of interest-rate swaps might have remained on this he-said, she-said level for some time. It can be boiled down to this: Critics suspected that issuers were paying too much for swaps and other derivatives, and that most of them were getting involved in things whose risks they were incapable of evaluating. Bankers responded that public officials were fully capable of understanding the risks and rewards, and that all issuers, even the smallest, ought to be able to benefit from the sophisticated products Wall Street had on offer. The products were not risky, proponents said; they hedged risk.

The subprime crisis showed what could go wrong. In the fall of 2007, dealers already flooded with auction-rate securities inventory began letting certain auctions fail. Rates began climbing. In January 2008, yields on some securities almost doubled as investors fretted about the health of the insurers backing so much of the debt. When the guarantors were downgraded as a result of their losses on subprime securities—in Jefferson County's case, FGIC (downgraded by Standard & Poor's on January 31 to AA from AAA) and XL Capital (downgraded by Moody's to A3 a week later)—yields shot higher. In February, the auction-rate securities market froze when dealers stopped supporting auctions. Yields on the county's variable-rate debt went to 10 percent from 3.09 percent; on the auction-rate debt, to 6.25 percent from 3.92 percent. The cost to the county: $6 million in interest alone. Annual debt-service costs eventually rose to $460 million, more than double the sewer system's annual revenue of $190 million. The swaps were not protecting the county, because while auction and variable rates climbed, the benchmark rates banks paid to the county—the London Interbank Offered Rate (LIBOR) and the Bond Market Association (BMA) index—fell.

The county was not alone; the same thing happened to issuers everywhere who also used swaps, including Harvard University, for example.

On February 27, Moody's answered the question that inevitably arises in times of municipal financial stress: how many more municipalities out there are in the same boat as X? In cutting the county's debt to Baa3 from A3 and placing it on review, "reflecting concern about the county's ability to manage its 'highly leveraged' debt portfolio," the rating company said, "Moody's is unaware of any other municipalities or governmental enterprises that have used variable rate and hedging tools to this extent."

Moody's continued, "We believe that the degree of risk that this poses to Jefferson County as a result of current disruptions is likely to be unique and not replicated in the vast majority of other municipal entities."

The county put out a material-event notice on February 29, which stated that it might be unable to pay banks holding its floating-rate debt or make collateral payments on its interest-rate swaps. The move might force the county to buy back $847 million of floating-rate debt and terminate the swaps at a cost of $184 million. Even if the banks did not demand immediate payment, the floating-rate debt would become accelerated bank debt, with the county having to make 16 quarterly payments of as much as $53 million. At around this time, the county started talking about reaching a forbearance agreement with its banks. Market participants brought up the possibility that the county might have to declare bankruptcy.

Jefferson County's descent into the financial abyss might have dominated the headlines were it not for the near collapse of the financial system in 2008. In March, Bear Stearns imploded and was sold to JPMorgan Chase & Company. The stock market swooned, and in September, conditions deteriorated still further with the Lehman Brothers bankruptcy. The county was pushed off the front page as it attempted to muddle through. Nobody seemed eager for the county to declare bankruptcy. But neither did the state step in and attempt to sort things out.

This is essentially where the county is today, working to resolve a crisis not entirely of its own making.

The later the hour, the more interesting the stories became, as more and more behind-the-scenes details were revealed. In March 2008, for example, Goldman, Sachs & Company and Birmingham-based Sterne Agee & Leech in a restructuring proposal advised the county to unwind all its swaps. "The amount of risk the system has incurred is well beyond what is considered acceptable in the municipal marketplace," the firms wrote. "These swaps are essentially bets on the market that are not germane to the operation of a sewer system."

In April 2008, the Securities and Exchange Commission charged Larry Langford (ex-president of the county commission and former mayor of Birmingham), banker William Blount, and lobbyist Albert LaPierre with fraud in connection with an "undisclosed payment scheme," where Langford ensured that Blount's firm was involved in all of the county's bond and swap transactions in exchange for $241,000 in bribes. Langford was sentenced to 15 years in prison, Blount to 52 months, and LaPierre to four years.

In September, JPMorgan Chase & Company said it would stop selling interest-rate swaps to governmental borrowers. "The risk/return profile of this business is such that the returns no longer justify the level of resources we have allocated to it," the firm said in a memo to employees.

Finally, in November 2009, the SEC charged J.P. Morgan Securities and two of its former managing directors for their roles in an "unlawful payment scheme that enabled them to win business involving municipal bond offerings and swap agreement transactions" in the county. In settling with the SEC, the firm paid $50 million to the county, forfeited $647 million in termination fees it claimed the county owed it under the swap transactions, and paid $25 million to compensate "harmed investors and the county." The bankers said they would fight the charges. On March 1, 2011, the U.S. Justice Department said it planned to move for a stay of all depositions involved in the case. The reason? Justice was conducting its own investigation into the county's sewer financing. In September of 2011, the county approved an agreement with creditors that included $1.1 billion in concessions, sale of new bonds, and a series of sewer rate increases.

*See also* auction-rate securities; bid rigging; pay-to-play; swaps.

*Sources:*

Blackledge, Brett J., and Eric Velasco. "Smoot Contacts Get Bond Contracts, Jeffco Commissioner Defends Finance Deals." *Birmingham News*, October 24, 2004.

Braun, Martin Z. "SEC Probes Alabama County's Bond, Derivatives Deals." Bloomberg News, December 20, 2006.

Braun, Martin Z. "U.S. Looking into Jefferson County Sewer Deals, Banker Says." Bloomberg News, March 24, 2011.

Braun, Martin Z., Darrell Preston, and Liz Willen. "JPMorgan Swaps Roil Alabama on Secret Finance Deals." Bloomberg News, August 3, 2005.

"Hey, Wait a Minute." *Grant's Municipal Bond Observer*, September 5, 1997.

Hume, Lynn, and Shelly Sigo. "SEC Asks Jefferson Co., Alabama, about $4 Billion of Swaps, Warrants." *Bond Buyer*, September 24, 2004.

In the Matter of J.P. Morgan Securities Inc. Administrative Proceeding, Securities and Exchange Commission, November 4, 2009.

Jefferson County, Alabama, Swap Portfolio Report, Porter, White & Co., January 23, 2007.

Jefferson County Commission, 2nd Investor Relations Forum, September 22–24, 2004, brochure.

Jefferson County Program Review, Final Report, BE&K Engineering Co., CH2M HILL, Public Affairs Research Council of Alabama (Parca), Porter, White & Co., September 2003.

Keefe, John. "Anatomy of a Swap." *Grant's Municipal Bond Issuer*, November 20, 1997.

Richardson, Karen. "Sweet Hedge Alabama: A County Defends Rate-Swap Strategy." *Wall Street Journal*, June 8, 2005.

*Securities and Exchange Commission v. Charles E. LeCroy and Douglas W. MacFaddin*, November 4, 2009.

*Securities and Exchange Commission v. Larry P. Langford, William B. Blount, Blount Parrish & Co. Inc. and Albert W. LaPierre*, April 30, 2008.

White, James H., III. "Financing Plans for the Jefferson County Sewer System: Issues and Mistakes." *Cumberland Law Review* 40, no. 3 (2009–2010).

# K

## Kentucky Department of Finance v. Davis

Most states tax the tax-exempt interest earned on the bonds sold by other states. In April 2003, a couple in Louisville, Kentucky, George and Catherine Davis, decided to challenge this policy, saying it violated the Commerce Clause of the U.S. Constitution, which prohibits states from discriminating against interstate trade.

Of the 50 states, 41 tax the interest earned on the bonds of other states; four—Illinois, Iowa, Oklahoma, and Wisconsin—tax some of their own. In practice, what this means is that investors who live in a state with high taxes, such as California, Hawaii, New York, New Jersey, North Carolina, Ohio, Oregon, and Vermont (called by bond dealers "specialty states"), among others, invest in bonds sold by their states in order to get the best bang for the buck, or buy shares in mutual funds that do so (single-state funds). Those states, in turn, do not have to pay as much to borrow money in the bond market, because of the captive audience for their bonds.

A decision for the bondholders would mean that states would no longer be able to discriminate between in-state and out-of-state bonds, and would have to decide to drop such taxes altogether or tax all municipal bond interest in the same way. (Kentucky at the time estimated that the tax brought in between $1 million and $4 million a year.) Such a decision would also transform the market from one that is fragmented and regional to one that is national and consistent. A decision for the bondholders would also probably result in the dozens of single-state bond funds being merged into national funds.

The lawsuit made its way through the courts. In 2004, the Jefferson County Circuit Court found for the state; the Kentucky Court of Appeals ruled for the Davises in 2006. Kentucky's own Supreme Court declined to hear an appeal, and the state petitioned the U.S. Supreme Court to review the matter.

The Supreme Court decided the case on May 19, 2008. The court ruled for the state, saying that "the differential tax scheme is critical to the operation of an identifiable segment of the municipal financial market as it currently functions, and this fact alone demonstrates that the unanimous desire of the States to preserve the tax feature is a far cry from the private protectionism that has driven the development of the dormant Commerce Clause."

*Sources:*

*Department of Revenue of Kentucky, et al., Petitioners v. George W. Davis et ux.* Opinion of the Court, Supreme Court of the United States, No. 06-666, 553 U.S. 328, May 19, 2008.

Mintz Levin Public Finance Advisory, March 4, 2006, and March 22, 2007; Mintz Levin Public Finance Alert, May 21, 2007.

# L

## laddering

Using an investment strategy known as laddering, a bond buyer purchases securities maturing in incremental steps over a short time horizon. If the investor has $1 million, for example, he or she would buy $200,000 in bonds coming due in two years, four years, six years, eight years, and 10 years. If inflation rises, the thinking goes, the owner reinvests the money from the maturing bonds at progressively higher interest rates.

This is perhaps the most popular strategy recommended by brokers to individual investors. Not everyone believes in this cautious approach. For those looking to maximize their stream of tax-exempt income, buying bonds now with a 15-, 20-, or 25-year maturity may make more sense, because they can double their income. Shorter maturities typically carry much lower yields, in the 1 percent to 3 percent range. Go a little further out on the yield curve, and coupons increase to 4 percent to 6 percent.

Does it ever make sense for the typical buy-and-hold investor to wait for more clarity or certainty regarding the direction of interest rates? And if investors do wait, can they possibly make up the income they lost? It's harder than investors may think to catch up. These are the questions investors have to address in considering a laddering strategy. Over the past 20 years, a period of generally declining rates, the answer would have been no.

## last looks

The practice by some brokers of offering those bidding for business a look at a winning bid to see if they want to improve their own bid and so win the business. Usually used in conjunction with the reinvestment of bond proceeds; the practice came up during the original yield-burning investigation in 1995, and again in the "anticompetitive practices" bid-rigging inquiry that was announced in November 2006.

*See also* bid rigging; yield burning.

## lease financings

Lease financings gained in popularity as tax-cap fever spread in the 1980s and 1990s, and municipalities sought to finance projects without voter approval, with borrowing that would not count against any debt limits. The kinds of obligations associated with such financings are usually termed certificates of participation, the buyer receiving an interest in lease payments made by a municipality to an authority that sold the securities to finance construction, usually of a school or an office building. These payments are usually backed by a promise to appropriate, not an obligation to do so, and so are marginally less secure than general obligation, full faith and credit securities.

*See also* certificates of participation; risk factors.

## legal opinion

A law firm's opinion that a bond is validly issued, and is tax-exempt or taxable, as the case may be.

The role of bond counsel was defined after the Civil War, as states and localities repudiated debt sold during the war and Reconstruction, as well as debt sold in connection with railroad development. "In 1876, Judge John Forest Dillon published his important article, 'The Law of Municipal Bonds,' 2 Southern Law Rev. (N.S.) 437 (1876), in which he discussed the power of municipalities to issue securities in the light of existing court decisions," according to James Spiotto, a partner at Chapman & Cutler. "Earlier, as the Chief Justice of the Iowa Supreme Court, Judge Dillon also authored two seminal opinions establishing a modern rule of law by which the powers of local government are evaluated. He had also authored a treatise on municipal corporations which was an essential book on the topic." Both purchasers and underwriters of municipal bonds began seeking the opinion of Judge Dillon, and other lawyers began to specialize in the work, and the role of bond counsel was born.

*See also* bond counsel; tax-exemption.

*Source:*

Spiotto, James E. E-mail from James E. Spiotto, Esq., Chapman & Cutler Inc., July 19, 2010.

## letters of credit

A letter of credit (LOC) is a form of credit enhancement, typically used to backstop variable-rate demand obligations (VRDOs). If holders of this kind of debt tender their securities to the issuer's remarketing agent, the remarketing agent either retains them in inventory for sale in the future or puts them back to the LOC bank, at which time the VRDOs convert to so-called bank debt and become payable on an accelerated schedule, in four or five years instead of the originally stated 30 or 40 years. Issuers typically sell variable-rate debt with an ultimate maturity of 30 or 40 years, while the letters of credit usually run for only three or five years, requiring the issuer to seek extensions of the LOCs or new liquidity facilities.

*See also* auction-rate securities; variable-rate demand obligations.

## liens

A lien is a claim on an asset or a piece of property. Many bond issuers, for example, give bondholders a lien on a property being financed, exactly like a mortgage. In the event the borrower defaults on bond payments, the trustee can seize the property and sell it to satisfy the claims of those holding the debt.

## limited obligation

Limited obligation bonds have less than 100 percent of the backing of a state or municipality, as opposed to those that have the unlimited, general obligation, full faith and credit taxing power of a state or municipality behind them. This occurs when the issuers have only restricted access to their tax bases, such as when the amounts by which they may increase taxes are capped.

*See also* general obligation; initiative and referendum; Orange County, California.

# M

## market activity

Daily trading activity may be tracked through the Municipal Securities Rulemaking Board (MSRB)'s Electronic Municipal Market Access (EMMA) website. Transaction reporting in municipals has been available only since 1995. Before that, estimates of market activity were largely fictions, based on anecdotal reporting and the facts of how new issues were priced in the primary market, combined with a look at dealer inventory carried in a publication called the Blue List.

EMMA carries details of all transactions, including sales by customers, purchases by customers, and interdealer trades. Between 15,000 and 20,000 separate issues trade on a given day; volume ranges between $10 billion and $20 billion. The MSRB's website ranks "most actively traded" bonds by number of trades. This can differ significantly from the most actively traded bonds by dollar value, which can only be traced a week after a day's trading activity.

"A trade whose principal value (par value or face value) is one million dollars or more is shown as '1MM+' for the first week after trade date," explained Jennifer Galloway of the MSRB. "Reporting the exact value of these large trades, which typically are done by institutional investors, could reveal the identity of the investor, since some market members may know who owns large blocks of a bond. This could make investors less likely to do large trades, which in turn could adversely affect the liquidity of the bond. After one week, the 1MM+ indicator is replaced by the exact value of each such trade on EMMA."

So, for example, if an investor examined the most active trades by volume, as carried on Bloomberg, of October 29, 2010, the 2003 Illinois taxable pension 5.10 percent bonds due in 2033 topped the list, with 85 trades totaling $6,765,000. Checking back a week later, our investor would have seen that on October 29, the San Diego County Regional Transportation Commission's 5.911 percent revenue bonds due in 2048 actually ranked first, with 31 trades totaling $383,710,000. The San Diego bonds were priced on October 25, and the October 29 trades featured the sales of the new bonds, and included numerous sales of $10 million to $35 million blocks.

Most trading activity occurs within the first 30 days of pricing, after which, as the market axiom has it, "all bonds go to heaven," or into final investors' hands, these being predominantly buy-and-hold investors. Most daily transaction activity is concentrated in a small number of securities sold by a relatively small number of issuers, according to a 2004 report by the Securities and Exchange Commission's Office of Economic Analysis and the Office of Municipal Securities. "About 70% of municipal securities did not trade between December 12, 1999, and November 5, 2000," the report said. "Less than 1% of securities accounted for half of transaction activity during this period."

This report also compared the municipal market with the stock market. At the time, there were about one million municipal securities totaling $2 trillion, compared with 13,450 equities worth about $18 trillion. Average daily volume in the muni market, at $10.4 billion, was dwarfed by the $134.2 billion daily volume in the stock market.

The municipal market is almost overwhelmingly dominated by small issues, this study found: almost three-quarters of the securities outstanding had principal amounts of $1 million or less. About one-quarter of the fixed-rate market carried no ratings at all.

*See also* "All bonds go to heaven"; issuer concentration; Recalibration of 2010.

*Sources:*

Galloway, Jennifer. E-mail with MSRB's Jennifer Galloway, November 1, 2010.

*2009 Fact Book.* Municipal Securities Rulemaking Board, Arlington, VA, 2010.

Report on Transactions in Municipal Securities, Office of Economic Analysis, Office of Municipal Securities, Securities and Exchange Commission, July 1, 2004.

Taylor, Christopher. "Milestones in Municipal Securities Regulation 1975–2005." Municipal Securities Rulemaking Board, Arlington, VA, 2006.

## Marks-Roos

California's Marks-Roos Local Bond Pooling Act of 1985 allowed Joint Powers Authorities to sell bonds to finance capital improvements, education, hospital and health care facilities, housing, and redevelopment.

*Source:*

2007 Annual Report, California Debt and Investment Advisory Commission.

## Mello-Roos

California's Mello-Roos Community Facilities Act of 1982 allowed public agencies to set up community facilities districts to finance school facilities and capital improvements.

*Source:*

2007 Annual Report, California Debt and Investment Advisory Commission.

## mini bonds

Mini bonds are municipal bonds most often denominated as $500 or $1,000, below the $5,000 that is traditional in the market. Such mini bonds have in the past been marketed directly to individual investors, sometimes right out of an office in city hall.

## moral obligation

Moral obligation (MO) bonds were conceived by bond lawyer John Mitchell, who would go on to become Attorney General during the Nixon administration, to get around voter disapproval of bond issues during the first term of Governor Nelson A. Rockefeller of New York in 1960. Designed to enhance the marketability of state Housing Finance Agency bonds, the "moral obligation" was simply language added to the agency's indenture of the state's "legislative intent" to address shortfalls in order to meet principal and interest payments. The state had no legal obligation to assist the authority, and indeed a precursor of the New York City financial crisis of 1975 was a default by the state's Urban Development Corporation on notes after the state failed to appropriate the debt service. The default was later cured.

Other states quickly followed suit, and moral obligation bonds are a common feature of the market. Moral obligation pledges are generally used by states as a form of credit enhancement. "The most common form of moral obligation security is a nonmandatory debt-service reserve fund replenishment provision," Fitch Ratings wrote in 2005. "Under this structure, a debt service reserve fund is established and used if the underlying security is insufficient to make the needed payment. The MO provider is then notified of the DSRF draw and is asked to appropriate funds to replenish the reserve to the required level." Most moral obligation pledges were never called upon, Fitch said.

*See also* general obligation; New York City financial crisis of 1975.

*Sources:*

"A Conversation with John Mitchell." *Bond Buyer* Centennial Edition, August 1991.

"Rating Guidelines for Moral Obligations." Criteria Report, Fitch Ratings, November 28, 2005.

## mortgage bonds

Also known as mortgage revenue bonds or housing bonds, mortgage bonds are securities sold by state and local housing agencies to provide financing for both multifamily and single-family housing. Subject to the Alternative Minimum Tax (AMT), they are often guaranteed by the Federal National Mortgage Association, the Federal Home Loan Mortgage Corporation, the Government National Mortgage Association, or the Federal Housing Administration, and sometimes carry further monoline insurance on top of that. They often offer premiums between 20 and 40 basis points over other AMT bonds because of call risk or perceived call risk. "Any bond in the single family area can have as many as six different call options," observed analyst Kurt van Kuller in 1997. "They're freaks of the fixed-income world."

Such calls include prepayments, cross-calls (state housing agencies trans-ferring prepayments from one pool of loans or from one series of bonds to another), the typical optional call, unused proceeds call, surplus call, and collapsible call.

Most, but not all, housing bonds supported by agency-insured mort-gages carry triple-A ratings. Asked why there were issues without the top grade, Standard & Poor's replied in 2010 that monthly mortgage payments are deposited into accounts invested in short-term money-market securities, and that many bond issues rely on interest income from those accounts to cover debt service. "Standard & Poor's has found that if market interest rates are lower than what was assumed in the initial cash flow when the bonds were rated or last underwent a ratings review, there could be a shortfall of revenues available for full and timely bond debt service. Hence, if the credit enhancement on the mortgage does not cover bond debt service plus fees (if paid out of the trust estate), we believe there would be a gap in the trans-action to be covered."

*Sources:*

"Q&A: Kurt van Kuller." *Grant's Municipal Bond Observer*, June 27, 1997.
"The Rating Profile of Government-Enhanced Housing Bonds Is Still Pre-
    dominantly 'AAA' after Review." Standard & Poor's, November 9, 2010.
van Kuller, Kurt. "Housing Bubble: Implications for Municipal Bonds."
    Merrill Lynch, April 27, 2006.

## MSRB

The Municipal Securities Rulemaking Board (MSRB) regulates firms and banks that underwrite, trade, or sell municipal securities, as well as financial advisers who counsel issuers. The self-regulatory organization was estab-lished by Congress to oversee the market in 1975 after "several fraud actions were brought by the SEC against municipal securities professionals alleging improper and unethical trading and selling practices," according to the MSRB's Manual. The MSRB today also acts as the repository for official statements and disclosure notices, and is responsible for the collection and dissemination of real-time trading data, which it posts on its Electronic Municipal Market Access (EMMA) website. The organization is funded by fees on transactions of bonds, collected from dealers. Under provisions of the Dodd-Frank Wall Street Reform and Consumer Protection Act passed in 2010, the Board now also may collect half of enforcement penalties collected by the Securities and Exchange Commission (SEC) and a portion of the penalties collected by the Financial Industry Regulatory Authority (FINRA), and is permitted to impose fines of its own on dealers and advisers.

Based in Alexandria, Virginia, the MSRB has helped transform the municipal bond market from one that was small, with sales of $30 billion or $40 billion annually, and clubby, dominated by banks, insurance companies, and a relative handful of professionals, into the institution it is today, used by thousands of state and local governments to finance operations and capital projects. On the investor front, the MSRB has tamed a market that was opaque and obscure, where trading activity and prices were unknown, and where disclosure was spotty at best and nonexistent at worst. It has also curbed the pay-to-play practices that were rife in the 1990s as well as sounded early warnings on the necessity of full and adequate disclosure to investors, and on such things as the proliferation of swaps, yield burning, and bid rigging.

*See also* "Bond Daddies"; EMMA; escrowed to maturity; market activity.

*Sources:*

Ackerman, Andrew. "Regulation: SIFMA Critiques MSRB over Its Bid to Nearly Double Fees." *Bond Buyer*, December 6, 2010.

## Municipal Assistance Corporation

Entity established by the state of New York in 1975 to sell bonds on behalf of New York City, which at that time was frozen out of the municipal market by banks that would no longer underwrite its securities.

*See also* New York City financial crisis of 1975.

## municipal utility district

The Texas version of so-called dirt districts that sell bonds to encourage real estate development.

*See also* dirt bonds.

## mutual funds

Tax-exempt mutual funds offer investors who do not have the money to build a diversified portfolio of municipal bonds the opportunity to earn tax-exempt income in a convenient if sometimes costly way. Debuting in 1961, these funds contained $5.1 billion in assets two decades later, with money-market, or shorter-term, mutual funds at $4.4 billion, according to the Federal Reserve's Flow of Funds report. This was at a time when commercial banks (at $154 billion) were second only to households ($160.3 billion) in holdings of municipals. Market convention today combines both individual holdings and mutual funds as proxies to come up with the axiom that retail investors make up about 70 percent of the market. In 2010, for example, of the $2.85 trillion in municipal bonds outstanding, households owned the largest piece, $1.1 trillion. Money-market mutual funds, close-end funds, and exchange-traded funds accounted for a combined $954 billion.

The advantages of funds include the relatively small cost of entry—sometimes as little as $1,000. Then there is the benefit of having someone else do the research and manage credit and reinvestment risk. Finally, there is liquidity. Investors can cash in their mutual fund shares speedily. The disadvantage to funds is the fees that can eat up meager tax-exempt returns.

Professionals debate over the amount of money an investor needs before he or she buys individual bonds rather than funds. There is no definitive answer, although it is probably around $100,000. Investors looking to buy individual bonds are advised that munis are ideally a buy-and-hold investment and that liquidity is an issue; that is, it is not easy to sell bonds into the over-the-counter market for the same price an investor paid for them.

*See also* Fed Flow of Funds report; Heartland fund implosion; market activity; Who owns municipal bonds?

*Sources:*

Boyle, Nicholas. "Mutual Funds, from Backstage, Already Run the Show." *Bond Buyer* Centennial Edition, August 1991.
"Flow of Funds Accounts of the United States: Flows and Outstandings, Third Quarter 2010." Board of Governors of the Federal Reserve System, Washington, DC, December 9, 2010.

# N

## negotiated sale

With a negotiated sale, the dominant method of bond underwriting since 1976, issuers choose the underwriters who are going to sell their bonds and then sit down and discuss terms, either with or without a financial adviser at the table.

Thinking about it another way: with a competitive sale, bonds are bought by the underwriter, and then sold to investors. In a negotiated transaction, the bonds are sold—the underwriters pretty much know where all the bonds are going, and at what price—and then bought by the underwriters (in other words, the deal is closed). Underwriters say this is one of the benefits of negotiation: they can line up investors far in advance of the sale and can tailor bonds to suit the needs of investors.

In a competitive sale, the underwriter assumes the risk that it may not be able to sell all the bonds it has purchased at auction. Negotiation removes practically all of that risk from the transaction.

Once upon a time, negotiation was prescribed only for new issuers who were unfamiliar with the marketplace, credits with low ratings, and extremely large deals. Beginning in the 1970s, bankers began telling issuers that negotiation could be used effectively for all municipal bond sales. They succeeded. Negotiation outnumbered competitive sales in terms of dollar volume beginning in 1976.

Critics of negotiation say that two questions must be answered: First, what role is politics playing in the choice of the underwriter and other members of the financing team? And second, is the public really getting the best deal?

The Government Finance Officers Association (GFOA) has returned to the issue a number of times over the years. Acknowledging issuers' preference for the negotiated method of sale, the organization advocates that its members learn how to negotiate. Its latest "Best Practice" says: "Unlike a competitive sale, bond pricing in a negotiated sale requires a much greater degree of issuer involvement. The issuer negotiates both the yield on the bonds and the underwriters' compensation (also called the underwriter discount or gross spread), which includes the takedown (or sales commission), management fee, underwriting risk, and expenses. An issuer's success in negotiating the price of its bonds depends on its ability and willingness to devote sufficient time to understanding the market and the historical performance of its bonds."

Rather than engaging in a much greater degree of involvement, as recommended by the GFOA, many issuers seem to have abdicated most of their responsibilities to underwriters in a "leave the driving to us" fashion—that is, after their initial underwriter selection.

"In over 40 years of experience in public finance, I have found that the decision that causes the greatest controversy among members of the governing bodies of Alabama issuers is the selection of underwriters and other members of the financing team," wrote banker James H. White III in a 2010 study of Jefferson County, Alabama's sewer system financing. "For various reasons, elected officials generally pay more attention to who is going to provide financial services and products than they do to substantive aspects of a financing. In fact, selection of the financing team takes up so much time that there is little energy for more important details, because the bankers and lawyers pursue decision makers zealously and sometimes shower them with campaign contributions and gifts."

Some issuers, it is clear, believe that their work on a bond sale ends with the selection of professionals. Best practice indicates that hiring the help is not nearly enough.

Whom does the underwriter work for? Many issuers assume the underwriter works for them. In fact, the role is problematic. The underwriter tries to get the issuer the best price and at the same time move the bonds into investors' hands.

Then there is the matter of what might be termed professional longevity. Anecdotal evidence suggests that many issuers employ the same underwriters and bond lawyers for decades, either never putting out a Request for Proposal for services or doing so in only a perfunctory fashion. On the one hand, such professional loyalty seems charming. On the other, taxpayers have to wonder if they are getting the best level of service and the optimal borrowing terms when they head to the municipal market.

*See* competitive sale; Jefferson County, Alabama; market activity.

*Sources:*

"Pricing Bonds in a Negotiated Sale." GFOA Best Practice, October 15, 2010.

White, James H., III. "Financing Plans for the Jefferson County Sewer System: Issues and Mistakes." Text of a presentation at Samford University's Symposium on Jefferson County, January 29, 2010.

## net asset value

Net asset value (NAV) is the dollar value of a share in a mutual fund, determined by subtracting the liabilities from the portfolio value of a fund's securities, and dividing that by the number of outstanding shares.

## net interest cost

Net interest cost (NIC) represents the average coupon rate of a bond issue, weighted to reflect the term and adjusted for the premium or discount. It does not take into account the time value of money, as does the true interest cost (TIC) method.

## New Jersey pension obligation bonds of 1997

In January 1997, Governor Christine Todd Whitman of New Jersey proposed a $16.4 billion budget that included an unusual proposal to sell $3.4 billion in taxable bonds, the largest single issue in the state's history, to pay off an unfunded liability in the state's pension plan.

Municipalities had sold bonds to raise money for their pensions ever since Oakland, California, did so in 1985, but this was the first time a state planned to sell such an issue. What made this transaction novel was that it featured debt that seemed not to be needed and it was being championed by a Republican with conservative credentials seen by some as a possible presidential contender.

Combine this with almost tragic timing, and the New Jersey Pension Obligation Bond Issue of 1997 became an illustration of what not to do when it came to selling pension obligation bonds, probably discouraging other states and municipalities that might have sold such deals to good effect, and leaving New Jerseyans with a bitter aftertaste that still has not been overcome more than a decade later.

When the bond issue was originally conceived, New Jersey had pension assets of $45 billion, an unfunded 60-year liability calculated in March 1996 at $4.2 billion, and a separate surplus reserve of $2.3 billion. The plan was for New Jersey to sell $3.4 billion in taxable bonds and use a portion of the $2.3 billion surplus to fully fund the pension. The administration would then use the remainder of the freed-up surplus funds to help balance the state's budget for the next two years, in part by reducing its annual contribution to the pension fund.

The plan was not an immediate hit with either Democrats or Republicans. Most people saw it as a gimmick to avoid unpopular budget cuts or tax increases. Some expressed reservations about the state turning a soft obligation into a hard one, while some also observed that the state was giving up a bargaining chip with the public-sector unions. A few observers even questioned the risky nature of the transaction: the issuer was essentially going to take the money and bet that it could make more than whatever it paid to borrow the money in the taxable municipal market, presumably in the 7 percent range.

Then there was the question over whether it was needed at all. In March 1996, actuaries valued the state's pension assets at $45 billion. The next actuarial accounting would take place in March 1997. But a call to the director of pensions and investments revealed that on December 31, 1996, the market value of the state's pension assets had appreciated and amounted to $48 billion. As of January 31, 1997, they amounted to $49 billion, meaning that the unfunded liability was down to something like $200 million. Couldn't the state just ask the legislature to use some of that segregated reserve to top up the fund?

Criticism of the plan resulted in a reduction in the size of the deal, to $2.8 billion, but did not derail it. In June 1997, the New Jersey Economic Development Authority sold $2.8 billion in federally taxable (and state tax-exempt) state pension funding bonds in a variety of modes, with $1.28 billion priced at par to yield 7.424 percent. The schedule of debt-service payments showed that New Jerseyans would pay $10.3 billion over the life of the bonds, which mature in 2029.

It all worked out for a few years, and New Jersey lawmakers fattened up public employees' benefits by 9 percent in 2000. Then the stock market slumped, knocking off $13 billion of the pension system's market value. In 2002, *Pensions & Investments* magazine published an article headlined, "Lousy Timing: Pension Obligation Bonds Feel Pinch of Bad Market," which noted that New Jersey "has been unable since at least 1999 to outperform the 7.64% annual interest payments." The early 2000s were more or less a lost decade for the funds, concluding with the stock market collapse of 2007 to 2009.

There was a lesson to be learned. It was not that all pension obligation bonds were bad, but that a great deal of thought had to go into when a state or municipality sold them; that is, it is better to sell such bonds at the bottom of the business cycle or during a recession rather than when the economy is humming along and the upside is limited.

*See also* pension obligation bonds; pensions.

*Sources:*

McNichol, Dunstan. "Pension Funds Take a Dive—Billions Vanish as Market Falls." *Star-Ledger*, December 16, 2001.

Miller, Girard. E-mail exchange with Girard Miller, February 28, 2011.

"New Jersey Makes a Bet." *Grant's Municipal Bond Observer*, February 7, 1997.

Preston, Jennifer. "For Whitman, More Temporary Solutions." *New York Times*, January 25, 1997.

Preston, Jennifer. "Whitman Asks $16.4 Billion in New Budget." *New York Times*, January 30, 1997.

Preston, Jennifer. "Whitman Assailed on Idea of Bonds to Cover Pensions." *New York Times*, March 24, 1997.

Reynolds, Katherine, and Richard Richtmyer. "N.J.'s $3.4 Billion Pension Deal Would Be Nation's Largest Ever." *Bond Buyer*, January 14, 1997.

"Who Are They Kidding?" *Grant's Municipal Bond Observer*, February 21, 1997.

Williams, Fred. "Lousy Timing: Pension Obligation Bonds Feel Pinch of Bad Market." *Pensions & Investments*, August 19, 2002.

## New Jersey Turnpike scandal of 1993

A federal investigation launched in the spring of 1993 spotlighted political influence in the municipal bond market. The investigation centered on transactions between a big firm, Merrill Lynch, which was also lead manager on a $1.6 billion New Jersey Turnpike bond issue in 1991, and a small New Jersey company, Armacon Securities, which was co-owned by Nicholas Rudi, a banker and adviser to New Jersey Governor James Florio, and Joseph C. Salema, Governor Florio's chief of staff. Merrill said it had notified the U.S. Attorney's office after it had noticed there were trading "irregularities" in a joint account it had established with Armacon in 1991. The Turnpike sold a total of $2.9 billion in bonds in 1991 and 1992. Shortly after the investigation became public, Merrill placed three managing directors on administrative leave, Governor Florio signed an executive order requiring that the state and its agencies sell all their bond issues at auction rather than through negotiation (except for special circumstances), and chief of staff Salema resigned.

The Securities and Exchange Commission (SEC) began its own inquiry into the matter, and the market's various overseers were once again forced to examine why and how certain firms were awarded business. After a two-year investigation, Salema pleaded guilty to sharing in a kickback scheme designed to steer business, in this case a $237.5 million Camden County Municipal Utilities Authority transaction, to First Fidelity Securities Group of Newark, and settled charges with the SEC. Rudi pleaded not guilty and was later acquitted at a criminal trial, although he eventually settled with the SEC.

"The civil suit reveals how easy it was for deal-hungry bankers to use the complicated paperwork of large municipal bond deals to hide questionable payments," reporter Diana Henriques wrote in a *New York Times* article headlined, "Textbook Case in New Jersey: Political Art of Bond Deals."

Merrill Lynch was never charged with any wrongdoing. Two of the three managing directors at Merrill retired; one returned to the firm from administrative leave. The Florio order to sell most bonds at auction was superseded in 1994 by Florio's successor, Christine Todd Whitman.

*See* bid rigging; pay-to-play; underwriters; yield burning.

*Sources:*

Cohen, Laurie P., and Michael Siconolfi. "SEC Launches New Jersey Bond Investigation." *Wall Street Journal,* May 5, 1993.

Dickson, Steven. "N.J. Governor Bans Negotiated Underwriting at State Level." *Bond Buyer,* May 5, 1993.

Gray, Jerry. "Broker Suspends 3 over Bond Deal with New Jersey." *New York Times,* May 4, 1993.

Henriques, Diana B. "Textbook Case in New Jersey: Political Art of Bond Deals." *New York Times,* February 26, 1995.

## New York City financial crisis of 1975

"Ford to City: Drop Dead," a headline from the October 30, 1975, tabloid *New York Daily News*, summed things up for New York City in its financial crisis year of 1975. Long characterized as ungovernable, the city was now unlovely as well, beset by dirt, drugs, crime, pornography, poverty, graffiti-covered subways, racial tension, and white flight.

The story began in 1974, when banks questioned the city's reliance on short-term borrowing and the *New York Times* editorialized that the city was near bankruptcy. But it had really begun decades before, when urban planners and city elites, notably but not exclusively Robert Moses, decided to replace the chaotic, smelly, messy, but vibrant landscape with the glass boxes and highways that would symbolize the modern, slum-free, postindustrial city.

As author Joe Flood put it in his 2010 book, *The Fires*, Moses was energetic in "overseeing the destruction of hundreds of thousands of people's homes to build highways, parks, luxury housing, and office towers. All told, the city spent billions of dollars to tear down the houses of roughly a million of its own residents, and the jobs of hundreds of thousands more."

Moses was not alone. The Port of New York Authority, as it was then called, engaged in clearance of its own on 16 acres of lower Manhattan real estate to build the World Trade Center, the magnificent twin-tower office complex that remained almost empty for years after it opened in the early 1970s.

"New York had the largest, most competitive, most diverse industrial economy in the world," Flood continued. "It held more manufacturing jobs than the next two largest American cities combined, and spread them out in dozens of industries that were constantly growing, adapting and attracting bright new entrepreneurial minds." Slum clearance was common to many American cities at the time, "but industrial clearance was unique to New York. No other city in the country had the audacity to plow under its own economy."

The recession that began in November 1973 and lasted until September 1975 finished the job these visionaries had begun. The first cracks seen in the municipal bond market came in February 1975, when the New York State Urban Development Corporation, created in 1968 to build affordable housing, defaulted on some bond anticipation notes and the state failed to live up to its moral obligation to backstop the securities. The new administration of Governor Hugh L. Carey cured the default, but much worse was to come.

The short story of the New York City financial crisis—which spawned a shelf of urban history classics like Ken Auletta's *The Streets Were Paved with Gold* and Fred Ferretti's *The Year the Big Apple Went Bust*, among others—is that the city used money borrowed under its capital budget to cover operating expenses instead of raising taxes or cutting spending. And it did so mainly in the short-term debt market, leaving it vulnerable to rollover risk. Between 1966 and 1975, the city's short-term borrowing increased from under 10 percent of its indebtedness in 1966 to 36.9 percent in 1975. In May, banks refused to bid on any more city notes, and the city was faced with the prospect of default and insolvency.

The state, as described in Seymour P. Lachman and Robert Polner's *The Man Who Saved New York*, came to the rescue, setting up the Municipal Assistance Corporation (MAC) in June 1975 to borrow money on the city's behalf and in September, after bankers and critics in Albany and Washington complained that the administration of Mayor Abraham D. Beame was not moving fast enough to reform its finances, the Emergency Financial Control Board.

Key to the city's salvation was the willingness by its unions to buy bonds sold by MAC. Numerous accounts detail the last-minute agreement by the United Federation of Teachers to buy such bonds for its pension fund in mid-October, even as the city readied a petition for bankruptcy. Not everyone was opposed to such a move.

The headline that proved so durable (and perhaps second only to "Headless Body in Topless Bar" in popularity among the city's journalists) was published on October 30, after President Gerald R. Ford gave a speech at the National Press Club during which he said he would veto any bill to bail out New York City to prevent a bond default.

"Ford's line in the sand marked the beginning of a change arising in American political life, one that would be expressed in the angry citizen property-tax revolts a few years away," wrote Lachman and Polner. The New York City debate emphasized "the finite nature of the public purse, which liberalism, in its view of government as the principal vehicle of opportunity and advancement, had never really defined."

In mid-November, the state passed a moratorium on repaying $1.6 billion in city notes, offering investors the choice of 8 percent MAC bonds due in 10 years or a suspension of principal and reduction in interest payments for at least three years. The moratorium was struck down as illegal a year later, but it did buy the city and state more time and was counted as a default by the Ford administration, which then supported legislation making $2.3 billion in federal loans available to the city on an annual basis for three years.

The city would struggle through much of the next decade. Its brush with bankruptcy had a profound impact on the municipal bond market. "The New York City crisis led to neither massive default nor widespread political pressure for more regulation of municipal bonds," wrote bond lawyer Robert Dean Pope in 2001. "It did, however, attract the SEC's attention to the municipal market," and "encouraged the Securities Amendments of 1975, which created a new self-regulatory organization for municipal broker/dealers, the Municipal Securities Rulemaking Board, and expanded the applicability of the securities laws to the sale of municipal securities."

See also moral obligation; Rule 15c2-12; Tower Amendment.

*Sources:*

Auletta, Ken. *The Streets Were Paved with Gold.* New York: Random House, 1979.

Ferretti, Fred. *The Year the Big Apple Went Bust.* New York: Putnam, 1976.

Flood, Joe. *The Fires: How a Computer Formula, Big Ideas, and the Best of Intentions Burned Down New York City—And Determined the Future of Cities.* New York: Riverhead Books, 2010.

Lachman, Seymour P., and Robert Polner. *The Man Who Saved New York: Hugh Carey and the Great Fiscal Crisis of 1975.* Albany: State University of New York Press, 2010.

Pope, Robert Dean. *Making Good Disclosure: The Role and Responsibilities of State and Local Officials under the Federal Securities Laws.* Chicago: Government Finance Officers Association, 2001.

## NRO

In a bond pricing, underwriters will sometimes mark the column listing price or yield on a bond's maturity "NRO," which stands for Not Reoffered. This is usually done with a handful of maturities, but occasionally an entire transaction is so designated. Bond issuers using auction or competitive sale have long objected to the practice, saying it reduces transparency and hinders their ability to gauge the market, and so prevents them from knowing whether they are getting the best price for their new issues. Dealers have defended the use of the NRO designation, saying that in order to sell large amounts of certain maturities, not publicizing prices gives them a short-term advantage.

*Source:*

Allan, John H. "Puzzle to Be Solved." *Grant's Municipal Bond Issuer*, January 15, 1998.

## official statement

An official statement (OS) is a bond issue's offering document, containing everything a bond buyer needs to know before investing. The OS is filled with a great deal of legalistic language and is also repetitive, but it does reward close scrutiny.

The cover page includes a brief summary of the issue, the legal opinion, the amount of bonds sold, and the underwriters. Prices and yields are also listed on the cover, and are again detailed inside.

The OS contains the authorization for and purpose of the bond issue, estimated sources and uses of funds, security and sources of payment for the bonds, names of the issuer officials involved, and the names of the professional firms bringing the issue to market. The document also lays out the numerous calls and other redemption features of the bonds, as well as the debt-service schedule. There is also usually a lengthy discussion of the book-entry-only system, which long ago replaced receiving a physical security or bearer bond.

There may be a section on the risk factors involved in buying the bonds, especially if they are not general obligation (GO), tax-backed securities, and the OS may include a feasibility study if the bonds are for a project like a housing development or a convention center. GO issuers will provide an extensive overview of their organizations, economies, demographics, debt, and finances.

## OPEB

Other postemployment benefits (OPEB) promised to public pensioners, chiefly health care, are treated by states and municipalities as a pay-as-you-go obligation. OPEB first entered municipal bond investors' consciousness in 2004, when the Governmental Accounting Standards Board asked governments to calculate the potential cost of these benefits the same way they do their pension liabilities. In 2011, it was estimated that the total unfunded OPEB liability was about $2 trillion. Unlike pensions, which are relatively inelastic, other postemployment benefits may be changed or reduced.

See also pensions.

*Sources:*

Hampton, Ted, and Robert Kurtter. "Other Post-Employment Benefits." Moody's Investors Service, July 2005.

Miller, Girard. "Misplaced Pension Hysteria: The Real Monster Is OPEB, Not Pensions." *Governing*, February 3, 2011.

Young, Parry. "Reporting & Credit Implications of GASB 45 Statement on Other Postemployment Benefits." Standard & Poor's, December 1, 2004.

## open-end funds

See mutual funds.

## Orange County, California

On December 6, 1994, Orange County, California, filed for Chapter 9 municipal bankruptcy, having lost $1.6 billion in its investment pool. This was the biggest municipal bankruptcy ever (the county had net direct and overlapping debt of $3.9 billion) and, at the time, the most shocking, considering the county's wealth levels, location, and previously stellar credit ratings.

What astounded analysts and observers was that the county seemingly would not do what municipalities always did, and that was to do everything within its power to pay its debts. What was perhaps even more astonishing was that the county, because of the nature of California's numerous tax limitations, apparently *couldn't* do so. Nor did the state offer to bail the county out. This was stunning news in MuniLand.

The county certainly was not alone in losing money in 1994. As the Fed raised interest rates six times that year, from 3 percent to 5.5 percent by year-end, fixed-income investments in general declined in value. A lot of very sophisticated investors with winning records got burned. Before the year was out, it turned out that scores of municipalities from Florida to California racked up either actual or mark-to-market losses of several billion dollars, too, and this was a big surprise, because municipal investors as a group had always emphasized safety first, then liquidity, and then yield. In 1994, the market learned that in certain localities, the municipal treasury was being operated as a little profit center.

Orange County's losses were just the most spectacular, enhanced as they were by the use of leverage and culminating in bankruptcy when the county could not make a $1.25 billion collateral payment due its Wall Street lenders. Orange County was the first modern example of municipal bankruptcy by investment practice.

The county put part of its $7.5 billion investment pool in derivative securities and borrowed an additional $13 billion to further enhance its returns, which, Treasurer Robert Citron said, had averaged 10 percent annually since 1980. The real problem with the Orange County portfolio was not the various derivatives it held, although many of these were illiquid enough by the end, but the borrowing it had done to improve returns. In a phrase that was used again and again in 1994, Orange County borrowed short, bet long, and bet wrong. The county had lots of company.

Compounding the county's difficulties was the matter of whose money it was investing. The county invested money both for itself and for 187 entities, 88 of them in the county and, so good was the county's record of returns, 99 from outside (but still within the state of California). These included the usual operating and construction funds that typically reside in county investment pools, as well as money specifically borrowed to turn an arbitrage profit. In 1992, the county's pool had an average yield of 8.52 percent; the pool run by Los Angeles County, by comparison, earned 3.88 percent. The Orange County pool was also a comparative bargain, charging investors a management fee of 6 basis points, compared with between 10 and 20 basis points elsewhere.

Assistant Treasurer Matthew R. Raabe spelled out the county's basic investment strategy in a letter to the Newport Mesa Unified School District in July 1993. The Newport Mesa district had borrowed $46,960,000 in a taxable note offering and—along with several other municipalities—asked Orange County to invest the money so it could earn arbitrage profits.

"We have entered into a series of investment transactions designed to earn you an amount of interest that not only exceeds your interest costs, but earns you a reasonable arbitrage profit," wrote Raabe. "The investment strategy we have employed is called a 'reverse repurchase agreement' and it works as follows: We initially invested your debt proceeds by purchasing a United States of America government agency security. There are a number of these securities available on the open securities market, and they are excellent, safe investments. The particular security we purchased for you was issued by the Federal National Mortgage Association, commonly called a Fannie Mae (FNMA). That security, which matures in June, 1998, pays an interest rate of 5.40 percent.

"We then entered into a reverse repurchase agreement with a major brokerage firm in order to increase the yield on your investment. The broker lent us $46,079,030 at an interest rate of 3.32 percent and we turned over the FNMA security to them as collateral to guarantee that at the maturity of the reverse repurchase agreement we would pay them the principal and interest on the money we borrowed. (At the end of the agreed upon period, usually 180 days, we repay the moneys borrowed from the broker and they return the FNMA security to us. In the meantime, we continue to receive all the interest payments on the FNMA security.)

"Lastly, we reinvested the $46,079,000 that we had borrowed from the broker by purchasing a second FNMA security, this one paying an interest rate of 4.875 percent," wrote Raabe.

The earnings on the original FNMA totaled $2,514,708; the earnings on the second amounted to $2,227,633.13. They paid the broker $1,517,075.28. Interest earnings thus were $3,225,265.85. Subtracting the school district's borrowing costs (the 4.50 percent it paid on its note issue), Raabe calculated the projected arbitrage earnings at $1,112,065.85.

"When your debt comes due on June 15, 1994, we will buy the FNMA securities from you at the same price you originally paid. You will not share in any market gain nor have any risk of market loss on the sale of the securities. . . . There is no risk related to the $46,960,000 principal amount."

Raabe pointed out that the county had employed the strategy in its investment pool for many years, and added, "Our Treasurer, Mr. Citron, was responsible for introducing the legislation that added reverse repurchase agreements to the permitted investments listed in California Government Code Sections 53601 and 53635."

The county's investment strategy worked very well in times of relatively benign Federal Reserve policy. It did not work quite so well if rates were rising and the market value of its investments was falling, so that some of the more customized investments now cost more than they actually paid out, and some investors clamored for a return of some of their cash.

And that, in the end, is why Orange County declared bankruptcy: It ran out of cash. When Wall Street made its collateral call, the county had an estimated $350 million in cash on hand, down from $1.5 billion during the summer.

"Although the trades were complex, most of them—at their core—were bets that interest rates would stay low," wrote Frank Partnoy in his book *Infectious Greed* (2003), which chronicles the invention and rise in the use of derivative financial instruments, including those used by Orange County.

"Collectively, these managers had placed the largest secret bet in the history of financial markets," wrote Partnoy. "When the Fed raised rates on February 4, they lost."

These bets weren't so secret to everyone. Accountant John Moorlach and one of his advisers, investment banker Chriss Street, were warning everyone they could about the county's leveraged investment strategy in early 1994, and numerous press accounts appeared outlining the aggressive strategy. The reverse repurchase agreements, the derivative securities, the massive use of leverage—all these had been written about. Moorlach ran against Citron for treasurer on this basis, that Citron was mismanaging public funds, in June and lost.

Citron, who had been treasurer–tax collector for 24 years, was a popular man. Until paper losses became actual losses much later in the year, the issue of what he had invested in and why was pretty obscure to most people. Treasurer Citron was still considered almost a hero by a lot of local officials and their constituents, who had come to rely on outsized investment earnings to bolster their budgets without the tax increases they could no longer impose. At least six other California counties also pursued what were considered aggressive investment strategies.

A *New York Times* story called the county's bankruptcy "peculiar to California," observing, "The roots of the problem that erupted with such fury in Orange County in December can be traced back to 1978. That's when California voters overwhelmingly approved Proposition 13, a citizen referendum that rolled back local property taxes to 1 percent of market value and limited increases to no more than 2 percent a year." Almost two decades in the past, Proposition 13 had helped spawn a system of public finance "so arcane that only 15 people in the state understand it," the article quoted one analyst of the situation.

For his part, Citron ran, and won, even as a Democrat in a Republican stronghold, on his more than two-decade record of producing consistent high returns for his many constituents. He also took to lecturing the occasional Wall Street firm—including Goldman Sachs and Merrill Lynch (which had sold him many of the customized derivative securities that helped prove the county's undoing)—that suggested he might pare back his bets.

Citron later admitted that, in the end, he was just another unsophisticated investor pursuing an aggressive, risky strategy. His actual defense, to the extent that he ever used one, was that the county was a long-term investor, unconcerned with short-term moves in the market, and unconvinced that higher long-term interest rates were sustainable. The county's plan, he said, was to hold all investments, no matter how exotic, until they matured. As 1994 proceeded, and as the Fed kept raising rates, Citron kept buying securities and derivatives with longer and longer maturities.

This hold 'em part of the strategy unraveled when Citron's investors, 187 municipalities, started to demand at least some of their money back, as they were entitled to do. Like so many investors before him, Citron had not counted on a run on the bank, and on having to sell those investments, or trying to, prior to maturity. He urged them to sit tight. Most did so.

The Orange County bankruptcy was almost a punctuation mark, an exclamation point on a year that had already seen dozens of municipal investors admit to losses, and at least one, the Cuyahoga County, Ohio, Secured Assets Fund Earnings pool, shut down after losing $100 million for its 75 municipal investors. This was considered a spectacular blowup, until Orange County. After Orange County, analysts and observers perhaps inevitably wondered about "the next Orange County," and "how many Orange Counties are out there?" As well they might, because as is typical in MuniLand, nobody really had any idea. It was anyone's guess what municipal investment practices nationally might be. It turned out, for example, that 37 states did not regulate the maturity of municipal investments at all. The remainder had the usual crazy quilt of rules, prohibiting their cities and towns from buying investments with maturities longer than 12 months, three years, five years, 10 years, or "to the term of its availability," which meant that a municipal investor could not take money needed in 90 days and buy 10-year securities with it.

This would not be the first time that analysts seeking clarity and definition in public finance found that the rules pretty much depended on where you were. Much the same demand was later made in 2010, when investors started asking for the list of all municipalities that had entered into interest-rate swaps. No such list existed.

As for how many other Orange Counties were out there, it turned out (again as it so often does) that while there were other government investors and investment pools holding derivative securities and pursuing similar strategies (like borrowing money to increase the size of the bets), Orange County was indeed an outlier.

What really shook the public finance world more than anything else, though, was the county's rather swift filing for bankruptcy. Most observers thought Orange County would do what municipalities usually do when they run into financial straits: negotiate with their creditors, cut the budget, raise taxes and fees, borrow more money to restructure all outstanding debt, and seek some sort of relief or refuge from the state. Usually, municipalities take one or more of these steps; sometimes they take all of them, and often over the course of a year or more. But this did not happen in Orange County.

The first real indication that anything was amiss for most people was a little headline that Bloomberg News ran at 11:51 on the morning of December 1, 1994: "Orange County, Calif., to Meet with Moody's on Cash Situation." The story appeared at 12:08 p.m., the first paragraph stating, "Moody's Investors Service Inc. analysts will meet with officials of Orange County, California, next week amid concern that the county faces a cash crunch from investment losses." The story quoted a *Wall Street Journal* article from June that said treasurer Citron had leveraged a $7.3 billion portfolio to $21.7 billion, and that it included derivatives. The story quoted Karen Krop, a vice president at Moody's, saying that this was not an emergency meeting, and that the county's Aa1 rating was not under review. "When something is going on, it is important to sit down," Krop said.

That was the morning of December 1. Later that day, county officials finally disclosed that the value of the county's investments had declined by $1.5 billion. On Sunday, December 4, Citron was asked for his resignation. On Tuesday, December 6, the county filed for bankruptcy.

As Bruce Bennett, the chief architect of the county's bankruptcy, explained much later: It's different in California. The county couldn't just levy taxes and fees to raise more cash. "That logic is inapplicable in California, where there exist some serious restrictions on a municipality's ability to access its tax base," said Bennett.

The fact that the county filed for bankruptcy was shocking and even, to most non-California observers, inexplicable. To have such a large, and still wealthy, municipality say it was insolvent—this was new territory. What then infuriated MuniLand was the county's apparent insouciance about it all. The county turned down one early 1995 proposal (by J.P. Morgan

Securities) to create an independent authority that would sell $2 billion in variable-rate debt backed by a state intercept of sales taxes and motor vehicle licensing fees—because, officials said, it would tie up county revenue for too long. This bankerly proposal was, to most regular observers and participants in the market, entirely reasonable, almost a model solution of its kind. The county wanted no part of it.

Then there was the little matter of repudiation. County chief executive officer William Popejoy in March 1995 said the county reserved the "right" to challenge the validity of $600 million in taxable notes it had sold in July 1994 to invest in the fund. With the exception of the Washington Public Power Supply System default a decade before, the last time repudiation had been used in the municipal market was during the Gilded Age, when dozens of states and municipalities disavowed debt run up by the Confederacy and various carpetbag governments (in the South) and to aid railroads (in the West), a contagion that led to the rise of bond counsel.

In fact, the county would make holders of almost $2 billion in notes wait a year for repayment, although with a little extra yield. So, yes, Orange County defaulted on its debt.

And in June, voters there soundly defeated a measure to raise the sales tax by a half-cent to 8.25 percent from 7.75 percent for a period of 10 years, a move designed to raise the money to pay creditors.

This seeming intransigence was confounding. It was as if the conservatives of Orange County had run up the red flag and proclaimed a Bolshevik state, at least in the terms then generally understood by the municipal securities market.

"If borrowers become opportunistic, if lawyers can comb through the fine print and after the fact repudiate and invalidate debt, I think . . . this is going to be a much more skeptical, more cynical market, and a much tougher market to do business in, both for the issuer and the investor," said Dan Heimowitz, the head of public finance at Moody's, at a 1995 conference.

Heimowitz noted that the market had been very accommodating to those municipalities that wanted to sell bonds: "A great deal of the issues we rate at Moody's," he said, "are, in fact, instruments created to circumvent the voters, the constitutions, to get into the market and do the capital things that are necessary, with an expectation that they won't get challenged by the voters, that the politicians will strongly stand behind them. We come up with all kinds of rationales about essentiality and likelihood of payment in expectation that we understand that legal security is not perfect here."

And in testimony before the California Senate's special committee on local government investments, Heimowitz said: "Public finance in California is based on an extremely complicated web of legal theories, some of which are found in the statutes, many of which have evolved through court decisions over the past 100 years. About three-fourths of the public financing done in California, by the state itself as well as its cities, counties, school districts and special districts, is not defined by the constitution. By starting to pull on this one thread, it threatens to unravel the complicated fabric of California public finance."

Even in a market that seemed in many ways to be more candid then than it is now, Heimowitz was a very frank man.

In the end, it took Orange County more than 18 months to emerge from bankruptcy, a great deal of its recovery predicated upon making someone else, in this case Wall Street, pay. The county eventually recovered $1.1 billion, including $400 million from Merrill Lynch.

Treasurer Citron was later prosecuted by the county. He was fined and served a year in a work-release program. Assistant Treasurer Raabe was convicted of five felony counts, which were later overturned. John Moorlach was appointed to serve out Citron's term in March 1995. He ran in June 1996, in 1998, and in 2002, all without opposition. The county itself was chastised by the SEC for selling securities without disclosing the actual condition of the pool and the risks it ran to investors. The county eliminated the use of derivatives and reverse repurchase agreements in its investment policy, and now posts all its positions and trades on the Internet.

*See also* Chapter 9; default; disclosure; Washington Public Power Supply System.

*Sources:*

Hofmeister, Sallie. "A Bankruptcy Peculiar to California." *New York Times*, January 6, 1995.

Jereski, Laura. "How a Rescue Mission Failed, Just Barely, in Orange County." *Wall Street Journal*, December 22, 1994.

Jereski, Laura, G. Bruce Knecht, Thomas T. Vogel Jr., and Andy Pasztor. "Bitter Fruit: Orange County, Mired in Investment Mess, Files for Bankruptcy—Decision, Following Default on Reverse-Repo Deals, May Put Assets in Limbo—How County Got into This." *Wall Street Journal*, December 7, 1994.

"The Last Days of Pompeii." *Grant's Municipal Bond Observer*, June 2, 1995.

Margolick, David. "Ill-Fated Fund's Manager: Mr. Main St., Not Wall St." *New York Times*, December 11, 1994.

McCorry, John, and Dave Liedtka. "Orange County, Calif., to Meet with Moody's on Investment Losses." Bloomberg News, December 1, 1994.

"Of Credit Risk and Market Risk." *Grant's Municipal Bond Observer*, March 10, 1995.

"Orange Pulp." *Grant's Municipal Bond Observer*, December 9, 1994.

Partnoy, Frank. *Infectious Greed: How Deceit and Risk Corrupted the Financial Markets*. New York: Times Books, 2003.

Platte, Mark, and Debora Vrana. "Orange County's Fund Value Falls $1.5 Billion; Finance Officials Seek to Calm 180 Cities and Agencies and Prevent Run on Once High-Flying Portfolio." *Los Angeles Times*, December 2, 1994.

Raabe, Matthew R. Letter to Thomas Godley, assistant superintendent of Newport Mesa Unified School District, by Matthew R. Raabe, assistant treasurer of Orange County, July 13, 1993.

$600,000,000 County of Orange, California, 1994–1995 Taxable Notes, Official Statement, July 1, 1994.

"Uh-Oh." *Grant's Municipal Bond Observer*, October 28, 1994.

Wayne, Leslie. "Banging a Tin Cup with a Silver Spoon." *New York Times*, June 4, 1995.

Wayne, Leslie. "Orange County's Artful Dodger: The Creative Bankruptcy of Bruce Bennett." *New York Times*, August 4, 1995.

Wayne, Leslie, and Andrew Pollack. "The Master of Orange County: A Merrill Lynch Broker Survives Municipal Bankruptcy." *New York Times*, July 22, 1998.

## original issue discount

When a new bond is priced below par—say, at 98 instead of 100—this is known as an original issue discount. The capital gain on an original issue discount is not taxable, compared with the capital gain on a market discount, which is. The original issue discount is amortized over the life of a bond issue, and treated as tax-exempt interest.

*Source:*

MSRB online glossary at www.msrb.org.

## out-of-state authorities

In some states, authorities sell tax-exempt bonds for issuers in counties and cities well outside their own immediate geographic boundaries. In Arizona, Colorado, Florida, Virginia, and Wisconsin, there exist authorities that sell bonds for issuers in other states in return for fees. This rather limited and relatively benign phenomenon has, so far, escaped scrutiny and criticism.

*Sources:*

Rittner, Toby. "The CDFA Friday Special." Council of Development Finance Agencies, April 8, 2011.

Strom, Stephanie. "New York Nonprofits Turn to Out-of-State Options for Bonds." *New York Times*, January 25, 2011.

# P

## par

Par is 100 percent of the face value. A bond priced at par is priced at 100 percent, and the yield is the coupon rate.

## pay-to-play

Pay-to-play is the practice of transferring money or other goods or services to politicians in return for special consideration in the awarding of contracts. In state and local finance, this usually revolves around bond underwriting or money management work, including reinvestment of proceeds and pension business. As Jesse Unruh, the longtime speaker of the California House and later state treasurer, said, "Money is the mother's milk of politics."

The municipal bond market has grappled with the issue of pay-to-play over the years, the results only being diminished by the reach of the market's self-regulatory organization. The Municipal Securities Rulemaking Board (MSRB) governs only banks and securities firms, not lawyers, and, until recently, not financial advisers; so squeezing one part of a transaction only displaced the movement of cash, and then only for a while.

In 1991, after numerous articles had appeared describing banker contributions to various politicians running for office, the MSRB published a notice "warning that political contributions should not be made to issuer officials for the purpose of obtaining negotiated underwriting assignments," and said that rulemaking "might be necessary if current trends continued."

In 1993, the board proposed Rule G-37, prohibiting underwriters from making such contributions. The rule became effective in April 1994.

Underwriters and bankers were for the most part relieved, whereas elected officials were very annoyed at the rule, which shut off a lucrative source of campaign funding. Good-government supporters said that the new rule was too narrow to be effective, because bond counsel, financial advisers, and bond reinvestment brokers, among others, were not included. And then there was the use of consultants, sometimes firms or individuals with specific expertise, but more often politically connected individuals paid to help underwriters get business in particular states or localities.

In 1996, the board adopted Rule G-38, which required dealers to disclose their contracts with consultants hired to solicit bond underwriting business. In 2005, the rule was revised to ban the use of consultants entirely, forcing securities firms either to hire their consultants as employees or to do without their services entirely. The board said it took this step "after observing trends that showed increased usage of consultants, increased compensation of consultants, and increased political contributions by consultants."

In 2011, the MSRB gained oversight of financial advisers who assist municipalities in both financing and investing, and proposed a rule prohibiting such advisers from making most political contributions.

In August 1999, the Securities and Exchange Commission had proposed a similar rule covering investment advisers, Rule 206(4)-5, in response to a number of pay-to-play scandals involving public pensions. The rule went into effect in September 2010.

*See also* bid rigging; Ferber trial; Jefferson County, Alabama; Philadelphia trial; yield burning.

*Sources:*

Gasparino, Charles. "The Trouble with Consultants: The Market May Be Getting Serious about Campaign Contributions, but There's More Than One Way to Peddle Influence." *Bond Buyer*, November 16, 1993.

Taylor, Christopher. "Milestones in Municipal Securities Regulation." Municipal Securities Rulemaking Board, Arlington, VA, 2006.

## pension obligation bonds

Pension obligation bonds (POBs) are taxable municipal bonds whose proceeds are usually deposited in a state's or municipality's pension fund and invested. The issuer in essence bets that the funds will earn more than the interest rate payable on the bonds. This has usually proved a pretty good bet, because the long-term earnings in stocks have historically been higher than the 6 percent or 7 percent the issuer will pay in the taxable market to borrow money. In 2010, the National Association of State Retirement Administrators reported that over the past 25 years, median public-pension returns, typically invested in both bonds and stocks, were 9.3 percent; over the past 20 years, they were 8.1 percent, according to Callan Associates, a San Francisco-based investment consulting firm. Nevertheless, some times are better for selling pension obligation bonds than others, and issuers of these bonds can enhance their returns if they are smart about it.

Girard Miller, a consultant for Public Financial Management and a public pension expert, discussed the subject of bonding for fund pension and other postemployment benefits (OPEB) in a notable January 15, 2009, article for *Governing* magazine. "The real-world success of a benefits bond is primarily driven by equity market returns and therefore the point of entry into the equity markets is much more important than the spread between borrowing costs and assumed pension fund investment returns (usually the actuarial discount rate)," he wrote.

The old model of pension obligation bonds was driven primarily by public finance bankers interested in selling big bond issues; the new one ought to be determined by investment professionals, wrote Miller. Pension and OPEB obligations should only be sold to finance the equity portion of an issuer's portfolio, he wrote, because that's where the money is made. And such bonds "should only be issued during recessions or during the early stages of economic recovery, when stock prices are depressed," according to Miller.

How much to borrow? "It is foolhardy to fund more than 80 percent to 85 percent of total plan liabilities through a debt issue. In the past, under the old POB paradigm, issuers were encouraged to bond for 'full funding' of the plan's unfunded liabilities. There was a mistaken belief that this stratagem would 'fix' the underfunded plan once and for all. Instead, this approach perversely guaranteed that once the plan actually achieved the stock market returns it desired, the plan's funding ratio exceeded 100 percent and it was then deemed 'overfunded.' This inevitably brought the unions and retiree groups back to the table demanding benefits improvements—which then put the plans right back into unfunded positions in the next recession," wrote Miller.

Miller said that bond proceeds should be invested in equities for at least five years, after which small portions of the money would be allocated to fixed-income investments in order to achieve the plan's long-term asset allocation. He advocated establishing new and separate POB or OPEB trusts that would give the trustees the option of using sustained excess returns to reduce or defray future employer contributions or to redeem outstanding bonds. "As history has painfully shown, taxpayers then are far better served by reducing debt permanently than by increasing employee benefits permanently and irrevocably."

Miller suggested investing the proceeds primarily in broad-market institutional stock index funds or portfolios, to reduce costs as well as risks. He also favored diversifying market entry points over time, to take advantage of the next turn in the business cycle and the next recession.

*See also* New Jersey pension obligation bonds of 1997; pensions.

*Sources:*

"Evaluating the Use of Pension Obligation Bonds." Government Finance Officers Association Advisory, March 2005.

Miller, Girard. "Bonding for Benefits: POBs and 'OPEB-OBs': New Strategies to Shatter the Old POB Paradigm." *Governing*, January 15, 2009.

## pensions

Until the subject exploded into the nation's consciousness in 2010, few people concerned themselves with public pensions, either with the relative generosity of the pensions themselves, with the other postemployment benefits (OPEB)—chiefly health care—provided to some retirees and their families, or with the stock-market losses that produce gaping unfunded liabilities in so many state and local pension plans from time to time.

There had been discussions, of course, of the sales of taxable municipal bonds to raise money to deposit into pension funds depleted by those occasional stock-market losses or for other reasons—usually budgetary, often involving skipping the actuarially determined annual contributions states or municipalities were required to make to the funds. Then there was the 2004 decision by the Governmental Accounting Standards Board to have states and municipalities total up and account for those other postemployment benefit obligations on more than a pay-as-you-go basis, which was phased in over several years. But any discussions of such subjects were generally kept within the family of issuers, bankers, analysts, and institutional investors who make their livelihoods in the municipal bond market. Pensions were not the stuff of front-page headlines. Even rating-agency reports on the ballooning costs of other postemployment benefits, or on states and municipalities considering switching from their present defined-benefit plans to 401(k)-like defined-contribution plans, as important as they were, did not really garner much attention. There was a lot of good, very detailed work being done by a small coterie of analysts. The issue, however, seemed to be an acquired taste beyond academics, actuaries, and accountants.

A pretty good gauge of the public's growing interest in public pensions was the PensionTsunami website, founded in 2004 by the Fullerton Association of Concerned Taxpayers and acquired in 2010 by the California Public Policy Institute, an obviously politically interested organization that concerns itself, it says, with researching the impact of public unions on the government. When it was first founded, PensionTsunami collected a relative handful of articles a day, chiefly on California. By 2009, the site was typically posting a dozen or more stories every day—columns and editorials collected from around the nation, all dealing with the financial impact of pensions promised to generations of public-sector employees on state and local budgets. Pensions as a journalistic subject had gained traction.

The state and local government pension issue gained real visibility in 2010 with the publication of several studies and papers that outlined a problem that, by then, and primarily because of stock-market losses, had grown too big to ignore. In February of that year the Pew Center on the States, a division of the Pew Charitable Trusts of Philadelphia, produced "The Trillion-Dollar Gap: Underfunded State Retirement Systems and the Roads to Reform." This report marked the first time anyone had pegged the size of the gap between what states had on hand and what they owed their current and retired employees in pension, health care, and other retirement benefits; the report pegged the gap at $1 trillion, a number guaranteed to make headlines.

There was a reason: unfunded pension liabilities simply had not been an issue before. As Standard & Poor's had observed in a piece of commentary the previous year, in 2009, pensions did very well with their investments in the 1990s, and so-called funding ratios averaged more than 100 percent by 2000, compared with 80 percent a decade earlier. (Not surprisingly, such ratios may have contributed to the plans' undoing, with unions demanding, and politicians doling out, increases in benefits.) By 2007, the latest year for which data were then available, the funding ratio average had dropped to 83 percent, and more bad news was on the way as the stock market slumped.

The Pew report was a very reasonable, nonincendiary piece of analysis, both grading the states and urging them to take action. The report observed that even before the subprime crisis, some states had not been making the actuarially determined annual contributions to the plans that they ought, and continued, "the bill for public sector retirement benefits already threatens strained budgets." The report also said that its $1 trillion figure was likely conservative, as it did not include the big investment losses suffered by pensions in the second half of 2008.

The $1 trillion figure found its way into numerous stories and blog postings. What really caught commentators' attention nationwide, however, was the work of Robert Novy-Marx of the University of Rochester and Joshua D. Rauh of the Kellogg School of Management. In a series of papers, the authors showed that, if one calculated the states' collective unfunded liability using a Treasury security rate of return instead of the states' typical assumption of earnings at 8 percent or more, their actual liability swelled from about $1 trillion to $3.26 trillion, and that a number of states' plans could run dry within a few years, absent a big increase in contributions or a reduction in benefits. The papers were academic in style; only the numbers were provocative, but that was enough to focus the nation's, or at least the commentariat's, attention on what up until then had been a pretty dry and nonurgent topic. Such liabilities, coupled with bonded debt of both the general obligation and moral obligation variety, were surely "unsustainable" or "unmanageable," to use two words that achieved currency with critics, and must sink municipalities (and states, if they were only allowed to file) into bankruptcy, critics said.

Once these numbers were published, the press started looking more closely at the pensions and benefits provided to retirees. Backlash against the public sector was inevitable, and it turned out to be even harsher than the one against Wall Street in 2008, when a number of the banks and securities firms that had played such a role in the subprime crisis also announced that they would be giving out bonuses as usual in 2009, if only on a slightly more modest scale. That backlash, directed against those who collected Wall Street's lottery-like, lifestyle-changing windfalls on a regular basis, lasted barely a bonus season. The one directed against state and local government employee unions was destined to go on considerably longer, and perhaps with more palpable results.

The reasons weren't hard to fathom: Wall Street is a small, faraway community, whose relatively few highly compensated performers every few years seemed to inhabit the same media fantasyland as models, movie stars, artists, and top athletes. The media covered the doings of bankers not because of any visually apparent and appreciable talent, but because of their ability to put up big numbers in terms of earnings, and their possession of enough money to satisfy any desire.

Yet their actual ranks were small. In July 2009, then-attorney general Andrew M. Cuomo of New York produced a 22-page report on the "bank bonus culture," and found that the nine major banks that had received money from the Troubled Assets Relief Program in 2008, big names like Goldman Sachs and JPMorgan, had also paid 4,792 employees more than $1 million in bonuses. The numbers of bankers (a generic term for all those employed by securities firms) who collect significant bonuses can possibly be numbered in the tens of thousands; add in those in the hedge fund and money management business, and maybe the entire community of Wall Street–style bonus recipients is around 50,000, enough to fill a baseball stadium on a summer Sunday.

Main Street, however, is by definition home, and more a part of the real world of everyday experience than is Wall Street. And it seemed, to many Americans, that the public sector somehow did not participate in the Great Recession. State and local governments continued to hire long after private companies were firing what ultimately would amount to 8.5 million workers, or 7.3 percent of the 115.6 million-person workforce peak of December 2007. The 19.8 million-strong state and local government sector began layoffs only in August 2008, and then only very slowly.

Unlike the ranks of private-sector workers, whose retirement savings had been decimated by the recession, most government employees enjoyed full, guaranteed pensions and often lifetime health care benefits. Government workers could look forward to retiring at age 55 at a time when many Americans figured they would have to work until they were certainly well into their 60s or even older. More than one analyst said non-public-sector Americans were suffering from "pension envy." Unlike the case with Wall Street bankers, this time they, the taxpayers, could do something about it. The revelations that a Bell, California, city manager made more than $800,000 a year and that the ranks of the "$100,000 club" (that is, government retirees whose pensions topped $100,000 a year) were growing nationwide only intensified the scrutiny and subsequent resentment. Newspapers and especially the blogosphere sizzled with stories detailing obvious abuses of the system, such as spiking higher an employee's final year's salary, upon which the pension was based, through massive amounts of overtime. Such instances, even if relatively rare, became the stuff of urban legend.

The story had a very political aspect, at least on a national level. The public unions gave political campaign contributions overwhelmingly to

Democrats. The Democrats were routed in the midterm congressional elections in 2010 and lost control of a number of statehouses.

Conservatives, notably Newt Gingrich, championed the notion of allowing states to file Chapter 9 municipal bankruptcy so that they could renege specifically on their pension promises and thus gut the public labor unions' power. Republican members of Congress proposed legislation to force states to report pension liabilities at a lower discount rate consistent with Treasury bond yields or give up the ability to sell bonds on a tax-exempt basis. On the state level, Republicans, led by Governor Chris Christie of New Jersey and Governor Scott Walker of Wisconsin, eagerly joined battle against the unions, portraying them as greedy and out of touch with the fiscal realities confronting so many Americans and their own states of residence.

Political theater aside, the unions had consolidated their considerable gains in pension and other benefits incrementally over time, and with whatever party happened to be in power. Increases in salary and benefits were the price of political peace, and elected officials paid it. More than one commentator said that the taxpayers did not seem to be at the table during the negotiations with the unions, or even, for that matter, in the same room.

Unfunded pension liabilities and the backlash against public employee labor unions was a key part of the hysteria that in the fall of 2010 had at last gripped the municipal securities market, which is normally placid even in the face of bad news. Fed a continuous diet of sensationalistic headlines, news stories, and blog entries, investors pulled something like $40 billion from municipal bond mutual funds, about 10 percent of the total and the most ever, over a six-month period. The barrage of bad news culminated on December 19, 2010, when banking analyst Meredith Whitney stoked the mania with a prediction on a CBS *60 Minutes* segment entitled "Day of Reckoning" that 2011 would see 50 to 100 significant municipal bond defaults totaling "hundreds of billions" of dollars. This prediction finally stirred those who had more experience in terms of the municipal market and public finance to respond to the almost-two-years-long drumbeat of hyperventilating headlines and misguided stories.

As so often is the case in the municipal bond market, the public pension story is a very nuanced one, resisting both generalization and aggregate numbers like $1 trillion or $3 trillion. Some plans are fully funded, or almost so; some plans are not. As the Center for Retirement Research at Boston College (which, with the Center for State and Local Government Excellence, maintains an online database on most state and local pensions) pointed out, pension plans in the aggregate account for only 3.8 percent of state and local spending. The Center for Economic and Policy Research, a Washington think tank, called the discussions about pension shortfalls "misleading," adding that "the total shortfall for the pension funds is less than 0.2 percent of projected gross state product over the next 30 years for most states. Even in the cases of the states with the largest shortfalls, the gap is less than 0.5 percent of projected state product."

Another Washington research organization, the Center on Budget and Policy Priorities, which had been prominent for regularly announcing the multibillion-dollar budget deficits facing the states (which at least sounded very alarming), in January 2011 published a report of a very different stripe: "Misunderstandings Regarding State Debt, Pensions, and Retiree Health Costs Create Unnecessary Alarm." Regarding the assertions that public pensions would crush state and local economies, the report said, "Such claims overstate the fiscal problem, fail to acknowledge that severe problems are concentrated in a small number of states, and often promote extreme actions rather than more appropriate solutions."

And the National Conference of State Legislatures, among others, said that states, for their part, had not been feckless during the Great Recession, but in fact had wrestled with the subject of pensions and benefits for several years and with varying degrees of success, trimming future and sometimes existing benefits, raising employee contributions, and increasing eligibility requirements. "We think it is important to note that, rather than being passive, as has been implied in some media reporting on this matter, states have been actively addressing their pension funding issues using the tools available to them under state law," observed Chris Mauro of RBC Capital Markets in a research piece. Even Roubini Global Economics, in a report stating that the present value of unfunded state and local liabilities was really $7 trillion and that the market could experience $100 billion in defaults over five years, observed that the worst of the doomsayers "assume the *Titanic* is set on autopilot heading for the North Pole."

No one could doubt that public pensions and benefits had arrived as a subject for discussion and debate—and as a very visible factor in ratings, as well. In January 2011, Moody's produced a report combining debt and pension liabilities, saying this would improve "comparative credit assessments" of states.

In February, Fitch announced that it was enhancing its analysis of state and local government pension obligations, as well, and that this might well have an impact on credit ratings. Standard & Poor's, in downgrading New

Jersey to AA– from AA, cited the state's pension and health care obligations. Public pensions, now more or less transparent, were also now page one news.

*See also* New Jersey pension obligation bonds of 1997; OPEB; pension obligation bonds.

*Sources:*

Baker, Dean. "The Origins and Severity of the Public Pension Crisis." Center for Economic and Policy Research, February 2011.

Cohen, Natalie. "Bankruptcy and Public Pensions: Debunking Some Misconceptions." Wells Fargo Securities, February 25, 2011.

Cohen, Natalie. "Public Pension Primer." Wells Fargo Securities, November 23, 2010.

Cuomo, Andrew M. "No Rhyme or Reason: The 'Heads I Win, Tails You Lose' Bank Bonus Culture." Andrew M. Cuomo, Attorney General, State of New York, July 2009.

Hampton, Ted. "Combining Debt and Pension Liabilities of U.S. States Enhances Comparability." Moody's Investors Service, January 26, 2011.

Hampton, Ted, and Robert Kurtter. "Other Post-Employment Benefits (OPEB)." Special Comment, Moody's Investors Service, July 2005.

Lav, Iris J., and Elizabeth McNichol. "Misunderstandings Regarding State Debt, Pensions, and Retiree Health Costs Create Unnecessary Alarm." Center on Budget and Policy Priorities, January 20, 2011.

Mauro, Chris. "U.S. Municipal Focus: Legislative Changes to State Pension Funds." RBC Capital Markets, December 9, 2010.

Munnell, Alicia H., Jean-Pierre Aubry, and Laura Quinby. "The Impact of Public Pensions on State and Local Budgets." Center for Retirement Research at Boston College, October 2010.

Norris, Floyd. "Accounting for Public Pensions." *New York Times*, December 10, 2010.

Novy-Marx, Robert, and Joshua D. Rauh. "The Crisis in Local Government Pensions in the United States." October 2010.

Nowakowski, David, and Prajakta Bhide. "States of Despair." Roubini Global Economics, March 2, 2011.

Offerman, Douglas. "Enhancing the Analysis of U.S. State and Local Government Pension Obligations." Fitch Ratings, February 17, 2011.

O'Leary, Shawn P. "State and Local Pensions: A Primer for Municipal Investors." Nuveen Investments, September 2010.

Petek, Gabriel, and James Wiemken. "U.S. States and Municipalities Face Crises More of Policy Than Debt." Standard & Poor's, November 8, 2010.

Prunty, Robin. "Pension Funding and Policy Challenges Loom for U.S. States." Standard & Poor's, June 30, 2010.

Raphael, Richard. "U.S. State and Local Government Bond Credit Quality: More Sparks Than Fire." Fitch Ratings, November 16, 2010.

Rauh, Joshua D. "Are State Public Pensions Sustainable?" *National Tax Journal* 63, no. 10 (2010).

Smith, Robert G., III. "Gasping over GASB 45: OPEB Funding Challenges for Public Entities and U.S. Taxpayers." Sage Advisory Services, Austin, Texas, May 10, 2006.

"The Trillion-Dollar Gap: Underfunded State Retirement Systems and the Roads to Reform." Pew Center on the States, February 2010.

Walsh, Mary Williams. "Mounting Debts by States Stoke Fears of Crisis." *New York Times*, December 5, 2010.

Walsh, Mary Williams. "A Path Is Sought for States to Escape Debt Burdens." *New York Times*, January 21, 2011.

Walsh, Mary Williams. "State Debt Woes Grow Too Troubling to Camouflage." *New York Times*, March 30, 2010.

Young, Parry. "Funding OPEB Liabilities: Assessing the Options." Standard & Poor's, December 14, 2005.

Young, Parry. "How Big U.S. Cities Are Faring with the Pension Fund Meltdown." Standard & Poor's, August 11, 2006.

Young, Parry. "Public Employers Are Exploring a Switch to Defined Contribution Pension Plans." Standard & Poor's, November 16, 2005.

Young, Parry. "Reporting & Credit Implications of GASB 45 Statement on Other Postemployment Benefits." Standard & Poor's, December 1, 2004.

Young, Parry. "Rising U.S. State Unfunded Pension Liabilities Are Causing Budgetary Stress." Standard & Poor's, February 22, 2006.

## "People don't buy municipal bonds to get rich; they buy municipal bonds to stay rich"

This is a market axiom demonstrating that municipal bonds are investments designed to preserve capital, primarily, and to produce tax-free income, secondarily. They are not speculative investments purchased in hopes of price appreciation, although their prices may indeed go up if they are prerefunded.

*See also* "All bonds go to heaven"; refunding.

## Philadelphia trial

In June 2004, the municipal bond market got a chance to look at pay-to-play, big-city style. It wasn't pretty.

*United States of America v. Ronald A. White, Corey Kemp, et al.* was all about steering municipal bond business to favored underwriting firms in return for business, cash, or political contributions. The indictment contained 56 counts for everything from conspiracy to commit honest services fraud to wire fraud, mail fraud, extortion, and making false statements to the Federal Bureau of Investigation (FBI). As the U.S. attorney said at a news conference announcing the indictment, "This is an indictment not only of the defendants but of a 'pay-to-play' culture that can only breed corruption."

The lawsuit against Ronald White (a lawyer and fund-raiser for Mayor John Street of Philadelphia), Corey Kemp (the city's treasurer), and others, including bankers from J.P. Morgan Securities and Commerce Bank, was 150 pages long and read a little bit like a novel, the result of dozens of quotes from judicially authorized wiretaps. Mayor Street was not indicted. FBI listening devices had been discovered in his office the previous October, short-circuiting the investigation.

The indictment began:

"Defendant Ronald A. White was a private attorney licensed to practice in the Commonwealth of Pennsylvania. White sought employment as an attorney participating in the issuance of bonds of the City of Philadelphia and related agencies, and also sought in those deals the award of printing contracts to a printing company nominally owned by his paramour, defendant Janice Renee Knight.

"White also acted as an advocate on behalf of financial services companies seeking to do business with the City, in exchange for which assistance White sought and obtained lucrative legal fees and other remuneration, business for Knight's printing company, and substantial political and other contributions to causes favored by White, including the re-election of the Mayor of Philadelphia.

"The Mayor instructed his staff that, if White or firms he touted appeared to be qualified, the staff members should award the City business White sought, and provide White with inside information he sought regarding the operations of City agencies otherwise unavailable to the public."

White died in November 2004. The trial began in February 2005. Kemp was convicted in May, and in July was sentenced to 10 years in prison, the most of any of the defendants.

Particularly noteworthy for those interested in public finance nationally were copies of interviews conducted by J.P. Morgan lawyers with bankers Charles LeCroy and Anthony Snell, who pleaded guilty to federal charges in the case. The interviews gave a rare behind-the-scenes look at what bankers call a "relationship business" and why certain parties are paid on transactions, even if they perform no actual work—"a common approach in the industry," according to one of the bankers, LeCroy, who would also figure in the Jefferson County, Alabama, story.

*See also* Jefferson County, Alabama; pay-to-play.

*Sources:*

"Interview with Anthony Snell." Memorandum, Morgan Lewis & Bockius, April 19, 2004.

"Interview with Charles LeCroy." Memorandum, Morgan Lewis & Bockius LLP, April 19, 2004.

"March 4 Interview with Charles LeCroy." Memorandum, Morgan Lewis & Bockius, April 19, 2004.

"March 4, 2004 Conversation with Anthony Snell." Memorandum, Morgan Lewis & Bockius, April 19, 2004.

Milford, Phil, and Andrew Pratt. "Former Philadelphia Treasurer Sentenced to 10 Years." Bloomberg News, July 19, 2005.

Mysak, Joe. "MuniLand Has a Must-Read—Philadelphia Wiretaps." Bloomberg News, January 26, 2005.

*United States v. Ronald A. White, Corey Kemp, et al.,* U.S. District Court for the Eastern District of Pennsylvania, June 29, 2004.

## PIT bonds

In 2001, the state of New York established state Personal Income Tax Revenue Bonds, which are backed by the first 25 percent of the receipts from the state's personal income tax (PIT). Legislation authorized five issuers to sell such PIT bonds: the Dormitory Authority, the Environmental Facilities Corporation, the Housing Finance Agency, the Thruway Authority, and the Urban Development Corporation. Critics of the creation said carving out the tax diminished the value of the state's general obligation pledge.

## preliminary official statement

A bond's official statement in near-final condition, often lacking only the pricing details and sources and uses of funds, was also called a red herring because the document was marked as "Preliminary" in red ink on the cover.

*See also* official statement.

## premium bonds

Premium bonds are priced at an excess of par. Such pricing results in more production, or money, to the issuers, because they are getting, for example, $106 instead of $100 for their bonds.

## premium laundering

Premium laundering is a phenomenon first described by an Internal Revenue Service (IRS) whistle-blower in the summer of 2008 as a deliberate violation of Rule 171a, which does not allow buyers of tax-exempt bonds to amortize the premiums paid on those bonds. They may amortize the premiums paid on taxable bonds, but many banks' accounting software apparently did not make the distinction. This was not much of an issue when most investment banks did not hold lots of municipal bonds, and most bonds were priced around par. As the whistle-blower wrote to the IRS: "Banks now hold massive proprietary positions of municipal bonds through their treasury, tender-option bond, and arbitrage trading desks. Due to market conditions and investor preference, nearly all tax-exempt bonds are now issued at a premium, sometimes at a significant premium." This was why, he explained, some very interesting pricings were observable, particularly in 2003 and 2004. The earliest maturities of bonds, sold mainly in the competitive market but also in the negotiated market, were being priced with 6 percent coupons well in excess of $100, and not being reoffered. The whistle-blower called what was happening "bond-premium laundering."

Asked to define the term, he replied: "What I mean is that non-deductible basis adjustments are mixed in and 'laundered' with truly deductible mark-to-market losses. The nature of the loss gets re-characterized via the use of daily mark-to-market accounting, and the amortization component is hidden in the daily ups and downs of market rates, and mixed in with all the other, taxable bonds."

Here's how this scheme worked: A bank buys a $70 million tax-exempt note issue maturing in less than nine months, pricing it with a 6 percent coupon at 103.557, which yields 1.04 percent. The bank pays $72,489,900 for the bonds, plus an additional $523,538 to finance the position. At maturity, the bank gets back $70 million, plus $3,033,000 in tax-exempt interest. The bank makes a $19,000 profit. "But who in their right minds would tie up $70 million for a $19,000 profit?" asked the whistle-blower. If the bank also treats the bond premium, $2,489,900, as a deduction, the bank gets to avoid $871,465 in taxes at the 35 percent rate, so this trade "made" $890,465.

He explained it a little further: When you buy a muni bond, the tax-exempt interest you are entitled to is the yield, not the coupon. Buying a 6 percent coupon bond at a yield of 1.04 percent, on your tax return you can avoid paying tax on the 1.04 percent, not on the 6 percent. Bond accounting systems were designed in the main for taxable bonds, and accrue interest daily at the 6 percent rate on the bond. The market value of the bonds drops daily due to the premium amortization. An above-market coupon is accrued while the deductible amortization losses flow through to the mark-to-market line. If the bond is tax-exempt, the dealer can split the daily 6 percent accrual into tax-exempt (1.04 percent) and taxable (4.96 percent), or let the 6 percent go entirely into the tax-exempt interest line and adjust the tax basis of the bond downward each day. Either choice is correct. What is not correct is to do nothing and look the other way.

How this ended was apparently with one bank, frustrated at losing some big deals, alerting another bank's tax department that something was amiss. The high-coupon structure on the earliest maturities of issues seemed to disappear. The industry probably thought it had settled this matter by itself. Not too long after, the IRS came calling.

*See also* yield burning.

*Sources:*

Mysak, Joe. "Bond Traders Didn't Care If Muni Deals Were Illegal." Bloomberg News, September 16, 2008.

Mysak, Joe. "Whistleblower Offers Tips on Bond-Premium Laundering." Bloomberg News, September 9, 2008.

Mysak, Joe. "Whistleblower Says Dealers 'Laundered' Bond Prices." Bloomberg News, September 2, 2008.

## prerefunded bonds

Bonds that have been refunded in advance of their first call are said to be prerefunded. The proceeds of a new bond issue are invested in a portfolio of U.S. Treasury securities or other triple-A-rated collateral, with the payment stream matching that of the bonds being refunded, usually until the first call date. This usually occurs within five years. The prerefunded bonds are rated triple-A, and often sell for higher prices than they did originally.

About 78.5 percent of prerefunded bonds are escrowed with Treasury obligations, with another 21 percent escrowed with federal agency securities, Bank of America Merrill Lynch municipal research strategist John Hallacy estimated in 2010. "The rate of advance refundings has varied widely through time," Hallacy wrote. "The savings to the issuer, the usual driver of an advance refunding, is a function of the level of interest rates and the amount of negative arbitrage in the escrow."

He continued, "If short-term taxable escrow yields are below longer-term tax-exempt yields, the escrow securities will produce negative arbitrage. This negative arbitrage must be subtracted from any interest rate savings produced by a decline in tax-exempt rates."

*See also* escrow churning; escrowed to maturity; refunding.

*Source:*

Hallacy, John. "Waiting for Godot or QE2?" Muni Commentary, Bank of America Merrill Lynch, October 29, 2010.

## price to the par call

The price to the par call pricing structure was popular from early 1998 to 2008, providing investors, typically mutual funds, some protection against rising interest rates.

The structure featured bonds that carried coupons anywhere from 25 to 50 basis points higher than normal in the 10- to 15-year maturity range. The bonds would be priced at a premium, lowering the yield to expected levels, with the expectation that the issuer will call them at the earliest opportunity. If the issuer does not exercise the call, the buyer winds up with extra income in the form of the higher coupon.

## pricing

Pricing refers to the terms the issuer is supposed to negotiate in a negotiated sale. In a competitive sale, the pricing of the bonds—the bid made by underwriters—is take it or leave it; the issuer decides to accept it or reject it. In a negotiated pricing, there is supposed to be room for give-and-take. Not all issuers realize that the underwriter is actually in an adversarial relationship with them at this point; that is, the underwriter wants to price the bonds to sell, whereas the issuer, meanwhile, wants to get the best price, the lowest borrowing cost. The very least the issuer should do is compare how its bonds are priced to how they were priced before, by simply looking at a triple-A scale and seeing how many basis points more than the triple-A scale its bonds have been priced. All else being equal—that is, if the credit is the same as it was before—the pricing should be about the same or, it is hoped, better. Unlike the competitive sale, this is not a one-shot process. The underwriters can go back and reprice the issue depending upon market demand. If issuers are taking the process at all seriously, few will choose to go it alone, instead making sure to have a financial adviser on their side.

Far from the "leave the driving to us" service advocated by some bankers, issuers would be well-advised to get involved with the process intimately. "Unlike a competitive sale, bond pricing in a negotiated sale requires a much greater degree of issuer involvement," the Government Finance Officers Association says in the Best Practice it produced in 1996 and updated in 2000 and 2010. "The issuer negotiates both the yield on the bonds and the underwriters' compensation (also called underwriter discount or gross spread), which includes the takedown (or sales commission), management fee, underwriting risk, and expenses. An issuer's success in negotiating the price of its bonds depends on its ability and willingness to devote sufficient time to understanding the market and the historical performance of its bonds."

*See also* competitive sale; flipping; negotiated sale; underwriters.

*Source:*

"Pricing Bonds in a Negotiated Sale." Best Practice, Government Finance Officers Association, 1996, 2000, 2010.

## principal

The principal is the face amount of a bond issue, disregarding the interest payments. For example, the Carbondale Area School District in Lackawanna

County, Pennsylvania, on October 15, 2010, sold $6,680,000 in general obligation bonds. The $6,680,000 is the principal amount. The interest the school district pays amounts to an additional $1,150,411.95, paid over the life of the debt.

## private placements

Private placements are transactions that are neither negotiated nor competitive, but placed directly with one or two investors, usually local banks.

## Proposition 2½

*See* initiative and referendum.

## Proposition 13

*See* initiative and referendum.

## public–private partnerships

There was a time when toll roads and public transportation were in the main privately owned. That time may return, if advocates of public–private partnerships (PPPs) have their way.

The concept of PPP deals, in which states and municipalities lease toll roads and other assets to private companies in return for up-front payments, gained some traction in 2005 after Chicago leased its Skyway, a 7.8-mile-long elevated highway that connects the Dan Ryan Expressway with the Indiana Toll Road, for 99 years in return for $1.8 billion. In 2006, Indiana leased the Toll Road, a 157-mile highway across the northern part of the state that runs from Illinois to Ohio, for 75 years for $3.8 billion. The two transactions sparked a lot of discussion, if not emulation. The idea of selling the streets, and other public assets, including bridges and airports, is still foreign to most Americans. Public officials, for their part, were reluctant to sell assets for what might be criticized as too low a price.

The PPP idea was a simple one. In return for a big cash payment, governmental entities could get out of something that was not part of their core mission and distance themselves from the political fallout that would result from big increases in user fees. The private company now in charge of the asset could run it using modern efficiencies to improve service and make a profit after increasing fees and tolls to more realistic levels. As many as half of the states were said to be looking at PPP deals as the Great Recession and its aftermath reduced their revenue and made it harder and harder to maintain transportation infrastructure. But such deals were slow in coming.

The possibility of PPP deals offered bond investors some intriguing opportunities. Buying the debt of an underperforming bridge or toll road could lead to a bonanza if it was sold and that debt redeemed. Investors had to decide if this was an opportunity, or merely the illusion of one.

*Sources:*

Baeb, Eddie. "Macquarie-Cintra's Purchase of Indiana Road Approved." Bloomberg News, March 15, 2006.
George, Cherian, et al. "U.S. Toll Road Privatizations: Seeking the Right Balance." Fitch Ratings, March 22, 2006.
Matesanz, Maria, et al. "Toll Road Privatization Trends in the U.S.: An Assessment of the Credit Benefits and Risks." Moody's Investors Service, September 2006.
Villaluz, Philip. "U.S. Toll Road Privatization: The Stakes Are High—Bond Investors Take Another Look." Merrill Lynch, March 20, 2006.

## Puerto Rico

The bonds of the commonwealth, along with those of American territories, are triple-tax-exempt, that is, free of all city, state, and federal taxes in all jurisdictions, making them a popular investment nationally, especially for funds.

## pyramid bonds

A term dating from the 1980s used to describe certain kinds of abusive reimbursement financings, where issuers sold bonds to recover expenditures made with public funds and invested the proceeds in taxable securities to earn arbitrage. Tax officials termed some of these kinds of deals pyramid bonds because they were designed to reimburse issuers for expenditures made long before. The result of the pyramid bond imbroglio, which stret-ched for several years, was the promulgation of regulations under the tax code to restrict the ability of borrowers to use bond proceeds to reimburse themselves for prior expenditures. "Borrowers routinely pass 'reimburse-ment resolutions' now to preserve the ability to make such reimbursements, but there is a general three-year limit on reimbursement, with some exceptions," according to Dean Pope, a bond attorney with Hunton & Williams. "Thus a city can no longer decide to finance for the first time today a school it built 10 years ago."

*See also* arbitrage.

*Sources:*

Pope, Dean. E-mail, September 2, 2011, In Re: Pyramid Bonds.
Pryde, Joan. "Bond Lawyers Warn Issuers to Shun 'Pyramid Bonds,'" *Bond Buyer*, September 2, 1987.

## Qualified School Construction Bonds; Qualified Zone Academy Bonds

*See* taxable municipals.

# R

## ratings

The system of letters and symbols used by the ratings agencies (usually paid by the issuer) to grade securities. About one-quarter of the number of issues in the municipal market are not rated at all, chiefly speculative offerings that would not be rated investment grade and very small, infrequent issues for which the cost might be prohibitive.

*See also* Recalibration of 2010.

*Source:*

"Report on Transactions in Municipal Securities," Office of Economic Analysis and Office of Municipal Securities, Division of Market Regulation, United States Securities and Exchange Commission, July 1, 2004.

## the ratio

The ratio represents how much tax-exempt municipals yield compared to U.S. Treasury bonds, which are taxable. Bonds are considered cheap when the ratio is above 90 percent or 95 percent, and expensive when the ratio is in the 80 percent area.

The ratio on 10-year maturities shot up in 2008 as the subprime credit crisis exploded, almost all of the bond insurers lost their triple-A ratings, and even municipal bonds were not considered safe enough for the most conservative investors. In March, it rose to almost 120 percent with the collapse of the auction-rate security (ARS) market, when dealers ceased backstopping the sales of ARS with their own bids. It spiked toward the end of the year after the failure of Lehman Brothers, rising to a record high of 195 percent.

*See also* auction-rate securities.

*Source:*

Bloomberg data.

## Recalibration of 2010

In March 2007, Moody's Investors Service published a dense, 58-page paper on "The U.S. Municipal Bond Rating Scale: Mapping to the Global Rating Scale and Assigning Global Scale Ratings to Municipal Obligations."

"To improve the transparency of U.S. long-term municipal bond ratings, Moody's is implementing a new analytical approach for mapping these ratings to the global scale used to rate all bonds outside of the U.S. public finance market," the ratings company opened.

This unpromising beginning launched a revolution in the municipal bond market.

It was, seen in retrospect, almost inadvertent. The revolution took three years and featured letter-writing campaigns, congressional hearings, and lawsuits. It was played out amid a stock market crash, the longest and deepest recession since the Great Depression, the freeze-up of the auction-rate securities market, and the annihilation of most of the major bond insurers. And when this revolution concluded, investors everywhere finally could look at their city or state or county or school district and see if it was as creditworthy as the Coca-Cola Company.

Of course, it didn't start that way. Moody's in 2007 said it was going to map taxable municipal ratings to the global scale because there were more "crossover" buyers of state and local bonds—nontraditional investors who normally sought out only corporate debt, and international investors who bought taxable municipals for portfolio diversification. To accommodate these new entrants, Moody's would provide "Global Scale Ratings."

Because of municipalities' very low probability of default, Moody's acknowledged that most would be rated higher on the global scale. On page 13 of the report, issuers got a chance to see exactly what this meant: states rated A1, Aa3, Aa2, or Aa1 would be rated Aaa, for example. Those rated Baa1, A3, or A2 would be rated Aa1. And so on.

Moody's said it would continue using a separate municipal rating scale—in use, it later said, since 1918—"because many municipal investors and issuers place a high value on the fine gradations of risk" provided by the scale.

The "new methodology" announced by Moody's touched off a mutiny by certain state and local officials, who apparently had not been aware that the analysts at Moody's were judging them by a double standard.

"To the extent that the ratings increase debt service cost and are not truly a reflection of the risk, taxpayers come out on the short end of the stick," Tom Dresslar, a spokesman for California Treasurer Bill Lockyer, told Bloomberg News in May 2007.

The controversy simmered along, perhaps fed by a 24/7 news cycle, and in June 2007 Moody's published a "Frequently Asked Questions" paper concerning the new global scale. "If at some point in the future the market's preference shifts toward migrating municipal ratings onto the global scale, we will reconsider our position" on using two scales, said the ratings company.

Neither of the other two major ratings companies followed Moody's lead. For its part, Standard & Poor's maintained that it had always used a single scale to assess credit. As early as 1999, Fitch Ratings had called municipal bonds "underrated," and had embarked on a series of upgrades beginning in 2000.

In the fall of 2007, two things happened that made the existence of a dual rating scale no longer a topic of almost academic discussion and instead a matter of some urgency. As subprime losses mounted, investors became worried about the financial condition of the monoline bond insurers, which had guaranteed so much of the municipal market. And then auction-rate securities sales began to fail. Both auction-rate and variable-rate borrowing costs rose.

"With at least $2 billion of annual taxpayer savings possible, we urge issuers to act," advised Matt Fabian, a managing director at Municipal Market Advisors, in a January 2008 commentary. That same month, Fitch cut Ambac's and FGIC's triple-A ratings. They were the first of the major bond insurers to lose their top grade.

In February, the dealers who had always acted as buyers of last resort stopped bidding for auction-rate paper altogether. On March 4, California Treasurer Bill Lockyer and 14 of his colleagues in state and local government sent the three ratings companies a five-page letter urging them to create a new rating standard for municipal debt.

"For investors, the current system greatly inflates the risk of investing in municipal bonds relative to alternative investments, leading to investment decisions that are not based on the best information," the letter said. "For municipalities, the dual standard has cost our taxpayers and ratepayers billions of dollars in increased interest costs and bond insurance premiums." The letter noted that the bond insurance industry "exists in large part because of your municipal rating scales."

One week later, on March 12, the House Financial Services Committee held a hearing on how the credit crisis was affecting state and local governments. Public officials urged Congress to pressure the ratings companies to move to a global scale that would acknowledge their very low default rate when compared with corporate borrowers. Chairman Barney Frank sided with the officials, and advised the ratings companies that they had a month to fix the problem—or else.

On March 20, Fitch announced that Chief Credit Officer Robert Grossman would focus on the "harmonization" of corporate and public finance ratings. That same day, Moody's published a Request for Comment on assigning global ratings to tax-exempt municipal obligations. The company said that in May it planned to assign both the municipal and the global scale ratings to municipal issues. It still did not say it was doing away with the two scales.

On May 31, Connecticut Attorney General Richard Blumenthal sent a letter to Christopher Cox, chairman of the Securities and Exchange Commission (SEC), asking him to "take action to reform the credit rating industry," and for good measure copied Barney Frank and Christopher Dodd, chairman of the Senate Banking Committee.

"Our investigation has revealed that as far back as 1999, the ratings agencies have knowingly and systematically given state, municipal, and other public entities lower credit ratings than other forms of debt, such as corporate and structured securities, with similar or even worse rates of default," wrote Blumenthal.

Two of the biggest bond insurers, Ambac Financial Group Inc. and MBIA Inc., lost their triple-A ratings on June 5, with Standard & Poor's cutting both to AA.

On June 12, Moody's said it had heard from 150 market participants—this counts as a large number in the municipal market—and was extending the comment period for its March global scale request. At the same time, the company proposed "to proceed with a single rating scale for our public finance issuers, and to transition our public finance ratings to our global scale." The market participants it had heard from, Moody's said, found the existence of the dual rating scale "confusing."

This apparent capitulation did not stop Connecticut Attorney General Blumenthal from suing the three ratings companies for the "unfair, deceptive and illegal business practice of systematically and intentionally giving lower credit ratings" to states and localities than they did to corporate and other forms of debt with similar or worse rates of default. The lawsuits were still wending their way through the courts in mid-2011.

Fitch followed Moody's lead, on July 31 saying that after holding roundtable discussions with 44 issuers, investors, and what it termed "intermediaries," it was proposing "a recalibration of its municipal ratings so they denote a comparable level of credit risk as its international rating scale for corporate, sovereign, and other entities."

The Fitch announcement marked the first appearance of the word *recalibration* in the ratings saga. Fitch, which also called recalibrations "a normal part of the rating process," estimated that the move would result in the percentage of governmental issuers rated AA going from 47 percent to 70 percent, and those rated AAA from 11 percent to 16 percent.

The municipal market is nothing if not deliberative. On September 2, 2008, Moody's put out an announcement of its own. It would "begin to recalibrate its U.S. public finance ratings and migrate them to its global scale," beginning in October. The process, "prompted by recent market events and a shift in market sentiment," as well as comments from "more than 200 market participants," would take three months.

Not so fast. In mid-September, Lehman Brothers declared bankruptcy, and Merrill Lynch & Company sold itself to Bank of America. On September 15, the Dow Jones Industrial Average fell 504.48 points. The next day, it went up 141.51 points; the following day, it fell 449.36 points. Such swings became commonplace in the days ahead, and on October 7 both Fitch and Moody's postponed the move to a global scale until more settled conditions prevailed. The Recalibration was tabled.

The Great Recalibration, announced again in March 2010, finally took place in April and May. In all, Fitch moved 13,500 bond issues to the global scale; Moody's moved 70,000. The new ratings affected 1.24 million separate CUSIP numbers, which are assigned to each maturity of a bond issue, according to Bloomberg data.

Both Fitch and Moody's denied that the move reflected anything more than an adjustment: it "does not represent a change in our opinion of the credit quality of the affected issuers," said Moody's; it "should not be interpreted as an improvement in credit quality," said Fitch.

That's not how most municipal bond issuers saw it.

*See also* auction-rate securities; insurance; variable-rate demand obligations.

*Sources:*

Blumenthal, Richard. Letter to Christopher Cox, Chairman of the Securities and Exchange Commission, May 31, 2008.

"Corporate Ratings for Munis." Municipal Market Advisors, January 17, 2008.

"Exposure Draft: Reassessment of Municipal Ratings Framework." Fitch Ratings, July 31, 2008.

Lockyer, Bill, et al. Letter to ratings companies, March 4, 2008.

"Mapping of Moody's Municipal Ratings to the Global Scale: Frequently Asked Questions." Special Comment, Moody's Investors Service, June 2007.

"Moody's Extends Comment Period for U.S. Public Finance Rating Scale." Moody's Investors Service, June 12, 2008.

"Moody's to Offer Global Scale Ratings for all Taxable Municipal Debt." Press release, March 1, 2007.

"Request for Comment: Assignment of Global Ratings to Tax-Exempt Municipal Obligations." Moody's Investors Service, March 20, 2008.

Richard, Christine. "Moody's Double-Talk May Cost Taxpayers $3.6 Billion." Bloomberg, May 18, 2007.

*State of Connecticut v. Moody's Corporation, Fitch, Inc., The McGraw Hill Companies Inc.*, July 30, 2008.

"The U.S. Municipal Bond Rating Scale: Mapping to the Global Rating Scale and Assigning Global Scale Ratings to Municipal Obligations." Rating Methodology, Moody's Investors Service, March 2007.

Vekshin, Alison, and William Selway. "House's Frank Says Muni Ratings 'Ridiculous.'" Bloomberg, March 12, 2008.

## redemption

Issuers may retire their bonds prior to maturity through a variety of calls, sinking fund payments, and mandatory and optional redemptions. These are spelled out in detail in the official statement (OS).

## refunding

Municipalities most often refund their bonds to take advantage of lower interest rates. A current refunding takes place when older bonds are retired within 90 days after new refunding bonds are sold. An advance refunding occurs when the refunded bonds remain outstanding for more than 90 days, usually three to five years, until a call date or their maturity. The issuer sells new bonds and invests the proceeds in Treasury or agency securities that are placed into an escrow account dedicated to paying off the old bonds. The old bonds are said to be prerefunded and now no longer rely on the issuer for repayment, but instead rely on a pot of Treasury securities, and so may earn an upgrade to triple-A, should the issuer desire to get the bonds rerated.

After numerous abuses in the 1970s and early 1980s, tax-law writers tightened the rules governing refunding, including restricting the yield earned in the escrow account and limiting issuers to one advance refunding per bond issue. Refunding typically accounts for between 10 percent and 25 percent of the amount of bond sales in a given year.

*See also* escrowed to maturity.

*Sources:*

*The Bond Buyer/Thomson Finance 2005 Yearbook.* New York: Sourcemedia, 2005.

Hallacy, John. "Waiting for Godot or QE2?" Bank of America Merrill Lynch Muni Commentary, October 29, 2010.

## repudiation

Repudiation occurs when a bond issuer disowns the validity of debt it has sold in the past and refuses to repay it. The great heyday of American bond repudiation was the 1870s and 1880s, after the Civil War and the boom in railroad building that marked the Gilded Age. Municipalities, mainly in the South and West, repudiated debt sold during the Civil War, debt by carpetbag governments after the war, and debt sold to aid railroad development. This in turn led to the rise of bond counsel, lawyers who delivered an opinion that bonds were legal and valid obligations of an issuer.

*See also* bond counsel; Chapter 9; default; ultra vires.

## reserve fund

The reserve fund is also known as the debt-service reserve fund. Usually established at the time of issuance and funded with bond proceeds, this is a fund that contains money to be used to pay debt service in the event pledged revenue is insufficient. Tapping such reserve funds usually, but not always, constitutes an event of default. These funds typically contain enough to pay a year or two of debt service before they are depleted.

## retail order periods

Retail order periods were introduced in the 1990s to guarantee that some bonds find their way into local, individual investors' hands, and are now commonly used by large, frequent borrowers.

## revenue bonds

Said to date from 1885, revenue bonds are backed by user fees and other payments not connected to an issuer's tax base. They typically yield more than tax-backed bonds. At certain periods of fiscal stress, investors may actually prefer revenue bonds, reasoning that their claim on a specific, dedicated revenue stream may be stronger than a weakened tax base that may be further compromised by political considerations. The majority of bonds sold every year are revenue bonds.

*See also* Chapter 9; default; general obligation.

## RFPs

A request for proposal (RFP) is put out by bond issuers when they are looking to engage the services of underwriters, financial advisers, and the like. The RFP typically requires those who respond to provide anywhere from 10 to 20 pages (or more) about their professional qualifications; many underwriters provide detailed pitch books explaining how they would structure and sell particular bonds for the issuer. One or two rounds of interviews generally follow receipt of the RFPs. These documents are excellent sources of information about the design and structure of bond issues, as well as the qualifications and intentions of underwriters.

## risk factors

The most important section of an official statement after the "security for the bonds" is described lists the risk factors. In this section, the issuer details what might go wrong and imperil repayment of a bond issue, or doom it altogether.

Under "Certain Investment Considerations," for example, the Raleigh-Durham, North Carolina, Airport Authority said that the airport's ability to repay the revenue refunding bonds it was selling in August 2010 "depends on sufficient levels of aviation activity and passenger traffic at the Airport." It cited "many factors," many of which were not subject to its control: the economy; domestic and international affairs; air transportation disruptions; the threat of terrorism; health crises; the cost structure of airlines, including labor and aviation fuel; and federal regulation and federal legislation.

The town of Telluride, Colorado, in the official statement (OS) for the certificates of participation it sold to refund some previously issued bonds in August 2010, had a very different tale to tell.

The certificates, it said, were secured by the town's lease payments for various properties, including its city hall, administrative, and public works buildings. The lease is payable from all the general revenue of the town, "although no particular revenues of the Town are pledged to the Lease."

The town also notes that the certificates do not constitute indebtedness, and are subject to appropriation. "There is no assurance that the Town Council will appropriate sufficient funds to renew the Lease each year and the Town has no obligation to do so," says the OS.

The town also points to three proposed fiscal initiatives on the November 2010 election ballots: Proposition 101, which would reduce fees and taxes; Amendment 60, which would place further limitations on property taxes; and Amendment 61, which would "prohibit the State from issuing debt and entering into other types of borrowings or financings whatsoever, and limit local governments' " ability to enter into such transactions. "It is likely that this would include transactions such as the Series 2010 Certificates and other lease-purchase financings previously undertaken by the Town," says the OS.

*Sources:*

$9,785,000 Certificates of Participation, Series 2010, Evidencing Proportionate Interest in the Base Rentals and Other Revenues under an Annually Renewable Lease Agreement Dated as of August 25, 2010, between Wells Fargo Bank, N.A., Solely in Its Capacity as Trustee under the Indenture, as Lessor, and the Town of Telluride, Colorado, as Lessee. Official Statement dated August 10, 2010.

Raleigh-Durham Airport Authority, $242,365,000 Airport Revenue Refunding Bonds Series 2010A (Non-AMT), $94,080,000 Airport Revenue Refunding Bonds Series 2010A (Non-AMT), August 6, 2010.

## rollover

One of the nonexistent risks to state bonds cited by inexpert commentators during the great hysteria of 2009–2010 was rollover. These observers said that states facing deteriorating finances would be unable to obtain new funding when they had to repay their debts. Some seemed positively gleeful at the prospect, asserting that a day of reckoning was at hand for profligate spendthrifts. As with so much of the great hysteria, these people did not know what they were talking about. States and localities structure their debt with long maturities. It is self-amortizing, principal and interest being paid annually, and comes due every year, rather than in single-bullet maturities. Debt-service costs as a percentage of annual spending range between 4 percent and 8 percent. "These attributes allow Municipalities to retire debt uniformly over time, which greatly reduces 'rollover risk' that is often associated with corporate or sovereign debt," wrote analyst Vikram Rai of Citigroup in a special report published in 2011, "Rollover Risk in Municipals: Not an Issue."

The rollover risk that did exist in the municipal bond market was not a threat to states, but to small or weak credits that might not be able to renew bank liquidity, either letters of credit or standby purchase agreements, on their variable-rate demand obligations.

*See also* variable-rate demand obligations.

*Source:*

Rai, Vikram. "Rollover Risk in Municipals: Not an Issue." U.S. Municipal Strategy Notes, Citi Investment Research & Analysis, January 6, 2011.

## Rule 15c2-12

In June 1989, the Securities and Exchange Commission (SEC) adopted Exchange Act Rule 15c2-12, which says that underwriters cannot sell any bond over $1 million unless the issuer agrees to prepare an official statement to the transaction and produce it in a timely manner after the date of sale. The SEC also required underwriters to review the official statement to ensure that all key facts about an issue had been disclosed. The Municipal Securities Rulemaking Board then published its concept for a Municipal Securities Information Library as a repository for such documents, and adopted Rule G-36, requiring underwriters to send the documents to the repository. In 1994, the rule was amended to prohibit underwriters from buying bonds unless an issuer agreed to provide continuing disclosure.

*See also* "Deadly Sins"; disclosure; escrowed to maturity; Tower Amendment.

*Sources:*

Taylor, Christopher. "Milestones in Municipal Securities Regulation 1975–2005." Municipal Securities Rulemaking Board, Alexandria, VA, 2006.

Testimony before the Subcommittee on Telecommunications and Finance on Regulation of the Municipal Securities Market, September 9, 1993.

## rum bonds

The bonds sold by the U.S. Virgin Islands to build facilities used by the rum industry.

# S

## Saco, Maine

On January 16, 1979, the voters in Saco, Maine, upset by a 1978 property tax reevaluation that doubled and even trebled assessments, passed a measure that would cap property taxes at $3 million, allowing for an increase of 2 percent a year in the local budget. The previous year's levies had totaled $3.6 million, and the city of 13,000 went about firing policemen, letting teachers go, and cutting services. On December 31, the city defaulted on $2.1 million of tax anticipation notes (TANs), a rare and at the time notable instance of a general obligation default. The city failed in attempts to renegotiate the loan, and on January 3, 1980, a Superior Court attached the city's bank account, leaving it without funds for bills and payroll. Maine and Boston banks lent the city money, and Governor Joseph Brennen authorized the city to deposit all property tax revenues into an escrow account to repay the TANs. In April 1980, the chastened voters approved a referendum to repeal the property tax limit. "It seems here that there must be several ways to correct mismanagement without placing a city's fiscal affairs in a straitjacket and eliminating vital services," editorialized John J. Winders of *The Daily Bond Buyer* in January 1980.

*See also* initiative and referendum.

*Sources:*

"Saco, Maine, Referendum Repeals Controversial Property Tax Cap." *Daily Bond Buyer*, May 1, 1980.

174

Winders, John J. "Lifting the Gloom Comes Good News from Saco, Maine, and Skagway, Alaska." *Daily Bond Buyer*, May 5, 1980.
Winders, John J. "Tax Lid Advocates Might Take a Close Look at the Plight of Saco, Maine." *Daily Bond Buyer*, January 21, 1980.

## scales

Scales are another term for a yield curve, which shows what a bond issuer with a particular rating would pay to borrow money from three or six months out to 30 or 40 years, with a number for each year. It is common for issuers and their financial advisers to determine how their bonds are priced and have been priced in the past compared to a triple-A scale. This allows them to see how their bonds are perceived in the market over time. The issuer compares apples to apples (i.e., itself to itself).

## sealed bids

Issuers take sealed bids when they borrow money through competitive sales of their municipal bonds.

*See also* competitive sale.

## secondary market

The market for older bonds, compared with the new-issue, or primary, market. The secondary bond market may be tracked through the MSRB's Electronic Municipal Market Access (EMMA) website, and dealer inventories may be viewed on various electronic trading platforms, including the Bloomberg PICK service.

The municipal bond market is overwhelmingly a new-issue market. Most of the trading activity that takes place is in bonds that are about to be sold, trading on a when-issued basis, or that have just been sold. The MSRB has calculated that 36.7 percent of the total par value traded is composed of bonds no more than one month old. Between $10 billion and $20 billion in bonds are traded every day.

*See also* "All bonds go to heaven"; market activity.

*Source:*

Municipal Securities Rulemaking Board 2010 Fact Book. Alexandria, VA: MSRB, 2011.

## serial bonds

Serial bonds are bonds that mature consecutively by year, such as 2012, 2013, 2014, and 2015, and are a unique feature of the municipal bond market.

*See also* term bonds.

## William F. G. Shanks

William F. G. Shanks was an ex-Civil War correspondent, newspaper reporter, and magazine writer, who as proprietor of a news-clipping service found that he was receiving more and more requests for stories about railroad and municipal bonds. Based on this demand, he established a newspaper in 1891 called *The Daily Bond Buyer*, which reprinted such stories along with some original matter, chiefly editorials, as well as statistical material and news of proposed bond issues and results of sale. Born in 1837 in Shelbyville, Kentucky, Shanks died in Bermuda in 1905 and passed the newspaper along to his sons.

*Source:*

Mysak, Joe. "*The Bond Buyer* after 100 Years: W. F. G. Shanks Would Be Proud." *Bond Buyer* Centennial Edition, August 1991.

## stadiums

The value of stadiums as engines of economic activity has been debated at length, but as long as politicians are infected with the municipal edifice complex, cities will continue to help finance and build sports stadiums. Their willingness to tackle such projects appeared to diminish with the Great Recession, as some taxpayers expressed impatience with the idea of subsidizing wealthy team owners. To conclude that this temporary reluctance would become permanent is premature, however, and most cities threatened with the loss of their hometown teams and major league (or even minor league or spring training) status may be expected to fight such flights with everything at their disposal.

## state intercept programs

State intercept programs are popular means of helping smaller issuers, usually school districts, attain higher ratings and achieve lower borrowing costs. Should an issuer run into financial difficulty, a state with an intercept program promises to redirect the financial assistance it sends to the issuer to the bond trustee instead for payment of debt service. Participation in such programs usually raises the issuer's rating. More than half of the states have some sort of intercept program, again, usually for their school districts.

## swaps

A prominent if indeterminate feature of the municipal securities market since the late 1980s, interest-rate swaps came under fire in the early years of the new century as regulators and some observers became concerned that the instruments were being used by too many unsophisticated issuers who lacked the knowledge and expertise necessary to evaluate their costs and assess their risks. Suspicions about swaps ranged from their use to facilitate pay-to-play schemes to their speculative nature (issuers essentially making side bets on the future direction of interest rates) to the relatively high price to terminate them if the need arose. Government investigations in Philadelphia and Jefferson County, Alabama, and the credit-market meltdown that accompanied the subprime crisis seemed to validate these fears, in at least some cases. And so a legitimate financing technique turned politically and financially poisonous.

The biggest warning sign of the swaps conundrum was the conspiracy of silence that accompanied the instruments' use. The relatively small number of bankers who were pitching the things to state and local issuers wanted uncritical media coverage of the transactions or (more often, and at a later stage) none at all. To the extent swaps were discussed, it was as an advanced, money-saving technique that for years had been used by corporations, and now wasn't it at last time to allow governmental issuers the same opportunity? There the transparency ended. When asked how much a swap cost a municipal issuer, or how much the bank engaging in the swap had made on the deal, the banks involved claimed that such information was proprietary; the municipal issuers involved were unwilling or in most cases, it seemed, even unable to say.

The exact size of the market remains to this day a mystery. It was in the interest of those selling swaps to say that everyone was doing them, from the largest authorities to the smallest school districts, and they did so, at the confabs and conferences that periodically bring government finance officers, bankers, and analysts together. Yet to put a size on the market—on the number of municipalities that actually had engaged in swaps—proved an impossibility. The only entities that could have provided some clarity on this score, namely the ratings companies, were not helpful. In fact, there were only three instances where the usage of swaps was estimated (four if you count the SEC's intriguing if misleading mention of "derivatives").

That occurred first. In its July 1, 2004, "Report on Transactions in Municipal Securities," the SEC said that there were 14,000 derivatives issued in the secondary market, with a principal amount of about $61 billion. The agency did not specify the nature of the "derivatives," but later said they "traded," which indicates the agency was not talking about swaps at all but about such creations as floaters and inverse floaters in tender-option bond programs.

More promising was the July 30, 2007, Standard & Poor's report that said it had completed "Debt Derivative Profiles" that had turned up 750 swaps users, only 255 of which were state or local governments. This useful report seems never to have been updated. In October 2009, in a comment on the fallout of the financial crisis, Moody's said it had counted 500 users of swaps. Neither report put a figure on the outstanding notional amount or on the number of swaps that these users had engaged in, since a school district might enter one or two and an authority might enter a dozen or more. Even presuming there was no overlap between the Moody's and Standard & Poor's numbers, which supposition seems almost impossibly remote, it appears that only a small percentage of the almost 90,000 governments in the United States had ever used swaps.

The only other estimate of swaps usage by municipalities came in an April 2009 proposal by the Municipal Securities Rulemaking Board (MSRB), entitled "Unregulated Municipal Market Participants: A Case for Reform," in which the agency made its case for the oversight of financial advisers and investment brokers. The proposal stated: "Also problematic is the lack of available public information regarding the size of the municipal securities derivative market. Market participants have suggested that the market is between $100 billion and $300 billion, annually, in notional principal amount, but until these derivative transactions are formally tracked, the figures will be unreliable."

Here's how one of the most popular kinds of swaps worked. An issuer sells bonds whose interest rate is set at regular weekly or monthly intervals, in the auction-rate or variable-rate market, thus availing itself of the lowest rates possible. Very often, the issuer would get this transaction insured, and so rated triple-A. The issuer is thus paying short-term rates for 30-year debt. Then the issuer enters into an interest-rate swap agreement with a bank, agreeing to pay the bank a fixed rate and to receive from the bank a floating rate. The fixed rate is even lower than the issuer could get in the traditional long-term market. The issuer hopes (or bets) the floating rates it pays investors will be matched by the floating rates it receives from the bank. If the floating rate it receives rises above what it pays, the issuer saves. If the floating rate it receives sinks, the issuer winds up paying more than it first calculated. The more fawning articles on municipal swaps always pointed out how the issuer had "locked in" low borrowing costs on that "synthetic fixed-rate" portion of the deal.

Except that the issuer had locked in nothing. The overall cost was always at the mercy of the always-shifting swap payments. What happened during the subprime crisis was that issuers found themselves paying more on their floating-rate debt as a result of either failed auctions, downgraded insurers, or the movements in the variable-rate municipal market. At the same time, they collected a lot less from their swap counterparties, as the Federal Reserve slashed interest rates and banks' own short-term rates plummeted. As the costs rose, more and more issuers decided to stop the bleeding and refinance to straight long-term fixed-rate debt. To do so, they usually had to make termination payments to their counterparties, Bloomberg News calculating in 2010 that such payments had totaled $4 billion since 2008. Certain bond buyers and analysts inevitably asked if there were comprehensive lists of all issuers who had used swaps, and were answered, as always in the municipal bond market, in the negative. As issuers' infatuation with swaps came to an end, a few officials—probably too few—published scathing reports on municipalities' participation in this part of the market.

In 2009, for example, Pennsylvania Auditor General Jack Wagner, then running for governor, analyzed what had happened in the state after Pennsylvania authorized local governments to engage in swaps in 2003. They did so with apparent gusto, according to Wagner. Of the 501 school districts in the state, 107 entered into at least one Qualified Interest Rate Management

Agreement, the state's term for the usage of swaps and other derivative products. Another 86 local governments did the same. Between October 2003 and June 2009, the 193 entities made 626 filings related to $14.9 billion in debt. Wagner's report concluded that swaps were "highly risky and impenetrably complex transaction that, quite simply, amount to gambling with public money." He asked the state to forbid their use, and advised those issuers who did use them to terminate them immediately. In its October 2009 report, Moody's reported that Pennsylvania accounted for 22 percent of its universe of 500 issuers the firm rated that used swaps, followed by California and Texas (17 percent each) and then Tennessee (13 percent).

*See also* bid rigging; Jefferson County, Alabama.

*Sources:*

Block, Peter, and Justin Formas. "U.S. Public Finance Swap Activity Is Primed for Growth in Second-Half '07." Standard & Poor's, July 30, 2007.

Braun, Martin Z., and William Selway. "Hidden Swap fees by JPMorgan, Morgan Stanley Hit School Districts." Bloomberg News, February 1, 2008.

"Potential Risks of Variable Rate Debt and Interest Rate Swaps for U.S. State and Local Governments Are Heightened by Economic and Financial Crisis." Special Comment, Moody's Investors Service, October 2009.

"Report on Transactions in Municipal Securities." Office of Economic Analysis and Office of Municipal Securities, Division of Regulation, Securities and Exchange Commission, July 1, 2004.

"Unregulated Municipal Market Participants: A Case for Reform." Municipal Securities Rulemaking Board, Alexandria, VA, April 2009.

Van Natta, Don, Jr. "Firm Acted as Tutor as It Sold Risky Deals to Towns." *New York Times*, April 8, 2009.

Wagner, Jack. "A Special Investigation of the Bethlehem Area School District, Lehigh/Northampton Counties: A Case Study of the Use of Qualified Interest Rate Management Agreements ('Swaps') by Local Government Units in Pennsylvania, with Recommendations." Report by Jack Wagner, Auditor General, November 2009.

## synthetic fixed rates

*See* swaps.

# T

## take and pay, take or pay

Under take-and-pay contracts, buyers pay only for what they receive. Under take or pay, buyers pay no matter what. The contracts feature in bond sales related to public power and other energy transactions, such as gas prepayment deals. A ruling that the take-or-pay contracts signed by participants in the Washington Public Power Supply System were invalid led to the 1983 default on $2.25 billion in bonds, still the largest in the market's history.

*See also* Washington Public Power Supply System.

## takedown

The takedown is the sales commission or the underwriter's profit from a bond issue. A controversial subject in the 1990s was "Who owns the takedown?" Underwriters felt it was theirs, and issuers thought they could direct it as they saw fit to certain favored firms in a syndicate.

## tax anticipation notes

Also known as tax revenue anticipation notes (TRANs), tax anticipation notes (TANs) are sold by municipalities to raise money before taxes are collected.

*See also* bond anticipation notes.

## tax caps

Tax caps are voter-approved limitations on a governmental entity's ability to increase taxes, such as California's Proposition 13 and Massachusetts's Proposition 2½. They are viewed in the main negatively by analysts, who say that such restrictions limit issuers' financial flexibility.

*See also* elections; initiative and referendum; Saco, Maine.

## tax-exemption

On April 20, 1988, the Supreme Court decided that tax-exemption was not a constitutionally protected right naturally enjoyed by states and municipalities but rather a gift from the U.S. Congress. "The owners of state bonds have no constitutional entitlement not to pay taxes on income they earn from the bonds, and States have no constitutional entitlement to issue bonds paying lower interest rates than other issuers," said the Court in deciding *South Carolina v. Baker*, a case revolving around whether Congress had the right to compel municipal bond issuers to sell their securities in registered, as compared to bearer, form.

The Court ruled that Congress did have that right, and then went a step further, saying there was no constitutional basis for tax-exemption at all.

The idea that the interest paid on municipal bonds was tax-exempt derived from the doctrine of intergovernmental immunity, where federal and state governments refrain from abridging each other's sovereignty. Defenders of tax-exemption usually pointed to *Pollock v. Farmers Loan & Trust Co.* (1895) as the case that established the precedent that governmental debt obligations were immune from federal tax. In 1988 the Supreme Court said: "Under the intergovernmental tax immunity jurisprudence prevailing at Pollock's time, neither the Federal nor the State Governments could tax income that an individual directly derived from any contract with the other government. This general rule was based on the rationale that any tax on income a party received under a contract with the government was a tax on the contract, and thus a tax 'on' the government, because it burdened the government's power to enter into the contract. That rationale has been repudiated by modern intergovernmental tax immunity case law, and the government contract immunities have been, one by one, overruled."

Until the federal income tax was established in 1913, tax-exemption as such was not an issue. It became one almost immediately, however, as various members of Congress and the Treasury made the case that the tax-exemption should be abolished, either because it gave municipalities an unfair advantage over companies in raising capital, or because tax-exempt securities were purely a tax shelter for the wealthy, or because governmental issuers were abusing their own privilege by offering tax-exempt financing to corporate borrowers in the form of industrial development bonds. Assaults on tax-exemption, from both sides of the political aisle, became an almost annual feature of the Washington calendar.

An early, ardent opponent of tax-exemption was financier Andrew W. Mellon, secretary of the Treasury under Presidents Harding, Coolidge, and Hoover. "For it was clear to Mellon that with the prevailing high rates on individual income [in 1921, 65 percent], most of the rich were avoiding federal income tax by investing in 'tax-exempt' securities: state and municipal bonds sold whose interest the federal government could not legally tax," wrote his biographer David Cannadine. "If federal taxes were significantly reduced, Mellon reasoned, it would then become rational for the rich to move their investments out of tax-exempt securities, which produced low yields, and into taxable industrial stocks, on which the return was generally higher." Mellon proposed abolishing the tax-exemption in 1922 and 1924.

Franklin Delano Roosevelt, too, was no friend of tax-exemption, and proposed its abolition on the basis that municipal bonds were little more than a tax dodge for the rich. In 1941, the U.S. Treasury billed some investors in Port of New York Authority bonds for taxes, contending that the Authority was not really a political subdivision and so was not authorized to sell tax-exempt debt. The suit was appealed all the way to the Supreme Court, which in 1945 refused to hear the case, letting stand a Tax Court ruling that said, yes, such authorities were political subdivisions and so eligible to sell tax-exempt debt.

While there were a few forays made against municipals in the 1950s and 1960s, the most significant attack came only in the rewrites of the tax code that occurred in the mid-1980s, when congressional tax writers took a more comprehensive approach to perceived abuses of the tax-exemption. The U.S. Treasury, members of Congress, and Capitol Hill entities such as the Congressional Budget Office regularly propose killing the tax-exemption, sometimes as an element of overall tax reform, and sometimes just as part of recommendations on how the government can save money.

In "Reducing the Deficit: Spending and Revenue Options," for example, published in early 2011, the Congressional Budget Office (CBO) suggested as Revenue Option 13, "Replace the Tax Exclusion for Interest Income on State and Local Bonds with a Direct Subsidy for the Issuer." The

CBO suggested that Congress replace tax-exemption with a 15 percent subsidy paid to issuers. "The tax exclusion on interest income is less cost-effective because some of the federal revenue forgone through the tax exclusion goes to bondholders in higher tax brackets," the CBO said. Such a policy change would result in net savings to the government of $31 billion from 2012 through 2016 and $143 billion from 2012 through 2021, the CBO calculated. One disadvantage of the proposal would be higher borrowing costs, the CBO admitted, adding that the subsidy could be increased; 15 percent was just a starting point.

Opponents of ending tax-exemption argue that the current system works fine, and is as efficient as it needs to be. State and local officials have been an effective lobby when tax reform turns to the tax-exemption.

*See also* Mrs. Dodge.

*Sources:*

Cannadine, David. *Mellon: An American Life.* New York: Alfred A. Knopf, 2006.

Pryde, Joan. "The Ongoing Battle: Almost 70 Years of Assaults on Tax-Exempt Municipals." *Bond Buyer* Centennial Edition, August 1991.

*South Carolina v. Baker.* Opinion, U.S. Supreme Court, 485 U.S. 505, 1988.

## tax increment financing

Primarily used to encourage real estate development or improvement, these bonds are repaid from the growth in taxes generated by such additions.

## taxable municipals

Once a small portion of the market, the sale of municipal securities subject to the federal income tax has grown as the government prohibited the use of tax-exempt bonds for certain undertakings and encouraged the use of taxable bonds for others (e.g., the Build America Bonds program, which was authorized by the American Recovery and Reinvestment Act of 2009 and expired at the end of 2010).

Taxable issuance began in 1985 after tax writers began cracking down on what were perceived as abuses of the tax-exemption; issuance was at $326 million that year, and did not break $10 billion a year until 1995. It broke the $40 billion mark in 2003, and posted a high of $84.6 billion in 2009.

Congress has authorized various kinds of taxable municipals in recent years. These include Qualified School Construction Bonds, Qualified Zone Academy Bonds, Clean Renewable Energy Bonds, New Clean Renewable Energy Bonds, Recovery Zone Economic Development Bonds, Qualified Energy Conservation Bonds, Midwest Tax-Credit Bonds, and Qualified Forestry Conservation Bonds. Sold on a taxable basis, these securities feature interest-rate subsidies paid to issuers or tax-liability credits paid to investors. The only program that was an unqualified success was the Build America Bonds program. Issuers sold $187 billion of the bonds, which offered them a 35 percent subsidy on interest-rate payments, in the two years of the program.

*See also* Build America Bonds.

*Sources:*

*The Bond Buyer/Thomson Reuters 2010 Yearbook.* New York: Sourcemedia, 2010.

"IRS Announces New Rules Relating to Certain Qualified Tax Credit Bonds and Build America Bonds." Legal update by McGuire Woods LLP, May 20, 2010.

"Subsidizing Infrastructure Investment with Tax-Preferred Bonds." Joint study by the Congressional Budget Office and the Joint Committee on Taxation, October 2009.

## taxable tails

A taxable tail is a simultaneously offered taxable bond to finance the portion of a project's costs that may not be financed with tax-exempt bonds, such as issuance expenses for tax-exempt private activity bonds that exceed 2 percent of proceeds.

*Source:*

Weber, Fredric A., of Fulbright & Jaworski LLP, Houston, Texas.

## tender-option bond programs

Tender-option bond (TOB) programs were put together by investment banks and, later on, institutional investors such as hedge funds, which would borrow money to buy blocks of municipal bonds. Using a floater/inverse floater structure, these sponsors would put the bonds into a trust, and then sell floating-rate (lower-yielding) instruments to other investors.

The sponsors of the programs thus took advantage of the difference between short- and long-term yields. At the height of the mania for TOB programs in late 2006, observers estimated that as much as $180 billion in bonds had been put into such trusts.

"A typical tender-option bond program might consist of $20 million of municipal bonds yielding 4.25% deposited with a trust, producing $850,000 of interest per year," Michael Quint of Bloomberg News explained in December 2006. "The trust then sells $18 million of variable-rate notes yielding 3.5%, with interest payments of $630,000."

Quint continued: "After subtracting annual fees of about $50,000, the remaining interest of $170,000 goes to the $2 million security held by the hedge fund for a yield of 8.5%. The yield on this so-called residual rises if yields on the variable-rate notes fall, and falls if rates on the notes rise."

The tender-option floating-rate notes, whose rates were usually reset at periodic Dutch auctions, were usually backed by a bank letter of credit, and were puttable at par. They were a favored investment of tax-exempt money-market funds, which after the various tax reforms of the 1980s faced a dearth of high-quality tax-exempt notes.

The existence of the TOB programs enhanced liquidity in the market, as banks and hedge funds vied for $10 million and $20 million blocks of bonds.

The heyday of the TOB programs was from the late 1990s to 2006 and 2007, but variations on the theme date to the early 1980s.

*See also* floaters/inverse floaters.

*Sources:*

Hampton, Ted. "Standard & Poor's Will Start Rating 'Tender Options'; First One Soon." *Bond Buyer*, February 19, 1992.

Lauricella, Tom, and Liz Rappaport. "Fearful Investors Shy Away from 'Tender Option Bonds.'" *Wall Street Journal*, January 31, 2008.

Mysak, Joe. "Blame Hedge Funds for Decline in Muni Mutual Funds." Bloomberg News, August 24, 2007.

Quint, Michael. "Hedge Funds Help 'Stodgy' Municipals Beat Treasuries." Bloomberg News, December 18, 2006.

## term bonds

Term bonds are those coming due in a bullet maturity of 20 or 30 years or more. It is common practice for municipal bond issuers to structure their offerings with both serial bonds, which mature in consecutive years, and term bonds.

## Texas Permanent School Fund

Founded in 1854 to assist the state's schools, the Texas Permanent School Fund (PSF) has insured general obligation school bonds since 1983, guaranteeing by 2010 $50 billion of outstanding bonds sold by 781 Texas school districts. Rated triple-A, the fund has never had one of its bonds default. The fund has about $25.5 billion in assets, chiefly invested in stocks, but also including real estate and mineral rights. The PSF is one of the most famous and successful state-run credit enhancers; about half the states have such programs. From March 2009 to February 2010, the fund stopped insuring new bonds "due to declines in asset valuation as well as increased guarantees outstanding," according to Moody's Investors Service. The fund also contributes money to support public education in the state, in 2008 contributing $716 million to the schools, for example.

*See also* bond banks; insurance; state intercept programs.

*Sources:*

Preston, Darrell. "Texas School Bond Guarantee Fund Can't Back New Debt." Bloomberg News, March 5, 2009.

Preston, Darrell. "Texas $23 Billion School Fund Part-Time Bosses Face Revamp Call." Bloomberg News, October 29, 2010.

Rosenblatt, Robyn. "Texas Permanent School Fund." High Profile Ratings Update, Moody's Investors Service, April 2010.

## tobacco bonds

Backed in whole or in part by the tobacco industry's 1998 Master Settlement Agreement with 46 of the 50 states (Florida, Minnesota, Mississippi, and Texas reached separate agreements with the tobacco companies), tobacco bonds have been a high-yield fixture of the tax-exempt market since 1999. Fewer than half the states (and various political subdivisions) have sold about $40 billion in tobacco bonds. California and New York received the largest percentages of the settlement, nearly 13 percent apiece.

The settlement, paid to cover health-care costs incurred by the states, runs in perpetuity, or as long as a U.S. tobacco industry remains. The agreement was often referred to at the time as the "$206 billion settlement," an estimate of how much it was supposed to produce for the states in its first 20 years. "The target annual payments ranged from about $7 billion per year in 2000 to $9 billion annually in 2008 and thereafter in perpetuity," wrote Alan Schankel of Janney Montgomery Scott LLC in a 2010 research note. The annual payments are adjusted based on inflation and cigarette shipments, among other things, which led to actual payments "ranging between $5.8 billion and $7.6 billion since 2000."

In addition, the participating manufacturers can challenge how much they pay. Under the settlement agreement, participating manufacturers can ask for adjustments to compensate them for market-share losses to smaller, nonparticipating manufacturers. In 2011, Philip Morris USA, for example, made its annual Master Settlement Agreement payment of $3.5 billion, including $267 million paid into the Disputed Payments Account pending resolution of the 2008 Non-Participating Manufacturers Adjustment dispute.

Those states that wanted to take advantage of the tobacco settlement windfall created stand-alone trusts to which they transferred the revenue stream they received from the tobacco companies (thus insulating it from political interference) and sold asset-backed securities (the asset being this revenue). Most of the trusts have "tobacco settlement" or "tobacco securitization" in the name.

There was spirited debate at the beginning over whether governments should undertake such borrowing at all, or simply wait for the money to come in. This criticism was deflected by public officials who said that the tobacco revenue was a form of declining asset—cigarette consumption in the United States had been falling since its peak of 640 billion cigarettes in 1981. State officials were quite frank about transferring the risk to bondholders in exchange for cash up front. If cigarette smoking disappeared entirely, and with it, the annual installment of settlement money, bondholders just would not be paid, they said.

New York City sold the first tobacco bonds in 1999, using the proceeds to pay for capital projects. This was another matter of contention, of course, some people saying that the states should use the tobacco settlement money only on health care and on smoking-cessation programs, others saying that the money was really only reimbursement to states for what they had already spent and could be used for any purpose they deemed appropriate. The Government Accountability Office in 2005 found that states used about one-third of the money they received from the tobacco companies for health care, and almost one-quarter to pay for debt service.

The first iteration of tobacco bonds featured the usual serial and term maturities, capital appreciation bonds, and some very long-dated term bonds of 40 or 50 years, so-called turbo or super-sinker maturities, which were to be paid off with settlement money not used to make principal and interest payments. The real worry about tobacco bonds, it seemed, was not that everyone would stop smoking and the settlement money would disappear, but that the bonds would be paid off too soon.

This all changed, if briefly, after Standard & Poor's said the Altria Group, formerly known as Philip Morris, might have to declare bankruptcy if it had to post a $12 billion bond to appeal a class-action lawsuit in 2003. Issuers that wanted to sell tobacco bonds at the time had to promise they would make up shortfalls in debt-service payments. New York and California both sold such double-barreled deals. At the same time, attorneys general from 37 states filed a friend-of-the-court brief arguing that the bond should be reduced. It was, and Altria survived.

So did tobacco bonds. In May 2005, Virginia was able to sell a bond issue backed purely by settlement revenues again, and a number of other issuers followed suit. In 2010, Illinois's Railsplitter Tobacco Settlement Authority sold $1.5 billion in bonds that, because of their more traditional, conservative structuring, actually earned an A rating from Standard & Poor's.

Many risks were outlined in the "risk factors" sections of tobacco bond offerings—litigation, bankruptcy, the disputes over nonparticipating manufacturers—but none figures so large as the decline in cigarette consumption. That decline was exacerbated in 2009 by a 61-cent per pack increase in the federal tax on cigarettes, a rash of state and local tax increases, and continuing efforts to discourage smoking. In 2008, cigarette shipments declined 3.9 percent, according to the National Association of Attorneys General; in 2009, shipments dropped 10.3 percent. For intrepid investors, there were lots of interesting opportunities in tobacco bonds, especially among those issues with the longest final maturities.

*Sources:*

Hallacy, John. "The Promise of New Revenues." Municipal Bond Credit Monthly, Merrill Lynch & Co., February 23, 1999.

Hallacy, John. "Tobacco Settlement." Municipal Credit Research, Merrill Lynch & Co., June 29, 1999.

Larkin, Richard. "Tobacco Bonds Suffering from Consumption." JB Hanauer & Co., October 15, 2004.

Larkin, Richard P. "Exploding Cigarettes? Tobacco Payments Drop Sharply from Lower Shipments and NPM Disputes." Herbert J. Sims & Co., August 4, 2010.

"Philip Morris USA Makes Master Settlement Agreement Payment of Approximately $3.5 Billion." Press release, April 15, 2011.

"S&P Lowers 51 Tobacco Settlement-Backed Bond Ratings, 71 Ratings Affirmed." Standard & Poor's, November 11, 2010.

Schankel, Alan. "Tobacco Bonds." Janney Montgomery Scott LLC, December 6, 2010.

## toll roads

Highways that charge drivers to use them often tap the municipal bond market to pay for construction and maintenance. The risk that accompanies the bonds sold to finance new toll roads is that not enough drivers will use the roads and that toll revenue will be insufficient to repay the bonds. Investors would be well-advised to buy bonds being sold to build new roads only from geographic areas with which they are intimately familiar, defined as being knowledgeable about local traffic patterns, economic activity, and the use of reasonable alternative routes. Even then, it is notoriously difficult to forecast traffic and toll revenue for start-up roads with accuracy. The usual culprit is dependence upon economic activity that may or may not materialize.

The most recent cautionary tale concerning toll roads is the Southern Connector, a so-called public–private partnership that formed in 1996 as "Connector 2000" and sold more than $300 million in bonds to build a 16-mile toll road in Greenville County, South Carolina. Original projections were for the highway to get about 21,000 tolls a day. Actual yield was about 7,500, and the Southern Connector declared Chapter 9 bankruptcy in June 2010. The road restructured its debt, and bondholders owed $237.8 million received $126.9 million in new bonds with a priority of repayment, and $21.1 million in new bonds with a secondary priority of repayment. Owners of $90.9 million in subordinate bonds shared $2.2 million in new bonds junior to the two other series. The road emerged from bankruptcy in 2011.

*See also* public–private partnerships.

*Sources:*

Bathon, Michael. "Connector 2000 Wins Approval of Municipal Debt Restructuring." Bloomberg Municipal Market Brief, April 5, 2011.

In re: Connector 2000 Association Inc., Debtor, First Amended Plan for Adjustment of Debts, U.S. Bankruptcy Court in South Carolina, March 16, 2011.

## total return

Total return is an investment's current cash flow combined with gains or losses. Some individual investors, who have no intention of selling their bonds, contend that their coupon is their total return, because they disregard price movements in the secondary market.

## tourist attractions

No, no, no, no, no, no, and no. Aquariums, theme parks, glorified rest stops, and zoos have a checkered history in the municipal market, and have left a trail of defaults and heartbroken investors. The chief reason seems to be that such projects were uneconomical from the start, with municipalities and various conduit agencies entering territory where the private sector feared to tread, divining a market where none existed, beguiled by the illusion of opportunity. Numerous municipalities in the 1990s sold bonds for such speculative projects, their repayment almost entirely dependent upon the revenue from rising attendance.

Tourist attractions do not have taxing power. Unlike museums and cultural institutions, tourist attractions do not have endowment earnings to rely on, should attendance fail to materialize, as is so often the case. Nor, with municipal ownership, do they have access to the deep pockets and amounts of cash needed to spruce up the attraction with the regularity apparently demanded by visitors. The feasibility studies appended to the bond issues sold for these undertakings invariably show inflated and in retrospect implausible attendance expectations. As these things go, attendance may come close to projection in the first year. After the novelty wears off, attendance tends to dip, and dip, and has a hard fight to get anywhere near what the feasibility study says and the debt-service payment schedule demands. What distinguished so many tourist attraction bonds in the 1990s and 2000s was the relatively short fuse so many of them had. Baked into the cake was almost immediate success and profitability. The alternative was debt renegotiation, default, or bankruptcy.

Consider, for example, Edinburg, Texas, which in March 1998 sold $21.3 million in unrated revenue bonds through the city's Industrial Development Corporation to build the SuperSplash Adventure Water Park. The bonds carried a top tax-exempt yield of 8 percent, and were sold in minimum denominations of $100,000. On the sources and uses page, bond buyers could see that the city was making an equity contribution of $1.6 million; the state of Texas and the U.S. Economic Development Administration chipped in a combined $1.5 million in grant money. NOT SUITABLE FOR INVESTMENT BY UNSOPHISTICATED INVESTORS was marked on the cover of the limited offering memorandum.

Edinburg is located just north of the city of McAllen, about 14 miles from the Mexican border in the Rio Grande Valley. The city counted on visitors from south of the border: "Mexicans have a higher propensity to seek out recreation and entertainment and are more inclined to do so within the family unit," as it said in the feasibility study. They didn't show. Attendance was projected at 196,400 in 1998, 395,900 in 1999, and 449,200 by 2002. Actual attendance was about half that, and the park closed in September 2000. Investors eventually got around 15 cents on the dollar.

Then there is VisionLand, the grandly conceived theme park in Jefferson County, Alabama. "The overall theme of VisionLand will focus on the rich mining and iron and steel-producing history of the Birmingham area and will include iron and steel structures, rides in mining cars, and attractions styled after blast furnaces and other facilities familiar to residents of the Birmingham area," it said in the official statement to the West Jefferson Amusement and Public Park Authority's first mortgage revenue bonds, which initially carried yields of 7.75 percent and 8.25 percent when they were sold in 1997. The park was the brainchild of Mayor Larry Langford of Bessemer, who would later be jailed for corruption in financing the county's sewer system cleanup.

There was actually something to recommend these bonds. The 11 participating communities of the authority committed almost $3 million annually to the project for a period of five years, extended annually unless a municipality notified the authority it would not renew beyond its current five-year term. What's more, the commitment did not represent an annual appropriation, but a general obligation, full faith and credit debt.

The base case for VisionLand assumed attendance would be 720,000 in its first year, 1998, rising steadily to one million by 2006. In fact, 426,000 visited in 1998, 364,000 in 1999 (when the authority refunded the original bonds and borrowed more, in a deal totaling $90 million). In 2001, when attendance was expected to be 861,036, only 343,000 actually showed up. In June 2002, the park filed for bankruptcy, and was sold in 2003 for a little over $5 million. "A lesson that can be drawn from the expensive undertaking is that government really is ill-suited to run a business in such a competitive industry," the *Birmingham News* editorialized.

Finally, there is the Great Platte River Road Memorial Archway, financed by an unrated $60 million revenue bond issue in 1998 that carried yields of 7 percent. The Archway straddles Interstate 80 in Kearney, Nebraska, and resembles an enormous covered bridge, a "longitudinal, interactive, state of the art exhibit." Eight stories high, the Archway was designed to be a celebration of western history in general, and the Great Platte River Road trekked by pioneers in particular, arrayed on two levels. It was sort of a cross between a theme park and a rest stop. The feasibility study said that 906,000 people would visit the Archway during the first 12 months it was open, and rise steadily after that. A memorable sentence in the official statement to the bonds declared, "Given its prominence and potential to illustrate local history, it is thought that virtually every Nebraska resident will eventually visit the Archway in his or her lifetime." (Nebraska's population hovers around 1.7 million.) In fact, only 300,000 people visited the Archway in its first full year of operation. Attendance fell quickly after that. The bonds defaulted in 2002, and in 2003 the issuer exchanged new ones totaling $22 million for the original issue, in what is inelegantly known as a cram-down.

SuperSplash, VisionLand, and the Archway are hardly isolated examples. The high-yield municipal bond market flourished throughout the 1990s, each week bringing new examples of absurdity. It has never recovered.

*See also* Heartland fund implosion; Jefferson County, Alabama.

*Sources:*

$59,780,068.50 City of Kearney, Nebraska Industrial Development Revenue Bonds (The Great Platte River Road Memorial Foundation Project), Series 1998.

Mysak, Joe. "Archway Bonds Keep Spinning Never-Ending Tale of Woe." Bloomberg News, May 4, 2007.

"Phantom of the Open Hearth." *Grant's Municipal Bond Observer*, March 7, 1997.

Preston, Darrell. "Investors in Dry Texas Water Theme Park Get 15 Cents on the Dollar." Bloomberg News, November 8, 2001.

Preston, Darrell. "It May Not Be a Fun Summer in Bessemer: Rates of Return." Bloomberg News, May 15, 2002.

$21,315,000 Industrial Development Corporation of the City of Edinburg, Texas, Revenue Bonds, Series 1998A (Water Park Project).

"VisionLand Sale a Great Deal—For the Buyer." *Birmingham News*, October 25, 2002.

## Tower Amendment

Added to the Securities Exchange Act of 1934 in 1975, when Congress created the Municipal Securities Rulemaking Board (MSRB), the Tower Amendment has two parts, one that prohibits the MSRB and the Securities and Exchange Commission (SEC) from writing rules that directly or indirectly impose presale filing requirements for issues of municipal securities, and the second that prohibits the Board, but not the SEC, from adopting rules that directly or indirectly require issuers to produce documents or information for delivery to purchasers or to the Board. The Tower Amendment also specifically allows the MSRB to adopt requirements relating to disclosure documents or information as might be available from "a source other than the issuer."

In 1989, the SEC adopted Exchange Act Rule 15c2-12, which requires that issuers prepare official statements and produce them within seven days of a bond sale. The MSRB then adopted Rule G-36, which requires underwriters to submit official statements to the Board, and to create a central repository for official statements and advance refunding documents.

The Tower Amendment has been widely taken to mean that the SEC does not regulate municipal issuers. This isn't quite true, because the SEC's mandate is to protect investors, and it will prosecute fraud. Both San Diego and the state of New Jersey, for example, have been sued for fraud by the SEC, for misrepresenting the financial condition of their pension systems in their bond offering documents.

In practice what this has meant is a lag in the time municipalities file their financial statements. The SEC requires corporations to file their annual audited financials within 60 to 90 days after the close of the business year. States and localities sometimes take six months or more, although the Governmental Accounting Standards Board, the Government Finance Officers Association, and the Municipal Securities Rulemaking Board have all recommended more timely filing.

The average time it takes for an audit letter to be signed after the close of the business year between 2007 and 2009 was 146.6 days, Richard Ciccarone, president and CEO of Merritt Research Services LLC, found in a study published in 2010. An additional 30 days or more may be required for the issuing entity to release the document to the public. Ciccarone found that the speediest to release their financials were large, single-purpose wholesale electric agencies (such as the Bonneville Power Administration or the Northern Municipal Power Agency in Minnesota), which took a median time of just over three months to release their financials. State governments were the slowest, taking just under six months on average.

*See also* CAFR; "Deadly Sins"; disclosure; EMMA; escrowed to maturity; MSRB.

*Sources:*

Ciccarone, Richard. "Just How Slowly Do Municipal Bond Annual Audit Reports Waddle In after the Close of the Fiscal Year?" Merritt Research Services LLC, Hiawatha, IA, 2010.

"Report of the Municipal Securities Rulemaking Board on the Regulation of the Municipal Securities Market." Materials submitted before a Hearing on Regulation of the Municipal Securities Market, Subcommittee on Telecommunications and Finance, September 9, 1993.

## trick coupons

*See* competitive sale; 50 percent coupon; negotiated sale.

## true interest cost

True interest cost (TIC) is an underwriter's bid that represents both the total cash amount of the interest payments and the timing of the interest and principal payments; the true interest cost method of calculating interest cost takes into account the time value of money.

*See also* net interest cost.

## trustee

The trustee is a financial institution, usually a bank, which acts as a fiduciary on behalf of the bondholders.

# U

## ultra vires

This Latin term meaning "beyond the power of men" is used to describe bonds that have been invalidly issued. Municipalities often used such claims to repudiate debt in the nineteenth century, particularly in the Reconstruction South and in the railroad-mad West, which led to the growth of the bond counsel business. In modern times, the Washington Public Power Supply System default in 1983 was caused by a judge ruling that a majority of the participants in the system had entered into contracts without the specific authority to do so, thus invalidating the bond payments and causing the largest default, $2.25 billion, in the history of the municipal market.

*See also* bond counsel; Chapter 9; default; Washington Public Power Supply System.

*Source:*
John L. Kraft, Esq.

## underwriters

Underwriters are the securities firms and banks that specialize in buying and selling municipal bonds, divided between big, national concerns and regional firms that may do business in only a single state or region. The major Wall Street houses take different approaches to the business, some firms running old-style 300-person departments with offices throughout the country, participating in financings of all sizes, others concentrating on hiring a few rainmaker bankers and pursuing only the largest negotiated bond issues or programs. Some firms distribute to a vast base of retail investors, others cater to high-net-worth individuals with a minimum of $10 million (or more) to invest, and still others deal only with institutional customers like insurance companies and mutual funds.

Underwriters work for a spread, usually expressed either as a percentage or in number of dollars per $1,000 bond—a number that has shrunk from $20 or more in the 1970s to around $5 or less today.

Perhaps the biggest shock in the modern history of the industry occurred in 1987, when Salomon Brothers, the No. 1 municipal bond underwriting firm, decided to quit the business because it was not profitable enough compared with other lines. A number of banks followed suit, and to the present day it is not unheard-of for firms to quit underwriting municipal bonds, citing the relative lack of profitability. Even so, and even with the involuntary Recession-era departures of major firms—like Lehman Brothers, which declared bankruptcy in 2008; Bear, Stearns & Company, merged into JPMorgan Chase in 2008; and Merrill Lynch, acquired by Bank of America in 2008—the industry remains competitive. Underwriter compensation has not increased significantly.

In November 2008, Christopher Taylor, who had been executive director of the Municipal Securities Rulemaking Board for three decades, described what he called "The Muni Market Mess." The industry, he said, had been restructured by the Tax Reform Act of 1986, which all but eliminated banks and sharply curtailed property/casualty insurance companies as buyers of bonds, leaving individuals as the primary customers for municipal securities. This, he said, destroyed the business model the dealers were then using, which relied on trading with banks and insurers. Individuals tend to buy and hold their investments to maturity.

The new reality for underwriters was a fee-based world based on gaining negotiated business, where deal flow was all, and where the service they were offering—buying and reselling bonds—was hard to differentiate. The squeeze on profit margins led bankers to look elsewhere for new lines of business in addition to underwriting. This fueled the boom in helping issuers invest bond proceeds and the aggressive sales of interest-rate swaps and other derivative products, as well as variable-rate and auction-rate structures, all of which, while designed to lower issuers' borrowing costs, also offered the potential for more profits than the simple underwriting of new long-term, fixed-rate bond issues.

It remains to be seen how the industry will respond to the post-subprime-crisis world where states and localities are no longer interested in auction-rate and variable-rate transactions or interest-rate swaps. Heightened regulatory scrutiny, coupled with the ongoing bid-rigging investigation and the production of a number of major regulatory reports on the market, further clouds the picture. The one constant is that underwriting is a small business and growing smaller. In 2006, the top-10 underwriters handled 66 percent of the dollar volume of all deals sold. By 2010—after the financial crisis forced three of the top 10 into the arms of suitors while a fourth exited the business entirely—this proportion had grown to 71.7 percent.

*See also* auction-rate securities; bid rigging; yield burning.

*Sources:*

*The Bond Buyer 1990 Yearbook.* New York: Bond Buyer, 1990.
*The Bond Buyer 2005 Yearbook.* New York: Bond Buyer, 2005.
"Municipal Review: Underwriters & Financial Advisers, Yearend 2010." Thomson Reuters, 2010.
Taylor, Christopher A. "Milestones in Municipal Securities Regulation 1975–2005." Municipal Securities Rulemaking Board, Alexandria, VA, 2006.
Taylor, Christopher A. "The Muni Market Mess."

## unfunded pension liabilities

This is an actuarial estimate of the difference in how much a pension system may need to satisfy all of its obligations compared with what it has on hand plus what those assets may earn in the future. In flush times, these liabilities evaporate; in hard times, they balloon. Though long known as a potential source of worry by credit analysts, the issue of unfunded pension liabilities became a cause célèbre only after the Pew Center on the States published a report in February 2010 putting the unfunded number at $1 trillion.

*See also* pensions.

*Source:*

"The Trillion-Dollar Gap: Underfunded State Retirement Systems and the Roads to Reform." Pew Center on the States, February 2010.

# V

## value per capita

Also known as full value per capita and equalized value per capita, value per capita is the value of all taxable real property in a municipality divided by population, and a key measure of socioeconomic levels within a municipality, according to Moody's Investors Service. The national median full value per capita of all publicly rated cities in the United States is $100,304.

Connoisseurs of this gauge of municipal wealth (and creditworthiness) should look to places where the well-to-do enjoy second or third homes—Aspen, Colorado, for example, has a full value per capita of $2.6 million. Edgartown, Massachusetts, on the island of Martha's Vineyard, has an equalized value per capita of $1.93 million, while Nantucket's is $1.95 million. Quogue, on New York's Long Island, has a full value per capita of $3.2 million.

*Sources:*

New Issue—Aspen, Colorado, Moody's Investors Service, November 30, 2009.

New Issue—Edgartown, Massachusetts, Moody's Investors Service, November 23, 2010.

New Issue—Nantucket, Massachusetts, Moody's Investors Service, February 15, 2011.

Rating Update: Quogue Union Free School District, New York, March 12, 2009.

2009 U.S. Local Government Medians: Updated for Global Scale Ratings, Moody's Investors Service, July 28, 2010.
2010 State Debt Medians Report, Moody's Investors Service, May 2010.

## variable-rate demand obligations

Using this structure, issuers sell long-term bonds whose rates are reset periodically, daily, weekly, or monthly. The rates are usually based on some formula, such as a percentage of a Securities Industry and Financial Markets Association (SIFMA) index or a London Interbank Offered Rate (LIBOR). Unlike auction-rate securities, variable-rate demand obligations (VRDOs) carry a bank liquidity facility, such as a letter of credit or a standby purchase agreement, and are puttable back to the issuer, although remarketing agents often take the bonds that have been put back into inventory for resale. VRDOs that are put back to the issuer are presented to the bank providing the liquidity, and become so-called bank bonds, their repayment accelerated so that a bond with a maturity of 20 or 30 years becomes due in four or five years, with the municipality making quarterly payments.

In 2008, states and localities sold a record $128 billion in VRDOs as they refinanced both auction-rate and insured floating-rate debt, after dealers stopped supporting the auctions in the first case and insurers lost their triple-A ratings in the second case. Both events drove the rates paid by issuers of the debt higher.

Issuance fell in 2009 to $43 billion and in 2010 to $30 billion, the lowest in a decade, according to Moody's. At the same time, it became more expensive to sell these securities. "Before the crisis, liquidity support was available for 10–25 basis points," Moody's wrote in March 2011. "Its cost in the current market ranges from the 50 basis point range for high-quality essential service credits up to the 150 basis point range for weaker credits, down from 2009 highs but well above pre-crisis levels."

The letters of credit and standby purchase agreements usually run for a period of from three to five years, and must be extended upon expiration. There was some concern in 2010 and 2011 that certain issuers would not be able to renew expiring bank support and would be forced to convert their variable-rate debt to long-term, fixed-rate debt, and to make termination payments if they had coupled their VRDO issuance with an interest-rate swap, as so many did in order to lock in synthetic fixed rates. This financing structure was popular with issuers because it resulted in fixed rates that were lower than those available had they just sold regular fixed-rate securities to begin with.

Even if they could find bank liquidity, many issuers in 2010 and 2011 decided to refinance their variable-rate debt to rid themselves of the interest-rate swaps that were no longer performing because the plunge in the short-term rates that counterparties were paying them no longer matched the variable rates they were paying. "A lot of issuers are willing to refinance their debt even if it means a loss, because of the termination payment, just to get out from under the deal," Howard Cure, director of municipal research for Evercore Wealth Management LLC in New York, told Bloomberg News in 2011. Issuers "just don't want whatever risks and lack of flexibility comes with having a swap."

See also auction-rate securities; Jefferson County, Alabama; swaps.

*Sources:*

McDonald, Michael. "Wall Street Takes $4 Billion from Taxpayers as Swaps Backfire." Bloomberg News, November 10, 2010.

McGrail, Brendan A., and Matt Robinson. "Howard University Issues to Help End Goldman Swap: Muni Credit." Bloomberg News, April 4, 2011.

"U.S. Municipal Variable Rate Market: Review of 2010 Market Trends and Expected Developments in 2011." Moody's Investors Service, March 1, 2011.

## Washington Public Power Supply System

Formed by a group of public utilities in the state of Washington in 1957, the Washington Public Power Supply System (WPPSS) was responsible for the largest default in municipal market history: $2.25 billion in revenue bonds sold to build two nuclear power plants. The default occurred in August 1983, after trustee Chemical Bank demanded immediate, accelerated repayment of all so-called projects 4 and 5 bonds. This occurred after the Washington State Supreme Court ruled on June 15 that the state's public and municipal utilities had no legal authority to repay their 70 percent share of the debt. In July, WPPSS admitted it could no longer pay debt service, triggering Chemical's request. WPPSS missed its first actual coupon payment on January 1, 1984. The default sparked a series of lawsuits and an investigation by the Securities and Exchange Commission (SEC). The project had been beset by cost overruns, but the ruling that the bonds had been issued ultra vires was a shock.

The agency had its origins in the postwar electric power shortages in the Pacific Northwest, when it became apparent that the federal Bonneville Power Administration's hydroelectric program would be insufficient to meet demand.

"Public utilities had to find a way to raise millions of dollars to build their own sources of power," Howard Gleckman wrote in the *Bond Buyer*'s weekly Credit Markets in 1984. "They came up with the concept of a joint operating agency, a consortium of utilities that would finance and build power projects" using low-cost, tax-exempt financing.

Bonneville, prohibited from building new plants or buying power on its own by the federal government, encouraged the utilities with so-called net billing agreements, under which it in essence assumed the utilities' share of new construction in return for billing credits. In October 1968, Bonneville announced a 20-year regional power plan that featured the construction of two coal-fired and no fewer than 20 nuclear-powered plants. The first (10-year) phase included the two coal plants and five of the nuclear projects.

In 1972, the Internal Revenue Service killed the net billing arrangement, barring the use of tax-exempt finance for projects where the federal government purchased more than 25 percent of the power produced by a facility. WPPSS projects 1, 2, and 3, all underway (also over budget and behind schedule), were exempted. In 1974, WPPSS agreed with 88 public utilities to build projects 4 and 5. The participants signed take-or-pay contracts, under which they would be obligated to pay for the plants even if they never generated any power (the other kind of power contract, take and pay, only obligates participants to pay for what they use).

Cost overruns, bad management, a rise in conservation, a decline in demand for power, and rising interest rates (WPPSS eventually paid almost 15 percent to borrow money, as the Federal Reserve was raising interest rates) all helped doom the project. By May 1981, WPPSS said the five nuclear plants would cost $24 billion, six times the original estimate. In January 1982, projects 4 and 5 were canceled. Only project 2 would ever go into commercial operation.

The real key to the WPPSS default was the failure of the contracts tying the various utilities to the projects 4 and 5 bonds. "Although WPPSS was the first joint operating agency of its kind in the nation, its take-or-pay contracts were not unique in the Northwest; they had been used on other power projects," wrote Howard Gleckman in the *Bond Buyer*. "But unlike some other states, the concept was never tested in the courts of Washington, Oregon, Idaho or Montana."

Such test cases in state supreme courts or validations by state attorneys general are common today—a WPPSS legacy.

The federal bond fraud trial over the $2.25 billion default pitted 25,000 bondholders and trustee Chemical Bank against 100 various agencies, lawyers, underwriters, and consultants; it began on September 7, 1988. All the defendants reached settlements with the plaintiffs, totaling $700 million.

WPPSS is now known as Energy Northwest.

*Sources:*

Associated Press. "Last Defendant Settles in Bond Default Case." *New York Times*, December 23, 1988.

Gleckman, Howard. "WPPSS: From Dream to Default." Credit Markets, *Bond Buyer*, 1984.

Walters, Dennis. "The WPPSS Debacle." *Bond Buyer* Centennial Edition, August 1991, 43–44.

Walters, Dennis. "WPPSS Returns to Muni Market—at 5.95%." Bloomberg News, November 13, 2001.

## waste-to-energy facilities

Waste-to-energy facilities are plants designed to burn one kind of waste to produce electrical or steam power. Over the course of the municipal market's history, such plants have been designed to burn old tires (Illinois), the pulp left over from sugar refining (Florida), wood waste, and garbage. There was a boom in their construction in the early 1990s, after a typically overdone media scare about how the United States was running out of space to dump its garbage, epitomized by the day-by-day tracking of a barge with Long Island, New York, garbage journeying up and down the East Coast seeking someplace to dump its cargo.

These projects all sounded very good, because we like the idea of burning our garbage rather than dumping it at sea or burying it; the production of electrical or steam power also appealed to those who like the notion of civic self-sufficiency, a concept fueled by periodic press stories about small but idyllic cities, often in Scandinavia, that produce all the power they need by burning their own garbage.

But a word to the wise: it's harder than you might think to build and operate mills that turn one material into another, as investors in the municipal bonds sold for such enterprises have found to their chagrin.

*See also* garbage.

## Who owns municipal bonds?

Of the $2.8 trillion in municipal debt that the Federal Reserve figured was outstanding in mid-2010, households owned the largest chunk—just over

$1 trillion. Funds (mutual, money-market, and closed-end) owned a combined $947 billion. To round out the biggest holders of municipals, property/casualty insurance companies owned $369 billion, and commercial banks held $220 billion.

Individual investor domination of the market is a relatively new phenomenon. In 1965, for example, the household sector owned $36.5 billion of the $100 billion in municipal securities outstanding. Commercial banks owned $38.8 billion. A decade later, banks owned $102.9 billion in municipals, households $66.8 billion, and property/casualty insurance companies $33.3 billion. Household ownership surpassed that of banks only in 1981, $160 billion versus $154 billion. Insurance companies owned almost $84 billion. Municipal bond mutual funds, which had been introduced only in the 1970s, owned $5 billion.

This all changed dramatically with the passage of the 1986 tax act, which prohibited banks from deducting the cost of carry on their municipal bond investments except for those sold by small issuers or those who reasonably expected to sell only $10 million in bonds per year. This made municipals less attractive to banks, and they reduced their holdings accordingly. And this changed the complexion of the municipal bond business, transforming it from one that was primarily institutional and professional, or some would say clubby, to one that depended more and more on the individual investor. Over time, this shift reduced liquidity in the market, the consequences of which are still felt today.

The Internal Revenue Service, which only began asking taxpayers to list how much they earned in tax-exempt interest for the 1987 tax year, breaks down investor ownership in the winter issue of its quarterly *Statistics of Income Bulletin*. It presents an interesting picture of just how small the municipal market is, or perhaps of how municipal bonds aren't a significant part of the nation's financial culture. Of the 142 million tax returns filed by individuals and households in 2008, a total of 6.5 million claimed they received tax-exempt interest amounting to $79.8 billion. By comparison, 62 million returns claimed taxable interest of $223 billion, and 31 million claimed ordinary dividend income of $219 billion.

Those with adjusted gross incomes of $100,000 or more claimed $58.3 billion, or 73 percent of the tax-exempt interest pot. In 2007, this group took home 81 percent of the total, adding a new dimension to the market axiom that people buy municipal bonds not to become rich, but to stay rich. Perhaps people also buy municipal bonds to remain in the middle class.

The majority of tax-exempt interest (77 percent) was collected by tax-payers aged 55 and older, according to the IRS.

Not everyone was convinced that the Fed's estimate of munis outstanding was correct. In June 2011, George Friedlander of Citigroup wrote, "we have concluded that the Fed's data *dramatically* understates the amount of outstanding municipals," and that the figure was closer to $3.7 trillion, an estimate that was borne out by Bloomberg data.

*Sources:*

Federal Reserve Flow of Funds report, September 2010.
*Statistics of Income Bulletin*, Internal Revenue Service, Winter 2010.
Friedlander, George. "Special Focus: Is the Municipal Debt Outstanding Understated?" Citigroup Municipal Market Comment, June 3, 2011.

## willingness to pay

It is assumed that governments wish to or are willing to repay their obligations, and will do everything in their power to do so, and that if they default, it is because they lack the money to do so.

*See also* ability to pay.

## window bonds

Window bonds were developed by Citigroup Capital Markets after the auction-rate and variable-rate markets froze in February 2008, when most of the bond insurers lost their triple-A ratings, and the cost of standby liquidity facilities, such as bank letters of credit, skyrocketed.

The Window Variable-Rate Demand Bond (VRDB) has no third-party financial institution backing it; the issuer instead offers the buyer liquidity with a so-called dual-put feature through a Remarketing Window and a Funding Window.

After the investor in a window VRDB asks to tender his or her bonds, there is a 30-day Remarketing Window, during which a remarketing agent seeks a buyer. If the bonds cannot be remarketed, the window bonds enter a Funding Window with an unconditional mandatory tender. During the Funding Window, the issuer may call or convert the bonds.

In May 2009, Citigroup sought reassurances from the SEC that this structure would comply with Rule 2a-7, which restricts money-market funds to investing in securities with the top two grades, among other things. The SEC did accept it, but the structure did not become popular. Most issuers refinanced their auction- and variable-rate debt to long-term fixed-rate debt when they could.

*See also* auction-rate securities; variable-rate demand obligations.

# Y

## yield burning

On March 3, 1995, the front page of the *New York Times* business section carried a story headlined "Accuser in the Municipal Bond Industry." The story began: "In 14 years at Smith Barney, Michael R. Lissack earned millions of dollars. He advised local governments on bond issues worth tens of billions. And, he contends, he helped Wall Street line its pockets at the expense of taxpayers."

The story detailed what whistle-blower Lissack described as "yield burning," an almost inexplicably obscure process that might best be boiled down as the systematic overcharging banks and securities firms engaged in while putting together open-market Treasury escrow accounts for state and local municipal bond issuers. By marking up the prices on the securities, the firms "burned down" the yield to the levels allowed by tax law, and kept the profit.

"The extra markups were a big profit generator for many firms' municipal bond departments in the early 1990s, he says," the article continued. "But, he adds, those profits resulted in losses to the Treasury of hundreds of millions of dollars."

Thus began one of the darker episodes in the history of the municipal bond market, with a relatively high-ranking banker explaining how certain secretive aspects of the reinvestment of proceeds business worked to the advantage of those who ran the game. Lissack described the yield-burning process, and also detailed things like escrow churning and the practice of giving certain parties a last look at bids.

It took five years before the Securities and Exchange Commission (SEC) and the industry put together a global settlement with 12 underwriters, a $140 million agreement reached in April 2000. Lissack's lawyers, Phillips & Cohen of Washington, D.C., estimated that the government eventually received $250 million, including money from firms that were not part of the global settlement. As a whistle-blower who filed a *qui tam* lawsuit, Lissack was entitled to about 25 percent of the government's take.

The industry's first reaction to the revelation was to fight, saying that it was impossible to generalize about what the price of an open-market U.S. Treasury security might be without taking into consideration all facts and circumstances. They dismissed Lissack's claim that the prices listed in the *Wall Street Journal* for such securities could be any help at all in establishing prices, and seemed to rely on the notion that fair market value prices on open-market Treasury securities were pretty much what dealers said they were. This was not a very convincing argument.

Issuers, as John Connor of Dow Jones observed early on, were "complicit or clueless" about yield burning, mainly the latter, with perhaps a handful of public finance officers even able to evaluate the costs of their escrows. They relied instead on the representations of the bankers and lawyers who assisted them in their financings. This is what made the first yield-burning chapter so dark. The illusion that the nation's finance officers could trust their bankers implicitly was shattered. Yield burning was not something that occurred only with the uninformed and unsophisticated; no, as the SEC showed, the entire spectrum of issuers was affected, including the larger and more frequent issuers who should have known better.

As Kenneth Rust, director of the bureau of financial management in Portland, Oregon, said in 1999, "Underwriters are in the business of making money. You'd like to be able to trust them not to take advantage of you, but greed is a very big factor in this business. Your job is not over after the bond sale, no matter how good a job you did."

As with so many investigations into the market, this one was well along by the time it made its way into the press: Lissack had telephoned the FBI at the end of 1993. And as with so many incidents of wrongdoing in Muni-Land, it was difficult to categorize precisely what happened.

The essence of the crime revolved around tax law. Yield burning was wrong, the government said, because municipalities could not earn arbitrage profits when they sold tax-exempt bonds. Nor could they "deflect" those profits to a third party, like an underwriter. Yield burning was also wrong because it harmed the federal government, "which otherwise would have recovered any excess yield or excess profits on these transactions through the sale of special low interest bonds known as State and Local Government Series securities."

It was hard to make bond issuers care very much about yield burning, at least at the start. Indeed, as one banker pointed out at the time, if anything, issuers had an economic interest in allowing yield burning if it meant a reduction in underwriting costs. Part of the government's leverage in the case, though, was that it could just find deals where yield burning had occurred, challenge their tax-exempt status, and ask the issuers to pay up. The issuers would be left to sue underwriters, lawyers, and financial advisers. In 1996, the Internal Revenue Service took just that approach, announcing its Revenue Procedure 96-41, which stated, "The deflection of arbitrage through the purchase of investments at other than fair market value is prohibited," and then basically telling issuers to figure out if their bond proceeds had been involved in yield burning, calculate that amount, add interest, and send it in.

In 2000, after five contentious years, the yield-burning settlement was reached. In 2003, IRS officials said they had discovered that issuers were paying inflated prices for products used in the reinvestment of bond proceeds, such as guaranteed investment products. Yield burning, they said, had never ended. And so government regulators launched a new yield-burning investigation, the theme this time being "anticompetitive practices."

*See also* bid rigging.

*Sources:*

"Bombs Away!" *Grant's Municipal Bond Observer*, July 26, 1996.

"Das Ende. Das ist Das Ende." *Grant's Municipal Bond Observer*, September 8, 1995.

Mysak, Joe. "IRS's Anderson Sounds Alarm on Muni Derivatives." Bloomberg News, February 13, 2003.

Mysak, Joe. "The Man Who Cost Muni Bond Underwriters $150 Million." Bloomberg News, April 5, 2000.

"The Next Bombshell." *Grant's Municipal Bond Observer*, June 30, 1995.

Quint, Michael. "Accuser in the Municipal Bond Industry." *New York Times*, March 3, 1995.

"Required Reading." *Grant's Municipal Bond Observer*, May 17, 1996.

## yield curves

The graphic depiction of how much it costs to borrow money over time. The curve generally shows that it costs more to borrow for a longer period. When short-term interest rates are higher than long-term rates, the curve is said to be inverted.

*Source:*
*Bloomberg definition.*

## yield to maturity

Yield to maturity is the annualized percentage return of a bond held to maturity, taking into account its price, coupon, and interest income reinvested at the current yield.

# Z

## zero-coupon bonds

Zero-coupon bonds carry no interest and are sold at a deep discount; they pay an implied interest rate only at maturity. Zero-coupon bonds are popular vehicles to fund college educations and retirements.

# About the Author

Joe Mysak is editor of Bloomberg Brief Municipal Market. He has covered the municipal market since 1981, and is the author of *The Guidebook to Municipal Bonds: The History, the Industry, the Mechanics*, with George Marlin (1991); *Perpetual Motion: An Illustrated History of the Port Authority of New York and New Jersey*, with Judith Schiffer (1997); and *The Handbook for Muni-Bond Issuers* (1998). In 1998, he received the "Industry Contribution" award from the National Federation of Municipal Analysts. He and his wife live in Brooklyn, New York.